# CAFÉ
# NEANDERTAL

# CAFÉ NEANDERTAL

### EXCAVATING OUR PAST IN ONE OF
### EUROPE'S MOST ANCIENT PLACES

# BEEBE
# BAHRAMI

COUNTERPOINT
BERKELEY, CALIFORNIA

Library of Congress Cataloging-in-Publication data is available.


Cover design by Faceout Studios
Interior design by Neuwirth & Associates, Inc.

ISBN 978-1-6190-2777-0

COUNTERPOINT
2560 Ninth Street, Suite 318
Berkeley, CA 94710
www.counterpointpress.com

Printed in the United States of America
Distributed by Publishers Group West

10 9 8 7 6 5 4 3 2 1

# CONTENTS

*Author's Note*                                    IX

1  THE LA FERRASSIE SEVEN                             1

2  A BUNDLE OF SHALLOTS                              25

3  CHEZ LES NEANDERTALS                              51

4  THE INTERNATIONAL NEANDERTAL                      65

5  A DIFFERENT SORT OF PILGRIMAGE                    90

6  A MOVEABLE NEANDERTAL FEAST                      112

7  GATHERED AROUND THE HEARTH FIRE                  141

8  AS IF WRITTEN IN STONE                           166

9  PIPER AT THE GATES OF DAWN                       185

10 LOVE IN THE TIME OF NEANDERTALS                  206

11 A FOOT IN THE GRAVE                              234

12 MORPHING NEANDERTALS                             263


*Acknowledgments*                                  288

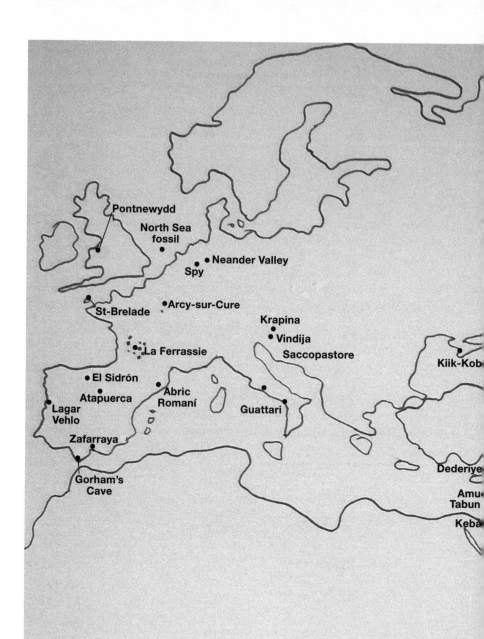

Pontnewydd

North Sea
fossil

Spy

Neander Valley

St-Brelade

Arcy-sur-Cure

La Ferrassie

Krapina

Vindija

Saccopastore

Kiik-Kob

El Sidrón

Atapuerca

Abric
Romaní

Guattari

Lagar
Vehlo

Zafarraya

Gorham's
Cave

Dederiye

Amu
Tabun

Keba

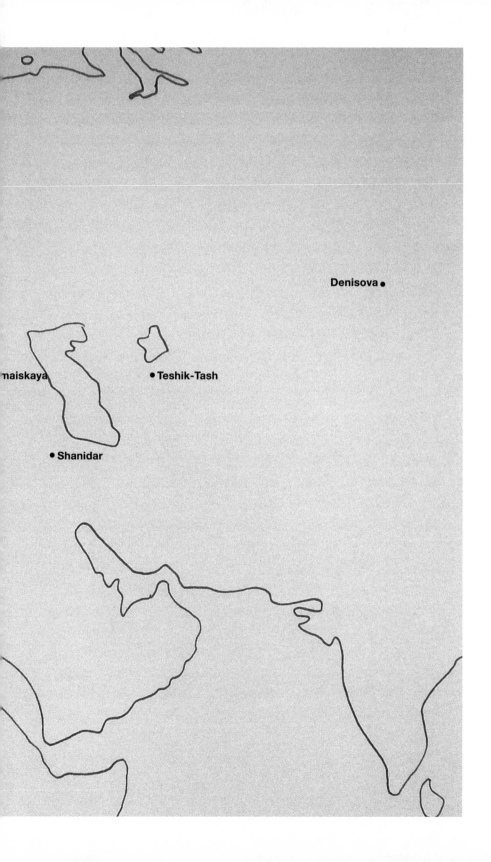

Denisova •

maiskaya

• Teshik-Tash

• Shanidar

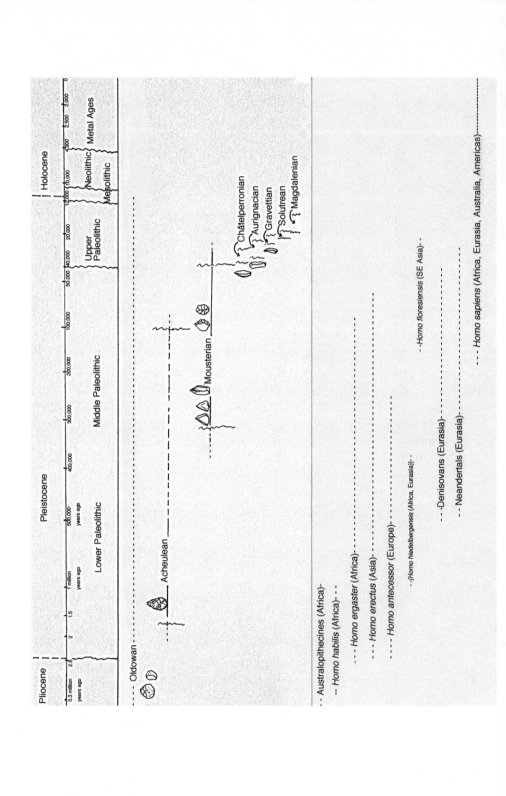

# AUTHOR'S NOTE

WITH SUCH A complex topic, involving so many people and places, past and present, I have made every effort to be meticulously accurate. If any errors have made their way in, they are wholly unintended. Also, at times I had to sacrifice the chronology of certain encounters to forefront clarity and present the wholeness and integrity of each chapter's topic. The events here cover the period from 2014 to 2015. The main dig featured, at La Ferrassie, went for five years, from 2010–2014. The summer after, in 2015, the key researchers met in Carsac to discuss the findings and possible interpretations based on the current body of evidence. That year I also did some long-distance trekking across southwestern France and northern Spain and visited other Neandertal sites. In all, I have remained true to the knowledge and experience of the encounters described herein. And lastly, I spell Neandertal without an "h" for a very particular reason, which I explain two-thirds of the way in. If you really want to know why before then, there is no harm in flipping ahead to find out.

# 1

# THE LA FERRASSIE SEVEN

**S**EVEN BODIES LAY scattered across the cave floor like leaves in the wind. Some were missing limbs or parts of their torsos or craniums. One's detached head had rolled a few feet away. Standing at the mouth of the cave, I made out the first body in the haphazard line of corpses beginning directly in front of my line of vision. There lay a large man in his forties. His lifeless arms and legs were folded in toward his body as if, in his last moments, he had been trying to keep warm. To the left of where he lay was a similarly positioned person, a woman in her late twenties or early thirties. Scanning to the right from both were the remaining five, all children, splayed helter-skelter, two not far from the man, one a little farther away, and the last separated from them all at the opposite end of the cave. The two oldest children had been ages ten and three. The remaining three were infants eight months and younger.

Even though this was a cold case, one that I was reconstructing from black-and-white photos while the actual bodies were now in a lab in Paris, it was hard not to feel the visceral presence of these seven. I immediately connected to their humanity through what I imagined were their emotions in their last moments of life. My thoughts burned with a single question. What had happened to them?

A comforting breeze picked up, evaporating the beads of sweat that gathered on my brow and rustling the leaves of the oak and hazel forest overhead. I looked up to take in the whole rock shelf under which the bodies had been found. It was hidden in the depth of a quiet forest on a remote hillside in an unindustrialized part of southwestern France. Cell phone reception was impossible. It was hardly an ideal spot for an emergency.

But everyone was here today, milling busily about, each focused on answering the same question. Investigators, crew, and local volunteers knowledgeable about the land and geography all worked within the large rock shelf, excavating, gathering samples, and looking for clues.

I watched mesmerized as one of the team of specialists, a veteran geologist, stared at the rock face for several long and considered moments as if he were seeing a movie play out on its surface. He next walked to a pile of just-dug-up dirt and pinched a bit from the top. He closed his eyes and rubbed the soil between his fingers, sensing something esoteric but material in the earth. He then held the soil up to his nose and like a master sommelier explored the bouquet. At last he opened his eyes and held the soil under the magnifying glass hanging around his neck to confirm or negate what he'd already learned from his own senses. He then casually returned the pinch back to its bucket and moved on to his next interrogation, carefully viewing, touching, and smelling rocks and dirt across our excavation zone. Was it more sand than clay? Did it have certain telltale minerals, burnt bits, bone? Did it belong more to one layer than another?

His answers would begin the most important foundational work of understanding the events that this earth had undergone by both natural and human causes. His presence marked a new science and the difference between the current team and those who had investigated here in the past. This team drew from a very diverse mix of specialists from across the sciences and across the world, bringing the best of knowledge and techniques to re-create the human and natural context in which these seven had lived, and died.

We even had a film crew, a two-person team that worked at the perimeter and wove in and out between the investigators, documenting every moment and every piece of unearthed evidence. They focused on paleoanthropologist Jean-Jacques Hublin, director of the Max Planck Institute's department of human evolution in Leipzig, Germany, who was visiting for the week. The lens zeroed in on his infectious broad smile and what he held in his right hand.

While the team already had been here for five dig seasons over five years, today, during the last two weeks of the fifth and last season, three paleoanthropologists—Isabelle Crevecoeur from Bordeaux, Asier Gómez-Olivencia from Bilbao, and Antoine Balzeau from Paris—found something of significance to the cold case. They had just reopened the original hole where the three-year-old child had been found, hoping to find more of the child's incomplete skeleton. Instead, they found an adult molar, and that in a part of the cave where no adults had ever been found, only children. It didn't seem likely that the tooth was associated with the two adults over fifteen meters away in a part of the cave where it seemed unlikely that it would have arrived by natural processes. A new question surfaced. Was another adult buried nearby, perhaps under all the rockfall that still had to be cleared away from deeper in the cave?

The camera rolled. Filmmaker Sophie Cattoire checked the lensing before asking her first question. Celebrated in the region for her talent and skill in bringing out the local life of the southwest—especially the personalities behind its prehistory—she and her partner both in life and in profession, Vincent Lesbros, were behind the film company Ferrassie TV—named after where we worked, the site of La Ferrassie. Today, against the sauna-like summer heat, she wore a low-cut dark blue spaghetti-strap top and had piled her long, flaming red hair atop her head, accentuated further by the cherry-toned lipstick that she pulled off with the easy elegance so common among French women.

She stepped back and regarded Jean-Jacques in his perfectly pressed cobalt blue summer shirt that brought out his engaging brown eyes. Because La Ferrassie derived its name from the iron-rich soil, *le fer ici*, "iron is here," being the most popular etymology offered by locals for the name, the burnt-orange earth that surrounded us popped with their blue tops. It was as if they'd planned this composition on a color wheel before enacting it. But like many things here, it was a part of the unplanned but perfect magic of the place, the people, and the work.

"*Alors*," began Sophie, "please tell us, Jean-Jacques, about the tooth you are holding."

"*Donc*, the tooth is probably the inferior molar of a Neandertal." He beamed an infectious smile into the camera, one that likely had been with him since boyhood when he first discovered the fascinating world of prehistory. He then paused and reached into his trouser pocket and pulled out two gigantic plastic models of teeth, a Neandertal tooth and a *Homo sapiens* tooth—like you do—both from adults, to demonstrate how obvious it was to him who the owner had been. These two model teeth had coincidentally arrived for him in the day's mail back at the dig house.

He pointed with his free hand and also explained that Neandertal molars tended to have larger pulp chambers, called taurodontism, a common feature in Neandertals and a rarer one among modern humans. Plus, the tooth had been found in a layer that preceded any modern humans to the area, so this was extra confirmation. He deftly held the models and the real tooth in his hands and offered the camera an extreme close-up.

While no one expected to find this adult tooth in the possible grave of a small child, what was in keeping with the known story of this cold case was that the tooth could only belong to a Neandertal because of the strata in which it was found, dating to between 50,000 and 70,000 years old—a date that the geologist was working hard to narrow down. This cold case was so old that it was perhaps one of France's oldest.

All seven found here were Neandertals. The site of La Ferrassie was famous and had long been called the Neandertal Cemetery for the fact that a good many archaeologists, as well as laypeople, viewed this as a place where intentional burials took place. Not everyone agreed though, for the evidence has a lot of holes, and in contrast they think these bodies could have been buried by natural causes, perhaps from a single natural disaster that took them all at once—such as hunger or extreme cold—and then their bodies were eventually buried through the process of natural sedimentation and rockfall. Yet others see a middle-of-the-way scenario: that the dead bodies were set aside here by other Neandertals but that natural causes covered them up.

La Ferrassie is in many ways a microcosm of the raging issues engulfing Neandertals, and us, in the broader field of paleoanthropology and the broader geographical contexts of Neandertals—who lived as far east as southern Siberia, as far west as Portugal's coast, as far south as Israel and Gibraltar, and as far north as Wales and the (now) island of Jersey. La Ferrassie is a site that concentrates not only the issues about whether Neandertals buried their dead but also issues about who they were as humans, especially those qualities we hold above all others as exceptionally human: our ability to think symbolically, to make complex tools, to speak languages, to create art, and along with these symbolic processes, the enactment of rituals such as burial, which implies a connection to the intangible, the afterlife, and the invisible spirit world.

La Ferrassie is in the Dordogne, not far from the town of Les Eyzies, and in the heart of the most concentrated region for human prehistory in Europe. Les Eyzies itself was a village whose rock shelves and prehistoric remains put it on the map and at the heart of European prehistory. It also became the natural location for France's national prehistory museum. One of Les Eyzies's rock shelves even gave us the name Cro-Magnon to refer to early modern humans, *Homo sapiens*. It was here in 1868, in the heart of the old village, where in the side yard of Monsieur Magnon road workers uncovered the burial site of five early modern humans who had lived here around 27,000 years ago. The Occitan word for hole, *cro,* was applied to the find. Occitan is an old Romance language originating in Latin and closely related to French and Spanish—the old language of the Troubadours—and was, and in many pockets remains, the region's dominant rural language.

Since then, the name Cro-Magnon, old Mr. Magnon's hole, has referred to the early *Homo sapiens* of the region, who arrived here perhaps around 45,000 years ago as a part of what is called "the transition" from Middle Paleolithic and Neandertals to the Upper Paleolithic and us. The Upper Paleolithic lasted until around 10,000 years ago. Neandertals disappeared from the fossil record around 35,000 years ago, the most dramatic event of the transition, one that seems to implicate us—this fast-moving, always innovating, environment-(over)manipulating version of humans, and the only one left walking the earth today. Around 100,000 years ago, there may have been at least six versions of humans walking the earth. Around 40,000 years ago, there were perhaps three, maybe four. Now it's just us, a fact that ought to strike one as weirder than there once having been six varieties or more. Look at canines or felines or spiders. Everyone but us has got many versions of their basic model. And we *Homo sapiens* are a remarkably homogenous species, no matter how different we think we look from each other across the globe. As a whole, we are less diverse than even the chimpanzees, who are living in smaller groups and in smaller and more compromised environments.

That's weird.

Neandertals lived in the Dordogne and across Eurasia long before any Cro-Magnons showed up. From the most recent estimates, they first emerged around 430,000 years ago (based on evidence from Atapuerca in Spain) and survived until around 35,000 years ago (in pockets all across Eurasia). The seven Neandertals from La Ferrassie probably lived between 50,000 and 70,000 years ago, around the time early modern humans began to leave Africa and at times were meeting and interbreeding with Neandertals. These encounters probably happened in Southwest

Asia. It is from many such meet-ups that we modern humans received somewhere from 0.7 percent to 2.1 percent of our genes from Neandertals. Eurasians today have on average about 1.5–2.1 percent Neandertal DNA within them, and Africans less than 1 percent.

(The picture is more complicated, though. Early modern humans made previous migrations out of Africa, somewhere between 200,000 and 100,000 years ago, that were less widespread but had impacts on populations of people living in the Levant. These folks most likely went extinct, but not before leaving some of their early, early modern human genes in Neandertals found in southern Siberia.)

Sometime after the La Ferrassie seven died—either at once or separately, depending on whose stance on the evidence you agree with—the rock shelf on which we stood had been a full-blown, fully covered, large cave. Its roof had crumbled and collapsed over several episodes, separated by thousands of years each time, due to cyclical fluctuations in glacial cooling and warming. The slow collapse eventually created a hill that supported the overgrowth of forest, further masking the original cave.

Yet that roof fall did something very convenient for future archaeologists. It sealed each level of human occupation that had existed in the cave, interspersing several human occupations over several thousands of years with sterile rock and dirt that sealed each in as a sort of Paleolithic Pompeii.

Above the large cave was a small cave, one that was still intact and also full of signs that other humans had been here long before us. It also naturally flowed into the lower and larger cave, making one imagine a duplex-like living space with upstairs sun and balcony and downstairs butchering, dining, tool crafting, and, uh, burying.

All told, there were at least eight separate human occupations at La Ferrassie, the first five associated with Neandertals from 90,000 to 50,000 years ago, and the last remaining two with early *Homo sapiens*, from around 38,000 to 22,000 years ago. That level six was playing games with everyone. Called the Châtelperronian level, it was occupied around

45,000 years ago and possessed a style of stone tools that partook more of *Homo sapiens* blade technologies but occurred in a time that overlapped with Neandertals and in some places seemed to be made by Neandertals. Some archaeologists think Neandertals made them and others think *Homo sapiens*. A few think both may have, in an innovative and hybridizing kind of overlap. The jury is still out on this but this matter is also an important piece for understanding who the Neandertals were, what became of them, and the nature of our relationship to them.

THE NEXT AFTERNOON, after the crew returned to work and the excitement over the new find was contained, Sophie asked Jean-Jacques for an extended interview in the forest, just above where we worked. They moved away from the center of activity to greater quiet, where only the occasional birdsong of the territorial red-throated European robin interrupted their conversation. I squinted up the hill, pricking up my ears to hear anything, but it was impossible. I could see Vincent quietly clicking production stills as Sophie coaxed prehistoric secrets from the grand master.

I remained curious as we retired to the village of Carsac, about twenty-eight miles away. This was where the archaeologists camped and pitched their tents in the large backyard where Harold Dibble, one of the key dig directors, had set up the camp and lab. My old archaeology professor in graduate school, he was the reason I was here. Harold had found a shack of a place in the village, an old tobacco-drying barn, a *séchoir à tabac*, and turned it into the archaeologists' home base for his digs throughout the area. While better than pure camping—the dig directors slept under the *séchoir's* roof while the crew pitched tents in what was an old farmer's field—it was still pretty rustic. Crew showers and latrines benefited from the shelter's hookup with indoor plumbing, but were so "prehistoric" that they had taken to painting Paleolithic designs of hands, bison, and a couple of shagging mammoths on the water closet walls.

The Dordogne had never been industrialized and to this day remains a place where people live close to the land. Once it had been famous for its high-quality tobacco, but today, with smoking falling out of fashion, other equally celebrated traditional crops have expanded into old tobacco fields, from corn and sunflowers to walnuts and wheat. It is a region also famous for the native black truffle, a seductive tuber we found at times growing just under the pebbles near oak tree roots at La Ferrassie when we cleared the ground to open a square. Once we even found a white truffle, near the surface of the back wall where the Neandertal man had been found. (Girolles and porcini also populated the forest, and I often saw the local volunteers using their break time to search for mushrooms for that night's meal. The forest was also rife with black and yellow salamanders and frogs the size of quarters, and rabbits, fox, wild boar, and red deer. Though nothing like the Paleolithic climate of the past, these rich natural realities made it hard not to think about what smart and clever people Neandertals had been to make this land their home.)

HAROLD HAD CONVERTED the wooden tobacco barn into a lab where the site sediment could be brought back, processed, catalogued, and analyzed before going into storage. He also renovated a small stone structure that had been added to one side of the barn and made it into his little bungalow, his pied–à-terre in *La France* so *profonde,* it included Neandertals. The house and lab sat on the edge of one of two main roads through the village, passing the twelfth-century Romanesque church and leading to the cemetery. His backyard tumbled downhill from the road toward where the Enéa Creek flowed nearby. That creek was a hint as to why this village was so central to prehistory.

The original human inhabitants along the Enéa had been Neandertals. They had most likely been attracted to good water and the limestone caves overhead carved by the tributary of the Dordogne. They had lived in three of four caves a stone's throw away on a ridge on the other side of the creek. They were collectively called Pech de l'Azé, with each cave distinguished with a number. Harold had dug at Pech IV with his mentors, François Bordes and Denise de Sonneville-Bordes. These two were the original Paleolithic archaeologist couple that had put Carsac on the map as an archaeologist's home base, a tradition Harold carried on after their passing.

Rather than camping in Harold's backyard, I was living in the Bordeses' old stone barn. I rented its loft from their daughter, Cécile. It sat across the garden from the main house, where I crossed to greet Cécile each morning and evening, plus her two dogs and three cats, and to use the facilities. It was a five-minute walk to Harold's dig house, along the same road that passed the church and led to the cemetery. There, François and Denise are buried in a limestone tomb covered by flint tools made by students who left them there as affectionate grave offerings, much as guitarists leave picks at the tombstone of Robert Johnson.

Carsac was so ideal and important in so many ways as an archaeological home base that it was worth the daily fifty-six-mile round-trip drive to La Ferrassie along sinuous country roads that made detours around the region's infinite limestone outcroppings and forests. Those limestone formations and those forests were the reason why this was one of Europe's most concentrated areas for prehistoric human habitations, as well as being a popular holiday destination for today's hominids hell-bent on the same things: good shelter, great food, and beautiful landscapes and climate. As the region's tourist office liked to advertise, the Dordogne has been "a vacation destination for 400,000 years." The good life has deep roots here. Just ask *Homo erectus,* our earlier ancestor who is related to both Neandertals and us, as he ventured into Europe.

An international team drawn from diverse places such as Australia, Iran, Canada, New Zealand, Portugal, Spain, Belgium, Holland, the USA, Greece, France, and England, the crew prepared the daily dinners that reflected their homelands' culinary inspirations. Harold also directed the menu plans and had his arsenal of tried and true recipes that made nearly everyone happy. These were French and American-style dishes he'd mastered and refined over decades of dig work. As the crew prepared dinner for thirty-five downhill in the backyard on outdoor gas burners and on an open fire, uphill, inside Harold's little stone house, the dig directors present that day gathered to decompress, review the day, and plan for the next one.

The team's directors were six scientists: Paleolithic archaeologists Harold Dibble from the University of Pennsylvania in Philadelphia, Alain Turq from the Musée National de Préhistoire in Les Eyzies, Shannon McPherron from the Max Planck Institute for Evolutionary Anthropology in Leipzig, Dennis Sandgathe from Simon Fraser University in Vancouver, and geoarchaeologists Paul Goldberg (aka the master soil sommelier) from Boston University and Vera Aldeias, also from the Max Planck in Leipzig. They also enjoyed input, collaboration, and visits from other respected scientists, such Jean-Jacques Hublin (Max Planck), Paul Mellars (Cambridge), Wil Roebroeks (Leiden University), and Gilliane Monnier (University of Minnesota), among many others.

Virginie Sinet-Mathiot, a bright rising star in paleoanthropology from Bordeaux, headed the lab. Her remarkable skills and unflappable cool kept it in remarkable order each day as it received numerous buckets of sediment from that day's work at La Ferrassie. These had to be carefully processed, catalogued, and stored in the next twenty-four hours so the lab crew would be ready for the next daily delivery, when it all began again. While she was often at the lab and so deprived of visiting La Ferrassie, where everyone felt the excitement was, Virginie knew something that few outside of this work know: most of the biggest discoveries in archaeology, especially Paleolithic archaeology, are made in the lab, not in the field. Excavators are too burdened with digging and documenting most of the time to realize what they are finding, especially when it is a small piece of bone or flint or a soil sample that needs a microscope and long hours of analysis. That just-discovered molar was an exception.

Thanks to a software program Harold and Shannon wrote, each artifact at the dig was shot in with a laser that then fed into the program and
noted the exact location of that item on a three-dimensional map of the
site. When something was found in the lab, the original location and
context could be pulled up through this program. The program also allowed a person to view the site in three dimensions and to begin to see
patterns of where more flint or broken animal bones lay or what the
spatial relationships of fire hearths were to each other, and the like.

Today five of the six core directors gathered upstairs along with our
special visitor, Jean-Jacques Hublin. I looked in on what was for dinner
downstairs—roast pork, sautéed red cabbage, a salad of greens, carrots,
tomatoes, and cucumbers, and garlicky green beans—and then went up
the hill and straight to Harold's cottage living room. In between, I received exuberant greetings and hand-lickings from Gary, the neighbor's
black Labrador, who had decided to live with us and escape his life with
three Shar-Pei. In his own way, he contributed to the work of the camp
by chasing down and devouring the apples that fell into the yard from
the two apple trees.

I myself was a sort of upstairs–downstairs person in the crew. My role
as journalist and anthropologist had afforded me precious equal access
to both worlds. And permission to drink, within reason, Harold's scotch.
I stepped inside his bungalow as he was pouring himself a scotch and
soda on ice. I sidled up shamelessly and poured mine neat. Outside of the
scintillation of touching Neandertal dirt, this was my favorite time of day.

Harold sat in his leather chair and swirled his drink before taking that
first rewarding sip. The sound of good ferment tumbling through ice was
as seductive as that tiny European robin in the forest, pleasingly punctu-
ating the cadence of rich conversation.

Jean-Jacques was already seated with an aperitif of white wine set before him on the coffee table. I took my glass and sat next to him.

"What, may I ask, did you and Sophie talk about in the forest?"

He flashed his engaging smile. "I told her that we are all storytellers,

and that we are drawn to origin stories. Of course, it is totally contradic-
tory to the concept of evolution, because there is no 'first' anything. But
people want the first stories. They want some sort of an Edenic moment.
Somehow, it reconciles with the biblical perspective, with all these theories about the African Eve and the Garden of Eden. We want a first something. And then it's also related to the notion of humans being different
from the animal world and somehow being separated by a trench. So you
have to be on one side of the trench or the other. I told her that this is the
problem with Neandertals." He took a sip of wine. "Neandertals for a
long time were on the other side of the trench. So we emphasized the
differences. But now somehow, they've passed over to this side of the
trench. Now we are erasing all differences because we want all humans
to be the same."

"How did she respond to your answer?" I asked, loving how in a few
breaths he'd summed up the root of most motivation, passion, and contention in the field. I had met Sophie through other prehistory circles
two years prior to becoming a crewmember at La Ferrassie, and knew
that her humanistic views of life included the Neandertals. Only the day
before she'd had another brief chance to interview Jean-Jacques and had
asked him about Neandertal and Cro-Magnon intermingling; the dreamy
idea of romance and wooing, a rainbow coalition, seemed to be implied
in the tone of her voice. He had disabused her of the idea. He explained
that there probably weren't any "flower bouquets and candlelight dinners," that we really have no idea what these interbreeding encounters
looked like, and that romance was less likely on the menu than fast food.
I thought I could see the air seep out of her sails and felt the sting myself,
for I too was a part of the rainbow coalition.

I confess I also carry a flame for the Neandertals. I even like to think
my percentage of DNA from Neandertals in modern humans, that estimated average of 1.5–2.1 percent among people of Eurasian ancestry, is
the full 2.1 percent. I even round it up to 3 percent. I liked them because
to an introvert in a society that encourages extroverts, they seemed to be

similar, living in smaller groups and possibly not needing to talk as much. We *Homo sapiens* are gabbing all the time, chasing away dinner without knowing it. I also noticed the same tendency among the local volunteers. One, Didier, even wore a T-shirt, black with white lettering, that simply said "*4 percent de Neandertal.*" (That was the top end of the percentage range when the genetic studies first came out, before they were later adjusted.) He and his fellow trench mate, Fabien, had confessed earlier their disenchantment with modern life as a big part of their draw toward prehistory; the world since the advent of agriculture some 10,000 years ago has been nothing but a hominid-made mess. As Vera succinctly said as we drove one morning to La Ferrassie, "Farming changed everything."

Three percent or not, at the same time I know that I have to keep my wishful emotions separate from the actual science and *let the evidence speak* (Harold's favorite mantra) about what was and was not possible. I also secretly suspected that everyone had their own dance with objective and subjective reality, and that those who were willing to admit it, the really honest ones, were best prepared not to mess up the actual data, or ignore the lack thereof. People jumped to conclusions with too little information and Jean-Jacques was right: this was rooted in our storytelling brain that desired origin stories.

Like Jean-Jacques, Harold was also deeply aware of and affected by this subjectivity in the field. When he called others on it, he was often criticized for not liking the Neandertals or for denying them their humanity, which was never his point. In fact, I'd found Harold far more sympathetic toward Neandertals than us *Homo sapiens*, a reality that would surprise many of his critics. Only two weeks earlier, at another "Scotch Time," as Harold affectionately calls these early evening sessions, he leaned passionately into this theme when someone brought up the idea that we moderns are inclined to like Neandertals because they were similar to us, because they were, in Jean-Jacques's language, on our side of the trench.

"Let's go with the evidence," Harold warmed into the topic with his familiar mantra, swirling the ice in his glass and rolling his eyes. "If the evidence shows Neandertals were like us, I'm all for it. But if the evidence does not show it, don't give me 'I like Neandertals.' Who cares if you like Neandertals? The question is, do we have the evidence to say that they're like us or not? Oh, and the other argument I just love is, 'Oh, we don't want to be mean to Neandertals, they're like brothers to us. Oh, Neandertals, you're just like us.' Meanwhile, Neandertals lived over 250,000 years. We've been around for maybe 160,000 years and I think we're going to extinction really fast. They didn't do that. So what are you going to tell a Neandertal when you meet him on the street? Are you going to say, 'Hey, aren't you happy to be just like one of us?' He's going to look you in the eyes and say, 'Fuck you. I don't want to be like you.' Why do you think it's a compliment to make them like us? We're not so great. I think it's pretty bad that the only compliment you can give a fossil ancestor is to be just like us."

"She was kind of amazed." Jean-Jacques brought me back to the present Scotch Time. "And she said, 'I didn't know scientists were interested in this kind of thing.' I said, 'Yes, I think the problem is that scientists do science and they think scientists of the nineteenth century were totally biased by their preconceptions about this and that, but it is in fact exactly the same today.' We project our fantasies about our values, nature, ecology, economy, family, and so forth onto what we study."

Harold listened, smiling appreciatively and taking another sip of his drink. He was fully relaxed; he wouldn't have to use his mantra, at least not today.

It was time to gather around the dinner tables in the backyard, but I was still mulling over this business of origins. It came up a lot, maybe a lot more than many researchers realized, in their own backstories.

I later caught up with Jean-Jacques to continue the conversation and asked if he wouldn't mind elaborating more on the subjective nature of stories and perhaps his own backstory. He was generously forthcoming and I learned that he was born in Algeria, and as a child he and his mother had been expelled back to France during a time of violent upheaval and turmoil. His parents already had been divorced, and he didn't see his father until he was a grown man. When he and his mother landed in Paris, they settled in the northern suburbs, in a pretty rough neighborhood. That childhood of separation, upheaval, and tough resettlement translated for him into issues of origins.

"Ancestry is a heavy question for me," he said. "I grew up in an absolutely ugly world. When we arrived in France, we were settled in the worst neighborhood around Paris. I was a preadolescent. I was already very interested in natural history and for me it was a sort of escape from this grim environment. It gave me access to the beauty of the world. The beauty of life. The beauty of everything. I was attracted to all fields of natural history. I think I sort of combined the interest in the remote past and the notion of ancestry with the interest for the living world in understanding the past world. It was a way to multiply the beauty of the present world by accessing the beauty of other worlds that came before. There was this sort of fascination for this lost world."

He paused for a moment and something else came to him. "This might sound funny, but doing something like paleontology has also something to do with the fear of death." He laughed as if he'd surprised himself in saying this aloud. "The need for fighting oblivion, fighting complete disappearance of a past life. I find it amazing that we can sort of—of course it's a sort of fantasy—to resuscitate it somehow, to take from death, from the ends of death, something that should have disappeared. To find a little piece of a human that lived a hundred thousand years ago, the tools he made, and the environment where he lived, to me, maybe it's a bit too psychoanalytic, but I see it as fighting death. It also meets my own anxiety because I have been exposed to death maybe more than others. It's a therapy." He laughed again at this admission, but I was touched by his willingness to share it, his openness to confess such things. If backstory influences how scientists see life, this backstory was going to assure impeccable research into the truth, as far as we could access it. It also made Voldemort look like such a ninny for not finding a more creative way to defy death.

"It's a way to say that even if you're dead," he concluded, "there is a chance somehow to survive, somehow, to extract from the nothing, the vacuum, the complete oblivion, things that are unknown."

THERE WAS A tradition in the American school of anthropology, in the branch of cultural anthropology, that before going out to the field, an ethnographer was encouraged to undergo psychotherapy. The whole reasoning behind this was to excavate one's own biases before heading into another cultural system where one risked becoming a mirror of one's unexamined psyche, and thus tainting the data, rather than becoming a receiver or mirror of the actual society one was studying. While I was limited in my view as an outside observer, I got the sense that this dynamic was rampant in paleoanthropology, a mix of both unexamined psyches and actual data, getting mirrored into the same frame.

IT WAS TWO twentieth-century excavations prior to ours that had discovered the skeletons at La Ferrassie. French archaeologists Louis Capitan and Denis Peyrony first uncovered six Neandertal skeletons between 1896 and 1922, and Henri Delporte found the seventh, the three-year-old's skeleton, during two separate seasons during excavations from 1968 to 1973.

The ancient human presence at La Ferrassie was exposed during roadwork in 1895 when workers cut open the side of the hill and uncovered stone tools and animal bones that implied a prehistoric human presence. The hill was already known for its iron-rich, ferrous earth, the soil the color of dark burnt orange. The upper cave had signs of an iron forge from the Middle Ages. It is essentially an orange, yellow, and brown layer cake of human evolution, from Neandertals to us.

The first excavation began a year later, in 1896, and cut deeply into the hill to open and pull off tons of stone from the collapsed cave ceiling. Though it applied the best excavation techniques of the time, it also jumbled and disrupted a good deal of strata, and hence, context about how people had lived and used this site. That precious data was lost. To their defense, it was and remains a tough site to excavate and the strata in the end may also have been jumbled by natural causes that geologists and archaeologists are still trying to reconstruct.

While the context was sacrificed in many key spots, the early excavators did succeed in uncovering perhaps the most intriguing elements, the rare skeletons of a past people both very much like us and sort of not like us, especially evident in the skull of the adult male. He had been someone with a very large brain, his cranium larger than that of nearly any living human male today. His body was so robust that even a modern-day professional wrestler should seriously question stepping onto the mat with him. He was someone who had wrestled woolly rhinoceros and mammoth for a living, using sophisticated and lethal spears effective only at extremely close range—including at times jumping on the animal's back and thrusting—as is evident in the sorts of injuries preserved on Neandertals' fossilized bones. Their hunts made today's bullfighting look like swimming laps in an indoor pool.

While the stone tools also were seen as significant, not all of them were selected for the final sample, some of certain shapes being cast off as insignificant. It was only many decades later, with more advances in paleoanthropology, that investigators realized that those cast-off flakes and chips were as important as the pieces that were kept.

Next, from 1968 to 1973, the second excavation directed by Delporte added to the cuts into the hill and also disturbed a lot of strata rich in context: stone tools, bones, and soil and their spatial relationships to each other. In 1972, Delporte found a portion of the cranium of the three-year-old child, the seventh of the seven skeletons. For reasons still unanswered, it took him until the next year, in the last month of digging, to find and uncover the child's body—even though it was only inches from its skull. The child's body was missing its arms and other fragments of its skeleton, a fact that led physical anthropologists collaborating with our team during this third La Ferrassie excavation to go back in and look for anything Delporte might have missed. They found nothing. Maybe the child's arms had been scavenged shortly after its death and dragged away by a hyena or wolf? But they did find that tooth that belonged to someone else.

In 1973, Delporte closed up the site for posterity and the next generation of archaeologists—which was Harold's team. It is an established reality in archaeology that future teams will likely have better techniques and insights and so it is a good idea at immense sites such as this one to excavate as far as one reasonably can and then preserve it for future archaeologists to take to the next level.

Harold's team opened La Ferrassie in 2010 and dug for five seasons, in the spring or summer, through to 2014, when they closed it up carefully for the next generation of archaeologists to reopen. They continue to work with the data and evidence they gathered during those five seasons, and they continue to puzzle through the haphazard records left by the prior two excavations from the twentieth century, a sort of archaeology of archaeology.

Archaeology from its beginnings has been and remains both an art and a science. In the sciences it suffers from what Dennis Sandgathe calls "crappy data." Crappy data comes from imperfect, often un-replicable data-gathering techniques that define so much of what archaeologists are able to gather at best, given the difficulty of extracting human data from the time-altered earth. Half the time you don't even know you're in an old occupation site until you've destroyed half of it and are standing on top of it, much like what happened in the early twentieth century at La Ferrassie. In other sciences, Dennis further elaborated, other scientists can replicate experiments to support or negate the original findings. That's rarely possible in archaeology, and when it is, there are missed opportunities because archaeologists aren't being trained to think in such a way. Which leads to the art side of the equation. As an art, archaeology is riddled with contentious debates about what it is to be human that sort of do but sort of don't stick to the crappy data, and that pull to the surface those uninvestigated beliefs and values to which Jean-Jacques referred.

La Ferrassie's history, again, and these seven skeletons, were a case in point. From the moment those first six skeletons were uncovered there, some began to call the site a Neandertal cemetery and the six were referred to as intentionally buried, not for any hard non-crappy evidence, but for the fact that to the twentieth-century and culturally embedded minds of the excavators, that was how it looked, because they assumed everyone *buried* their dead, and if a body was found in a hole in the ground, it was buried. Yet all the evidence to prove such a claim—the foundation of true science—had been swept away, dug, hauled, tossed, and was not well documented by the very people claiming they saw evidence for a human-made hole that preceded their own hole dug to get the skeleton out. If the skeletons had in fact been in holes intentionally dug by Neandertal hands, rather than being unintentionally covered by natural processes, or laid in a creekbed slowly filled in over time by sediment, well, we'll probably never know.

So why bother then? Because those skeletons exist, their stones and butchered animal bones exist, and La Ferrassie and sites like it exist and they still hold compelling pieces of the mystery of being human in the many forms that have been expressed on earth so far.

Harold calls La Ferrassie "the mother lode" of Neandertal sites in southwestern France and Europe, because of the skeletons and the burial debate. There are thirty or so nearly complete skeletons of Neandertals across the Old World—all other finds are small fragments of bones, such as a finger, a tooth, or a toe—and La Ferrassie has seven of those rare, nearly complete individual people.

La Ferrassie frames head-on numerous mysteries associated with Neandertals, especially those driving questions such as burial, fire use, fire-making, tool craft traditions, innovation and creativity, and the overlap, or transition, with us—because we *Homo sapiens*, we Cro-Magnons, show up at La Ferrassie at around 37,000 years ago. The current team's mission has been both to reinvestigate the burial question at this site and to apply much improved state-of-the-art excavation techniques since the time of the original excavations, many developed by Harold and Shannon. These would be used to reconstruct as well as possible the context of the site at areas the dig directors determined were still undisturbed, intact spots from the original Neandertal occupations.

THAT AFTERNOON, AFTER Sophie's camera stopped rolling and Jean-Jacques returned from the forest to look at the square that the just-uncovered adult molar had come from, I stood up from my excavation square and took another look at the whole scene: the golden yellow limestone rock wall before me with its sunspot-like lichen- and moss-speckled face, the imagined placement of the seven skeletons fitting together in my mind. And the new tooth. The breeze picked up again, only this time I shivered. As I looked pointedly at the remaining collapsed portions of the cave roof, new and demanding questions riddled my mind. Were there more undiscovered bodies here? What had their last days been like? What had happened to them and all their kin and friends and distant relations scattered across Europe and Asia? What had it been like to come into contact with early versions of us, newly arriving immigrants exploring the horizon beyond Africa starting perhaps around 120,000 years ago? *Homo sapiens*, who seemed to procreate more, move longer distances in one stretch, talk more, and use different technological traditions? What does all of this say about being human, and why are we, today, so particularly fascinated with the Neandertals? Was it because they were like us, or because they were not quite like us? Or because now that it is just us, the first time in hominid existence, we're feeling the rub? Who they were, then, becomes a more pressing, as well as a more exotic, question.

I returned to my square, my little Cro-Beebe, to finish out the afternoon of excavating. I was assigned this day to a spot at the sediment Level 1, identified as being around 90,000 years old and just above the cave's natural bedrock. Its top layer, which touched the 70,000-year occupation at Level 2, had a few Neandertal tools and butchered animal bones, signaling the possibility of a first Neandertal occupation at earlier than 70,000 years ago. My quadrant was just to the right of where the adult male, the forty-something Neandertal, had once lain. I'd recently held a replica of his nearly complete skull and felt intimidated by its magnitude. As I worked, I was always aware of him, as if his ghost hovered over my left shoulder, watching my work with amusement. I even began calling him Monsieur La Ferrassie to myself.

I was in heaven. I never got over the fact that as we excavated into undisturbed layers, ours were the first human hands to touch this same earth since these Neandertals had lived here, had breathed and died here. Over the many days, weeks, and eventually years—six years in all, with the fourth and fifth (2013 and 2014) as a crew member during the last two dig seasons at La Ferrassie, followed by a final data-analyzing post-dig summer season in 2015 in Carsac—I never got over the exhilaration of touching old dirt, bones, and stones. Each time, electricity shot through my fingertips with the knowledge that the last human hands to have touched that layer of soil had belonged to Neandertals. I could feel their fingertips fleetingly graze mine. Every time.

While here in my magical hole, I also noticed a lot of things about the culture of the natives, not just the Neandertals, but also the archaeologists and the local volunteers equally dedicated to them. They were as much a part of this story, and yet so often were left out of its telling. But it was they who influenced and defined very much how prehistoric research unfolded, not only here in one of France's most beautiful and ancient places, but also around the world at other sites. This was a good place to focus the lens on this dynamic given the remarkably international nature of the team. Furthermore, here was a region where local amateur passion for prehistory was the strongest I'd witnessed anywhere.

I'd spent over two decades in Iberia, also a part of Europe with an inordinate concentration of Paleolithic sites, and never found such local passion for prehistory in Spain or Portugal as I did here. One early morning as we drove to La Ferrassie, one of the crew from Belgium echoed my suspicions.

"The French have an unusual amateur affinity for prehistory," Jonathan said. "Other Europeans don't have it. I haven't seen it in Spain or Portugal or England. Pockets of Germany have it, but *all* of France has it." He had just mentioned some of the other heavy-hitters for Neandertal and Cro-Magnon sites in Europe, making the difference with the French all the more interesting. French prehistory buffs with deep experience and knowledge worked alongside us, weaving in and out at the dig site, the lab, and enriching our experience.

This local passion for the human prehistoric past was not only unusual but so prevalent here that I overheard it often in conversations during local afternoon gatherings at cafés and on market days when the community was out in force. All I had to do was plunk down at a café table and say, "So, how about those Neandertals?" and listen to the natives argue with animation, intelligence, and accuracy the latest findings and conjectures as if it were the latest rugby match. That's when I realized we all existed in a special place, one I called Café Neandertal.

The mixed objectivity and subjectivity of these natives—archaeologists and locals alike—turns out to contain in a microcosm a whole lot about what it is to be human. We think, we perceive, we feel things about others, whether they lived now or half a million years ago. It also reveals the workings of that mystery box between our ears, one guided as much by genes as by natural selection, the environment, and perception.

Equally intriguing in all this was the emerging reality that the world of Neandertals themselves was far more diverse than previously thought.

The Western European Neandertals, for whom we have more fossils, are a small group compared to the numerous populations represented by larger collections of smaller fragmented bones, such as from places like Krapina, Croatia, where some 1,200 fossil fragments represent about ninety individual Neandertals—something paleoanthropologist James Ahern from the University of Wyoming drew to my attention. We are becoming more aware that French and Iberian Neandertals were as diverse as Central Asian, Middle Eastern, and Balkan Neandertals, as are living modern humans across the globe today, perhaps more so. It was time to give them and their diversity the same measure of respect and awareness.

# A BUNDLE OF SHALLOTS

M Y ENTRY INTO the world of Neandertals in southwestern France was
thanks to a small bundle of French shallots. It was early May of 2010,
the year the excavation was opening at La Ferrassie for its first season of five, and I had rented a studio near the market square in the medieval town center of Sarlat-la-Canéda. I knew nothing about La Ferrassie
then, a little more about Carsac, but certainly had no idea I had landed
in the heart of Harold's world. I was already enamored with Neandertals,
but that is a lifelong affinity and a reason why I chose to explore this part
of France. Sarlat was the natural choice for a home base, a town five miles
north of Carsac and the administrative center of the corner of the Dordogne called the Périgord Noir. It is *noir* for its evergreen oak forests that
darken and hide the curves and contours of a complex landscape year-
round. It is *Périgord* for the ancient name of the region now called the
Dordogne because of the famous river that flows through it, from the
volcanic Massif Central in the east toward the Atlantic near Bordeaux in
the west. Like its oak forests, the Périgord Noir is an evergreen and mysterious landscape of our own deep dreams and deep ancestry, where
some of Europe's first hominids first arrived, stayed, and lived.

"France may one day exist no more, but the Dordogne will live on just as dreams live on and nourish the souls of men," Henry Miller wrote in his *The Colossus of Maroussi* from his visit to the region in the late 1930s. He'd felt it, too. There is something about being here that makes you feel an old energy pulling you deeper into your humanity.

I had been drawn to the area two winters prior to that May. I'd crossed the Pyrenees from northern Spain, a common pattern in my travels, for the Dordogne was a place that had long intrigued me for both its present cultural richness and its Paleolithic past. I was exploring spiritual experiences and sacred roots, and had several times walked different trails of the pilgrimage route to Santiago de Compostela in northwestern Spain that crisscrossed these mountains in many places as pilgrims from France forged paths into Iberia. But this time would be different. Drawn from my usual research in northern Spain, and desiring to explore parallels on the northern side of the mountains, I landed in Sarlat and found it had a pull on me like no region I'd ever inhabited. It was that pull about which Henry Miller had written many decades earlier.

It haunted me so much that I returned a year and a half later, determined to make this obsession into a viable effort as a freelance writer. My plan was to inhabit Sarlat for a few weeks, pitching story ideas to magazines as I explored and settled in. I had not expected how deeply I would connect to the place personally, beyond any intellectual or literary efforts. I actually felt as if I'd come *home*. I was profoundly happy. With that unprecedented joy, another magic took hold: nearly everything I pitched to editors sold. In the life of a freelance writer, that's pretty unusual. I knew that I had found one of those rare moments in life where passion and livelihood were intersecting. I settled deeply into local life and wrote.

One of the biweekly pleasures of my life in Sarlat was its market that set up every Wednesday and Saturday. It is a beautiful and well-restored medieval town, one that many have seen in at least one or two of the fifty-plus historical films shot here, such as *The Musketeer* or Michael Crichton's *Timeline*. Annually, some 2.5 million visitors alight upon the town of 6,000 and consume as many duck, goose, black truffle, and walnut culinary creations as possible. They then head out into Sarlat's vicinity to visit a few of the 1,200 castles and châteaux in the Dordogne or the few dozen Paleolithic caves still open to the public; before again gorging on more duck, goose, truffle, and walnut masterpieces—this time with more appreciation for the ancient hearth fires of times past that produced much the same local fare.

Saturdays tended to be the days when these many tourists converged on the market square, but Wednesdays brought in more locals getting the bulk of their weekly food shopping done; Sarlat's cafés overflowed with local conversations, some in French and some in Occitan, the mother tongue of most of southern France up through World War I.

I was finding more and more that common topics of conversation were as much about the prominent spiritual ideas in the culture as about the prehistory of the area. People fluidly and intelligently spoke about such things as the region's revived Catholicism with its feminist and New Age flavors, the Buddhist influence from the numerous Tibetan refugees in the region, power vortexes, dowsing, fairy tracks, healing spirit springs, and the like. As engagingly, they'd discuss ideas about the prehistory, such as new findings in paleogenetics, the fossil evidence, interpretations of Upper Paleolithic cave art, speculations over Neandertal language use and symbolic thought, the skill in the Paleolithic stone tools they had found in their fields, and so forth. More often than not, the two were connected: locals frequently explained that the contemporary spiritual expressions found in the Dordogne were deep precisely because of the region's prehistory and because early humans had lived here; they had laid the foundation for a profound connection to life, land, and spirit for all who came later.

Add to this that those who are born here, or moved here when little kids or as migrating adults, all feel a strong connection to that long human past. It is low key and earthy, organic. While no one here says they trace their lineage to local Neandertals or to local early Cro-Magnons—

because they understand that this would be naïve and outside current scientific thinking on the matter—they do speak of a profound connection to these prior inhabitants that surfaces spontaneously when farming or hunting or gathering wild foods such as berries and mushrooms. In that sense, it is ancestral.

Once, while I was deep in the forest learning how to read the signs given from the earth underneath oak trees in order to find truffles, my expert truffle hunter teacher said, "When I do this, I feel like I am entering the world of Cro-Magnon or the Neandertals. When I go into the forest and my mind shifts into the focus it needs to look for the signs of the truffle, I feel it. I feel they did this too, and I am a part of this long lineage of hunting and gathering. I am connected directly to it."

Another time, a farmer I stopped to speak with on the edge of his land told me, "I find Neandertal Mousterian hand axes in my field, just lying there on the surface. It's magic each time even though for here it's normal, right? But still it's incredible to find and to hold something that old. That person had crossed my field long before it was a field or I had been born."

There is a mystical quality in the eyes of these locals when they talk about these things.

Whether the scientists agree or not (some would not and most aren't even aware of this local romance with the past inhabitants, for they are often at a dig site, not a weekly market), it is a strong stream of feeling and emotion in the local culture and defines a good deal of native relationships with the people's own land and with the first residents: *Homo erectus*, Neandertals, and Cro-Magnon. And it has to be factored in, for these are the tendencies among the prehistory buffs and local volunteers, and their knowledge of this place is invaluable.

I was listening to all this rich folklore and noting it down, realizing in fact that my own sense of coming home was also connected to this ancestry. I think I must have had a mystical quality in my eyes, too, when they spoke to me.

As for the archaeologists, whatever their personal and professional stance, I'd noticed that they also felt profoundly connected to this land and to the subject matter they came here to study. While their focus was necessarily and strictly scientific, when gathered around the table after a long day of hard work in the hot Aquitaine summer sun, I'd see that same mystical quality in the eyes of many of them, too, as they would talk about the humans whose stone tools and butchered animal bones they'd just spent the day delicately uncovering and documenting.

In that first spring in the area, I had two daily research methods. One was to go for long treks into the countryside, where inevitably I would meet a gardener, farmer, horse trainer, goose raiser, or winemaker, often who first spoke Occitan with me. I would understand because of my efforts in learning both Spanish and French—and Occitan is somewhere in between the two even though it also evolved distinctly into its own language. But speak it, no. I would respond in French, and they would feel comfortable to keep speaking Occitan, and off we would go down a rich rabbit hole of local lore. A big part of that lore included the fact that they often found blades, flakes, and scrapers on their land and they felt a strong and daily affinity with peoples who had lived here long before them. Because of it, they thought about Neandertals and early modern humans a lot. It seemed to them, these ancient people were still present on the land and in the forest. I agreed. At times, I could feel it and the hair on my skin would stand up straight.

This explained the frequency of café conversations about prehistory during market days.

On those treks I also explored the region's wealth of once-occupied caves and met local guides who were deeply knowledgeable and willing to share not only their intellect but also the visceral experience of the place.

My second "research" method was to go to market day twice a week, starting early, both to get my own food shopping done and then to have the morning before me to mull about food stands and café tables as they formed and locals invited me to join in. My notebook began to fill with wonderful stories from their Occitan-preferring, Neandertal-loving lips.

On one particular spring morning in early May, I was simply enjoying the easy visceral pleasure of shopping at the Wednesday morning market, being a local, and piling the locally grown treasures into my pannier. I planned to make a shallot and kale linguine with the ingredients and needed only several good shallots, which I would sauté until caramelized and then toss with the rest.

Off to the dedicated shallot merchant's stand I went, where all he sold were dried shallots and garlic, their stems braided into decorative and functional bundles and hanging from his awning or arrayed in piles on the table before me. I selected a bundle of shallots and, as I handed the money to the vendor, I abruptly felt the air to my left ripple in a strange time-warping sort of way. Out of the corner of my eye I glimpsed a familiar robust figure flit past and disappear. I caught the flash of reddish-blond beard and a stomach that reminded me of gourmand tendencies, and then *poof*, gone. In that same blink of an eye I spied another man walking briskly with him, moving his arms in quick and animated conversation. They sped past garden stands, olive sellers, foie gras tables, jarred black truffles, and walnut liqueurs. The big man, I was sure, had a grin on his face. If I'd identified him correctly, this meant that the other man had just made a really brilliant point about something archaeological or had just cracked a really bad joke. The narrow labyrinthine passageways of the medieval town then absorbed them. Upon getting the change and tossing the shallots into my basket, no matter how quickly I tried to find them, they had entirely evaporated.

But that one figure, and that unpretentious and sudden grin and laugh, were engrained in my memory. In that square I found myself traveling twenty-three years back in time to my first year as a doctoral student in anthropology. I was in Harold Dibble and Alan Mann's human evolution courses at the University of Pennsylvania, where I'd first encountered that beard, figure, and wit. Harold was often the instigator of good-bad puns and often sprinkled his lectures with Paleolithic word-play, using *knap*, *stone*, *flint*, and *chip* in every imaginable double enten-dre. (His was such a variant of humor that he even named his sons, his only two children, Flint and Chip.) Alan would also add his quick wit to the levity and by the year's midpoint my classmates and I had dubbed the two Penn human evolution professors The Mandibles.

But I hadn't seen Harold in years. If he was here, it meant something really interesting was happening in the Dordogne. My heart pounded. My pulse quickened. I had to know. I rushed back to my studio, searched the internet for his contact information, and quickly wrote an email: "Hello Harold, Was that really you walking across the Place de la Liberté in Sar-lat, or is there someone else here in the Dordogne impersonating you?"

Impossible, I thought to myself as I wrote the words. Yet no one else in the world had that figure, an archaeologist-foodie's figure of a man unafraid of cooking with butter, cream, bacon, and duck fat, all in the same dish. Harold was famous for hosting digs where he cooked for ev-eryone and the wine flowed as if at the Wedding of Cana. He was fabled for making Excel spreadsheets to plan the entire season's lunches and dinners and prided himself in never repeating a meal. Moreover, he loved scotch. He loved big bowls of ice cream. He shared all these social-ly-gluing resources generously, creating his own ancestral hearth fires of gathered collaboration and contentment.

Harold also happened to be one of the world's experts on Paleolithic stone tools and the skilled flintknapper who had made authentic Nean-dertal stone tools for the movie based on Jean Auel's *Clan of the Cave Bear*. (He liked to add with Neandertalish humor that Daryl Hannah really liked his tool.) He also moved like a soccer player, which explains how he had disappeared so quickly.

All in all, he was a hard act to replicate, even though the nearby na-tional prehistory museum in Les Eyzies seemed to have used him as a model for their exhibit's reconstruction of an adult Neandertal, with its thick chest and red hair and beard.

I hit *send*.

By then I was sure I had seen a mirage. Impossible, I said again to myself. It had been over two decades since I'd sat in Harold's class. We all change. It seemed too uncanny. If in fact it was he, then it also would appear I was unintentionally stalking him, since all the places where I had done my own research and writing were all the places he too had done his—from France and Spain to Morocco, Egypt, and Iran. Even though I was pursuing more modern mysteries at the time, I was attracted to ancient lands where both Neandertals (in Europe and West Asia) and early archaic *Homo sapiens* (in North Africa) had lived. But the neat thing about training in anthropology in the North American tradition is that even if you are becoming a cultural anthropologist as I did, you still train in the other three subfields of the discipline, which are biological anthropology, linguistics, and archaeology. The idea is that they all relate to the study of humans past and present, and a serious anthropologist needs to be able to dig as much in the past as the present to understand a place and a people.

I checked my inbox and there sat a reply from Harold.

"What are you doing here?!"

It seemed perfectly natural that he, a Paleolithic archaeologist, would be here in one of the highest concentrations of Neandertal and early modern human sites in all of the world, but me? I was a writer and a cultural anthropologist. I studied living humans and normally non-Western ones, right? Nope. The western Mediterranean had become my favorite spot on earth just as it had for the Neandertals, and for good reason, and I wasn't budging.

I wrote back tout de suite, explaining that I was in the Dordogne for the same reason his ancient subjects came here: the great natural beauty, the food, the climate, and the culture. In fact, I really liked the locals and was writing about this part of France, including its passion for prehistory.

True to his reputation, Harold sent another quick reply and invited me, along with my landlady and friend, Nadiya, to lunch the next day.

Nadiya was in the building when I was experiencing the serendipity of shallots and she confessed her own passion for Neandertals. She offered to be the designated driver. Lunch implied wine, and archaeologists have a reputation for putting away a lot of it.

The next day we found ourselves settling in to a four-course lunch at the Hotel-Restaurant Delpeyrat in Carsac, five miles south and 180,000 years away, deeper into the heart of Café Neandertal. Carsac had been Harold's home base ever since he began excavating in the region in 1976 with François Bordes. As I took my seat, I felt as if I were sitting in the middle of the history of prehistory in France, at the same restaurant where Bordes's own crew dined during each of their many dig seasons.

In fact, in the Bordes's era, this was where everyone ate breakfast, lunch, and dinner. Then it had been a complete working farm, providing almost all the ingredients that went into the meals the restaurant served. Today, a kitchen garden still provided a good amount, but it was more restaurant and less farm while still serving excellent classic French cuisine.

Harold's colleague Dennis Sandgathe joined us. He was the same animated man I'd seen with Harold the day before, cracking jokes. I soon learned that their nicknames were Giggles and Smiles for this very reason.

Nadiya, a native of northern Thailand and now longtime resident of the Dordogne, had long been fascinated by prehistory, which was one reason why she also chose it as home. It was a story that many transplants, French and foreign alike, would give for coming here. The locals would of course just nod and say, "*Bien sûr*, it is the most natural thing to do in a place that has such a deep human ancestry."

We were shimmering with happiness over this encounter and for Harold's generosity as Philippe Delpeyrat, the father of this family operation, set before us the first course, bowls of fragrant chicken vegetable soup made that morning by Aline, his wife. Dennis filled our glasses with the local red wine.

This hominid life was pretty good when it was good.

I began asking my questions, starting with why Harold and Dennis were here right now. Each late spring or early summer, Harold explained, the two flew to France and opened up the barn, aka lab, and house and began setting things up in preparation for the excavation season before the crew of around thirty arrived to commence digging. This year they were also heading off for their dig in Morocco throughout May and then would return to Carsac in early June for the dig in France. I was intrigued. Neandertals had never lived in Africa, so, why Morocco?

It turned out that their Moroccan site, called Smugglers' Cave, Grotte des Contrabandiers, was an incredibly important part of the research because it was a Middle and Upper Paleolithic cave occupied by early modern humans from 120,000 to 10,000 years ago. They were early *Homo sapiens* but had lived in Africa at the same time Neandertals had lived in Europe and in Asia. Curiously, the cave was in Temara, only a few miles south of Rabat, where I too had once lived and had conducted research.

Our second course arrived, Aline's pork terrine. Dennis refilled our glasses with wine as I asked for more details about why two specialists of Neandertals in Europe were studying archaic early modern humans in Africa.

"There are a lot of debates about early modern physiology and behavior," Harold began, "so Smugglers' Cave allows us to look at a site contemporary with Neandertals in Europe but in Africa, indicating that they have not yet made contact with Neandertals and the behaviors found in Africa will be exemplary of modern human behavior."

It was for this same reason, he added, that they also had done work in Abydos, Egypt, looking for indications of what early modern behavior was like prior to humans leaving Africa and prior to any contact with Neandertals. "Because at some point," he said, "around one hundred fifty to one hundred sixty thousand years ago, early modern humans spread out from Africa. The Nile Valley was a natural corridor out. We were trying to find more direct evidence."

Their work was expansive, intense, demanding, and often left them feeling spread thin, but they were asking and exploring the linchpin questions at the heart of the mystery of Neandertals and us. What did we look and act like while still in Africa, and what did Neandertals in Europe and Asia look and behave like before we all crossed paths with each other?

Dennis poured more wine as the third and main course came out of the kitchen in the arms of Aurelie, the Delpeyrats' daughter. She set before us generous plates of roast beef with green beans, peas, potatoes, and asparagus cooked in a sauce of white wine, garlic, and olive oil. I knew Aurelie, a friend I'd made on the court during a hard night of badminton that first winter I'd come to the region. It had been thanks to Nadiya's insistence that I gave the deceptive game a try—a game she excels in and loves. The one redeeming part of that night was I began friendships with a handful of locals who would become more important in my life down the road. One was Aurelie, a master pastry and dessert chef who had also studied archaeology at university and was as familiar with archaeological strata as she was with *gâteau de millefeuille*. As she set down our plates, I saw her brother Sebastian peek out from the kitchen to be sure the other patrons were content. Harold had watched these two grow up and they were as much a part of his family as his own children.

Just as one course flowed into the next, and wine flowed from Dennis's carafe into our glasses (and to Nadiya's credit, she stopped drinking midway into the meal), the talk about their work in Morocco and Egypt flowed into asking about what happened soon after early modern humans left Africa for the first time. It was a more exciting topic than usual. The day before, when I saw Harold and Dennis flitting across the Place de la Liberté, *Science* had published the work of a vast international team of scientists on the successful nuclear DNA sequencing taken from Neandertal bone samples. Comparing it with DNA from a representative sampling of living humans from different parts of the world, they discovered that living people from Europe and Asian ancestries carried 1 percent to

4 percent Neandertal DNA. (This has recently been revised, with more research and a larger growing comparative database of both Neandertal and modern human genomes, to around 1.5 percent to 2.1 percent on average; with more ongoing research, this number may fluctuate in the future.)

"The new DNA study is no surprise," Harold said. "It is the much more logical possibility—that early modern humans and Neandertals interbred—and this study confirms it. The Middle East was the most likely place where interbreeding took place. But it's still exciting because this confirms it."

The new work in genetics on the Neandertal genome project added exciting possibilities in archaeological research. In some ways, it felt like it was surpassing what the field archaeologists could offer about the human past, but in fact, genetics and field archaeology are beautifully complementary. Genetics helps the archaeologist prove or discard certain theories about human migration patterns and mingling and even sets a time frame to when these things took place. But genetics can never re-create the ancient living context or the past behaviors. Field archaeology is still the only method that can do these things. Genetics also can't answer how or why Neandertals and modern humans got it on.

Aurelie brought out dessert, one of her signature creations, crème brulée topped with fresh raspberries just plucked from the kitchen garden. Dennis topped my glass off with enough red wine to pair with this delicacy. We all ordered espressos. Dessert was silent. We were too busy savoring the motivation all hominids have for living: food, drink, and good company in a warm, congenial place.

By the time we wrapped up lunch, Harold and Dennis had invited Nadiya and me to visit some of the Neandertal sites they'd already excavated, Roc de Marsal and Pech de l'Azé, when they returned from Morocco at the month's end. They also promised to have us over for dinner at Camp Carsac when some of the team began to arrive in early June.

A MONTH LATER, Nadiya and I climbed the rise on which stood the cave of Roc de Marsal, prime real estate in any epoch with its lush rolling hills, cliffs, and verdant valley below. I suddenly heard the slow, singular slide in time to see a thick-bodied *couleuvre*, a large black snake, slip off the path to my left. I tried to stifle a shiver and concentrated more fervently on staying on the narrow footpath. The *couleuvres* were still waking up from their winter slumber after an overlong, cool spring, and they moved like bleary-eyed people who had yet to drink their morning coffee. Less cautious than usual, sometimes they just blundered across a footpath, when during other times of the warm season they were shy and invisible. Then a hawk took flight from a branch right over our heads and the mood shifted again. Now it felt as if the ancient keepers of the earth and sky were here to take us fully back in time. As perfect timing would have it, we looked up and arrived at the foot of the hilltop cave and the long-ago residence of the valley's Neandertals.

Roc de Marsal is a Middle Paleolithic site north of Sarlat and Carsac and just south of Les Eyzies that was occupied by Neandertals around 80,000 to 40,000 years ago. The first human we saw was Harold, standing at the cave mouth and wearing that quintessential field hat, the Indiana Jones–style fedora. Standing farther inside, we saw he was chatting with two French colleagues, Guillaume Guerin, a physicist from the University of Bordeaux, and Alain Turq, who is a chief curator at the Musée National de Préhistoire in Les Eyzies. Deeper inside the small cave, Dennis was in full swing explaining the site in French to two amateur archaeology aficionados from the Loire who were here on a hiking holiday and who had made prehistory stops like this one all along their trek.

Nadiya and I joined them just as Dennis explained that during the past seven dig seasons the team had located thirty distinct fire hearths. This was proof positive that there was fire use during certain periods of its occupancy by Neandertals, but not during all the times they occupied Roc de Marsal. In fact, what they found at first defied the modern mind's logic. The fire hearths showed up only in strata connected to periods of warm climate. "There are no hearths in the strata during cold climatic periods," Dennis said, "telling us that the Neandertals could use fire, such as that gathered from a lightning strike during a spring storm, but not make it. This might explain why we see no fire hearths when the weather was particularly cold, a time you would imagine fire would be made if one could. But we don't think they could."

This picture turned out to be consistent with what they found when they were digging at Pech de l'Azé, the site near where we all now lived on the road between Sarlat and Carsac. They found evidence for fire use there as well, including evidence for controlling it and using it in discrete spaces, along with the accompanying burnt animal bone and flint tools in the hearths, but they found no evidence that Neandertals had actually made it.

We were all confused. How could you discern fire-making from fire-using? Harold had now stepped toward us to join our group. "The thing is," answered Dennis, "there's no evidence for fire when it was really cold. The fire strata at Roc de Marsal were during warm periods and warm periods had more lightning strikes." You just don't get lightning in the depth of a really cold winter. "The same is true at Pech de l'Azé. The correlation of the evidence for fire use at Neandertal sites and times when natural fire access was high [warm periods] is high."

Dennis paused. Harold finished the thought.

"We're pretty much on our own in thinking it was from lightning strikes, that Neandertals were controlling fire, just not making it."

I shivered. Cold winters would be when you really missed a warm fire, no matter how good roasting meat on a spit smells in the warm months. I thought about the cold winters they'd endured and how tough they had to have been. The experience of a warming fire was one of our most archetypal human images of comfort and home, especially in winter. I also realized that I had to work to suspend rampant ideas I had absorbed from the popular imagination that cast Neandertals as either entirely different from us or exactly like us, but that did not consider the entire range of evidence that supported or negated the image. What was wrong with them being exactly who they were, not better or worse, maybe different, maybe similar? Let the data speak first, not our romantic notions of being human! I was pulled briefly into this Harold-cheering headspace until I saw the look of sheer magic on Nadiya's face.

This was all new to her, and her Thai upbringing hadn't raised her with the same Victorian inheritance that European and North American kids got. To her, Neandertals were wondrous beings who had their own modus operandi. Rather than shiver, her Thai mind was also contemplating the potential of a spring fire, with new spring shoots and newly born fawns and baby boar to roast. I had learned that my friend was as much a city-bound hospitality expert (she had run hotels in Chang Mai, Bangkok, and Paris before arriving at this little rural outpost) as she was as a lifelong forager. When she was a child, she and her grandfather would leave the city and go into the surrounding forest and hills to gather wild foods to bring home and cook fresh over the flame.

Harold and Dennis brought me back to the present. They were now riffing about the coldest periods during the European Middle Paleolithic, which occurred around 120,000 to 130,000 years ago and again around 60,000 to 70,000 years ago. These were prime periods of Neandertal occupation and the temperatures could drop to around ten degrees Fahrenheit colder than today. If someone had the ability to make fire, they sure as heck would have. But they didn't. It's just not there in the strata.

Roc de Marsal was also famous for what had been called an intentional burial of a Neandertal infant. Back in the 1960s the amateur French archaeologist Jean Lafille excavated the site, and he came across the fossilized remains of a Neandertal child who died at around the age of two or three. The child was buried facedown in what looked like a pit. It was an exciting find and the infant and the sediment around which it had been found were carefully removed and taken to a lab in Paris for analysis. The find was viewed by both Lafille and by Harold's mentor, François Bordes, as evidence for intentional burial among Neandertals. After that, Roc de Marsal's infant became one of the most-cited cases for evidence of such behavior. But when Harold and the team reopened the site, studying the prior excavation records, data, and finds and applying new techniques and further excavation to the cave, two critical perspectives arose.

They discovered ancient subterranean water channels running through the rock in the cave that created holes and grooves throughout. "We went back to the original descriptions," Dennis said, "looking at field notes and very basic information. At the time, no one questioned that Neandertals buried their dead. But when you do look at the description, there's something that contradicts this, like digging a hole. The skeleton's hole was continuous with the sediment layer around it, therefore it wasn't a hole."

The Neandertal infant had been found in one of the water channels and it appeared that a hole had not been dug for him and that he had not been intentionally placed there. He was facedown and his limbs were splayed in awkward positions, an unusual orientation in comparison with human burials across time and space, which added to the sense that maybe this was an accidental burial; perhaps the infant fell into the channel and drowned or was placed in a natural grave and left there for natural forces to finish the work.

"Thinking that Neandertals buried their dead," offered Dennis, "makes them more human, more like us, so we like this idea. But there's not enough evidence to prove it. It's a case of emotion overriding science, which, however warm and fuzzy the feelings, must remain neutral and stick to the facts."

If Neandertals buried their dead, not only does it make them more human, as in like us—because we're the ones defining being "more human"—but also it offers us one aspect of their life not directly linked to simple physical survival. All the other issues archaeologists look at—fire, technology, diet, group size, even symbolic thought and language—have at their root physical survival. Burial is the one topic that transcends this and moves into more nonphysical, intangible areas of being human.

Burial also triggers a strong emotional response in us moderns, both scientist and layperson alike.

I recall when I first read about the flower burial of a Neandertal at Shanidar Cave in Iraq when I was nineteen years old, in an undergraduate anthropology course at the University of Colorado. I was reading that chapter late at night and it electrified me, thinking about the wonder of Neandertal burial. *They were just like us!* My hominid brain defaulted to this very thought that troubled Harold so much. But there's a reason this happens. I felt a deep emotional link. My heart, not my mind, was doing the thinking. I had turned directly to my emotions and connected as a family member to these long-gone cousins.

Years later, new investigations found that the flower burial was likely erroneous. It turned out that the flower pollens were probably not the remains of ancient bouquets laid on a grave of a loved one, but pollens possibly carried into the cave by bees or other insects, or the activity of seed- and flower-gathering rodents similar to gerbils, the Persian *jird*. While the science calls the modern mind's romantic image into question, I still found that I was reluctant to give up that original warm flush of emotion and connection I had felt long ago *because* it was born of the emotions, not the intellect. I think this happens more than people are willing to admit, even among scientists. No one gets so up in arms about bear evolution or ant evolution, even though they both shed a lot of light on us, simply because we don't see them as close enough in the tree of life to be "like us." As soon as you draw near a hominid, people get emotional.

It is hard not to connect directly and emotionally with people who buried their dead. It tells us right away, in shorthand, that they too felt the raw emotions of loss and the bite of being human, vulnerable, and mortal. This emotional connection makes it harder to stand back and say yes, but what does the evidence really seem to be saying? For that reason, all the more, we need constant vigilance in this emotionally invested work. It's a slippery slope when working with emotions and defending the integrity of the scientific method.

Humor helps.

The year before, the actor and filmmaker Alan Alda had visited Roc de Marsal to interview Harold, Shannon, and Dennis for his PBS special *The Human Spark*. With Harold's sense of humor stimulated by the great comic actor in the same place—a Neandertal site at that—I asked Dennis how the meeting went. "They hit it off immediately," he said.

"Can you give me an example?"

Harold overheard me asking and stepped in.

"We all went to the back part of the cave," Harold giggled, "and Alan sat down on a kind of shelf of sediment that was the leftover edge from where the block of sediment containing the Neandertal skeleton had been removed back in the 1960s. When he sat down, he crossed his legs so he had one foot sitting in the exact spot where the remains were found. I turned to him and said, 'Alan, I know you don't want to hear this at your age, but it looks to me like you've got one foot in the grave.'"

He busted out into laughter.

Having now been apprised of the off-camera jocularity, I wanted to see the official broadcast of the show. At one point, Alan asked the three, "Do you have a feeling for what essential thing differentiates us [from Neandertals]?" Shannon, Dennis, and Harold replied respectively: creativity to use resources differently; slightly more flexibility to adapt to different conditions; and language and symbolism that allowed large-scale communication.

Their answers addressed our particular *Homo sapiens* priority to carry more specialized innovations and ideas into the future, to pass them on through abstract communication that may have made the difference between us and our extinct cousins. It was less of difference than of the degree to which we dived into the more abstract cognitive world we shared with them and compared with them. For some reason, early modern humans took symbolic thinking into different, more evident directions. It doesn't mean it wasn't there with Neandertals, but that they didn't leave evidence for it as we do—that they didn't make it as material.

Soon I was going to also learn that words such as *creative* and *flexible* as well as "symbolic" really depended on how you framed things. Neandertals were all these things but in ways different enough that we're potentially blind to seeing them as easily.

Dennis later told me that he had elaborated on this very theme that day. He saw the difference between Neandertals and early modern humans as a difference in the need to communicate with others. Neandertals lived in smaller, more known groups whereas early modern humans were forming larger groups and occupying larger territories, meeting unknown people more frequently. Both communicating differently, and presenting oneself physically in a different fashion—such as with body markings and personal adornments with tribal and individual statements—may have become more necessary to navigate this universe. Even we more recent humans tend to really wear symbols of our individuality or affiliation only when we are navigating territory where we will encounter people from outside the family or close-knit inner circle. Just reflect on religious group, school, or sports team symbols and when you want to wear those icons most.

"As anthropologists we can see that when you examine human behavior across a range of different types of societies, from very simple foragers to city dwellers, and different levels of complexity in between, we see that one of the major things that changes with larger and more sedentary populations is the need for more complex ways to manage interpersonal and intergroup interactions—changes in social organization and communication. This requires different and more complex ways of organizing people in groups, and organizing subgroupings within larger groups." It comes down to how we use symbols and language to deal with this change in group size and population growth.

"A major factor in all this," he said, "is the place of the individual within the group. In very small-scale forager societies, an individual is interacting with a very small number of other people, a large percentage of whom are very closely related to [him or her]. There are no secrets between members of the group, every individual is overtly integral to the group, and there is a very strong sharing ethic—these factors strongly limit the need for symbolic behavior."

This most likely would have been the case for Neandertal groups. "By contrast," he added, "in larger and larger groups, the individual starts to disappear—it's easy for an individual identity to become lost in the masses of identities." He added that we're all hard-wired, a part of our collective primate inheritance, to assert our individual identities within the group. "In larger groups, this becomes more of an issue and the larger the group, the more work individuals have to put into asserting their identity and developing new ways to do this; symbolism is very effective for this."

But how did he see group size differences between Neandertals in Europe and the newer arriving early modern humans?

"From the archaeological record," he replied. "We know that modern human populations in Europe were around a magnitude larger than Neandertals'. There are around ten times the number of early modern human sites and these sites are much larger, in both area and in the quantities of stuff left there. In the Upper Paleolithic, groups had more people in them and there were more groups around. This would require changes in the way individuals interacted and the way groups interacted. For me, this easily explains the appearance of simple symbolic systems like personal ornamentation, mobiliary art, and cave art: it's about the *need* to develop more complex forms of communication." Neandertals didn't have that need.

That day in the cave at Roc de Marsal, Alan Alda concluded what the three archaeologists had just told him, "You might have had the beginnings of symbolism," with Neandertals, "but they wouldn't spread." It was there, but just not utilized. At least not visibly enough for us to find evidence of it in the physical archaeological record, and given what Dennis had told me, it was simply not *needed*. That's just it. The ability was there, but not the broad expression that you find with us. This was a perfect moment of truth because so often the debates are all-or-nothing, when the truth is in fact something more subtle and mingled.

Harold called this all-or-nothing contention the Neandertal pendulum, which swings between camps, with one end saying that Neandertals were like us and the other saying they were not like us. It is the trench that Jean-Jacques mentioned, only this image captures a whole spectrum of thought between these two extremes—even though it is the extremes that have affiliates who make the most noise, hence the all-or-nothing mood.

At one extreme are the staunch humanists and at the other end, the staunch scientists, and everyone—even the moderates in between—is debating fire, burial, language, symbolic thought, clothing, tools and technology, art, sex, group size, and relationships—the stuff that defines being human at its core. Any of them who want to publish or have a dialog with their colleagues find themselves, whether they like it or not, doing so on this spectrum.

The "humanists" tend to start with the position that Neandertals were human like us, which means full language, symbolic thought, art, and even ritual. These archaeologists (and others) seek evidence in the archaeological and genetic data to support this foundational assumption. It is an assumption so deep that when you speak to the humanists it is clear that to think otherwise—that Neandertals were not like us—verges on being seen as a simpleton, or worse, a racist.

The "scientists" start with the assumption that we know nothing from nothing and that so far Neandertals were definitely human, very smart, and technically sophisticated, but that still they were not quite like us. This is because so far the evidence looks iffy for language, for *sapiens*-like symbolic thought, art, and ritual. These are heated debates, often taken personally and sometimes with name-calling implying a range of accusations from racism to bad science.

Ironically, our romance with the Neandertals, when reflected in the media, seems spared this pendulum debate but it's an illusion because we the public are more humanists than scientists. We love the Neandertals and want to see them as being like us. We feed the human desire for origin stories, just as Jean-Jacques observed. *Once upon a time* is deeply engrained in us, whether it is with Cinderella or the infant of Roc de Marsal.

Is one camp right and the other wrong? I don't think so. I think storytelling stimulates the possibilities and defines the natural state of this work. I think it is a very human trait to involve emotions. But I am also profoundly aware that it is an undercurrent, a strong one, and in immersing myself into the subject matter, it is a current I must always be aware of. "You have to try and remain a scientist," Dennis told me, "and keep with the facts as much as it might be an emotional issue."

This mix is why I also seek out the perspective of the truffle hunter, the farmer, and the local who has lived here all his or her life. For starters, here there is no debate about whether evolution is a reality or not. The science is clear and accepted. In fact, with all this knowledge, most locals actually aren't saying one thing or another about the Neandertals and us. They are simply feeling a profoundly deep and, to them, magical but very different past. If they have any bias, it is that the Neandertals lived a fully immersed life in nature and did not alter their environment as we have. Their group sizes were too small to do so and their technology sophisticated but not to the point of allowing them to do anything other than hunting enough food for the moment. That does not reflect on their technology but on their choice for how to exist in the world. It is actually an indictment of us modern humans, who do not exist in balance in the world and who bend our technology to more than having enough to eat and afe shelter.

The local farmers and hunters are well aware of how hard life in nature was, but at the same time they look at the world we have altered so fundamentally and the environmental crises we've created, and they don't have too many good things to say for *Homo sapiens*. Except that after a day of gathering mushrooms, life sure is sweet when you return home and sauté them in butter and garlic and toss them with eggs and pour a local red, tear off a crust of chewy bread, and savor them with loved ones around a fire. If you asked them what it is to be human, it would be loving to hunt, gather, eat, sleep, make love, and sit by the fire. If so, then Neandertals were pretty much just like us except that we messed it up with more helpings of symbolic thought. Symbolic thought has gotten us into our current mess in the world.

Take Bernadette, an octogenarian friend I made through my many visits to Sarlat's market day and our ritual meeting over coffee after we'd each finished our food shopping. She talks only about deep stuff, her favorite being philosophy and mysticism. If you want to talk about retirement plans or health issues, she'll tell you something like she once she told me, "I don't talk to dead people anymore. *Je refuse*." She did this as she dropped a cube of sugar in her coffee and stirred. "Dead people are people who don't see that when this cube is dissolved, has lost its body, the sugar is still there, everywhere in the coffee. Just because you can't see something anymore doesn't mean the energy isn't still there. It's basic science. Einstein would agree." It was also her way of saying she doesn't suffer people who just fall into a routine and do what is expected of them, who don't think beyond their conditioning.

One day in the 2014 summer season, after working at La Ferrassie all week and enjoying our one day off, Saturday, I was sitting down to coffee with Bernadette during the weekly market. Her first question was, "What have you found, what have you learned so far, at La Ferrassie?"

I told her about all the animal bones and flint tools, that the concentration of stuff was more when we left the Neandertal strata and were digging into later occupations from the early modern humans, the Cro-Magnons, who'd also lived at La Ferrassie. I told her about the eight to nine possible different layers of different occupations. I told her about the raging debates concerning burial and fire and language.

She listened, she nodded, she thought for a while, and then she leaned forward with that cutting look similar to the one she'd had when she mentioned the living dead.

"Now I'll tell you what I see in all this. I see that Neandertals were more of nature, more in nature, and communicated without needing to speak the way we do. And they were not materialistic. That's why *Homo sapiens* sites have so much stuff, not because we have culture or are smarter. It's because we're hoarders, we're materialistic, and we never seem to have enough. They had enough. We're *Homo materialensis*. Look at all the debris we left then and all the debris we're leaving now. To what purpose? They were content to live in the present and not meddle so much with the rest."

*Voilà.* She sat back. Pleased. Other than market day to food shop and meet for a coffee or spending time in a friend's garden, she preferred the company of her books. She was presently reading Henri Corbin's very thick philosophical interpretations of Iranian mysticism in the Middle Ages. But what she had just stated was the way many of the prehistory-impassioned locals think, though I have to say, she cut to the quick with far less romance than most. But as much as one might want to see this as romanticism or escapism, she and others, such Didier and Fabien, two of the volunteers who worked with us, have actually put their finger on the very problem that may lead us current humans down the path of extinction long before we've had a chance to be on the planet as long as Neandertals had been, perhaps 400,000 years. At the most, we've been around for 160,000 to 200,000 years.

"WHAT YOU CAN'T deny about Neandertals," Harold concluded that day in the cave at Roc de Marsal in 2010, "is that they were extremely smart, made quality stone tools, and took care of each other. What's hard to show is if they had language, if they had symbols, if they wore clothing, if they made fire, and that they had burials. What Neandertals have the potential to do is show us that they're just like us except without [our] culture. What does that look like, to be human without culture?"

This way of saying it has gotten him into some twists with other paleoanthropologists because he doesn't always clarify what he means by *human* and *culture*, by which he just means *modern* human and *modern* culture. I'd heard him enough times, most in fact, referring to Neandertals as humans too, just different from *modern* humans—which genetics and the archaeological record largely show—but human nonetheless.

And when he used the word *culture*, he used it in the way cultural anthropologists do, to refer to contemporary cultures, and to Culture, the whole abstract world inside our heads that is saturated and dripping with language and symbol-making as also the product of modern human beings. Culture in these terms may be this messy, intangible survival tool inherent in all archaic humans, but that early modern humans may have tripped more into and opted to amp up outwardly and with material manifestations, toward manipulating our world more and surviving in it with new adaptations.

Culture also happens to be the adaptive strategy that once improved our survival odds and that is now the source of our survival problems, from warfare and famine to pollution, global warming, and genetically manipulated food sources, to those only motivated only by profit no matter what. The jury is out on us. But amping up on culture—the human version of it with all its symbols, languages, abstract concepts, and material products—is no better and no worse than any other adaptive strategy that members of our genus *Homo* have tapped into, and like other strategies, it very well may have reached its optimization point. The Neandertals had theirs and after a good long run, went extinct. What's to say we're not on that same path?

Other anthropologists, especially the physical anthropologists and the primatologists, tend to use the term *culture* more broadly to define any type of learned behavior that also is a part of shared group norms. This meaning can be applied to other social mammals, not only chimpanzees and us. This is where the misunderstanding arises. Harold always means modern human culture when he says "culture," which is a very recent development in human evolution, even if the capacity was there or expressions of it took on different, less materially obvious forms.

One Scotch Time during a predinner session of ruminating at Camp Carsac, when I waxed poetic about the creative spirit in all humanity, both Neandertals and us, Harold said, "That's fine, but the bottom line is this, all nature expects is that we reproduce and multiply. That's what it's all about, shagging and begetting."

Unless you're a single-celled creature, it is pretty much about shagging, begetting, and multiplying; extending yourself into the gene pool and allowing new possible genetic variations on a theme to emerge in the future toward dancing with survival versus extinction, all the while morphing the species into something more adapted to the new set of circumstances.

"Other than that, nature's pretty much neutral about all the rest," he added while swirling the ice in his glass.

# CHEZ LES NEANDERTALS

FEW DAYS AFTER visiting Roc de Marsal with Nadiya that first spring in 2010, I was back in Carsac. Harold was initiating me into my very first Scotch Time. He handed me a scotch and soda on the rocks as Dennis opened a bottle of red wine from the Pecharmant, a splendid little wine region in the heart of Bergerac to the west that makes Bordeaux-like wines that are almost never exported.

He set the opened vintage on Harold's kitchen counter, underneath a wall arrayed with high-quality stainless steel chef's knives on a magnet mount. It was museum worthy, much like the displays of flint blades I'd seen in the national prehistory museum in Les Eyzies. Clearly, Harold's passion was blade technology, period, whether it was Neandertal or contemporary. He loved to cook, and tonight he was cooking for the ten of us who had arrived at Camp Carsac. Another twenty were due in the next few days. It was a rare moment of quiet and calm.

In Sarlat, five miles north, the peak summer rental season was building momentum as the burgeoning swell of the region's 2.5 million annual visitors arrived. Nadiya managed several holiday rentals so was not able to join us. I doubted I would see her at all for the rest of my stay, which was nearing its end. With summer's swell came higher prices, and my modest writer's life had to shift camp soon to less pricey pastures.

But for now, life was simple and sweet. Drinks in hand, Dennis gave me a tour of the place. We began with the old barn. The lab was on the first level and the upper loft level had been converted into several places for the dig directors to sleep. Outside, between Harold's house and the barn, was a space large enough for two water closets and two reasonably private shower stands. That was when I saw someone's humor in the Lascaux-styled bison, deer, horses, hand stencils, and abstract symbols painted inside the toilet stalls; plus the penciled-in shagging mammoths, to Harold's point about nature, just above the toilet paper dispenser.

We went down the slight slope to the backyard, enjoying the expanse of cornfield to our right that swept to Carsac's beautiful golden sandstone twelfth-century Romanesque church. Local lore said that the church was built over a ritual gathering place of Druids in the old oak forest during the Iron Age some 2,500 years ago, right there at the transept. The magic of this land does not cease and the crew gazed at this Druidic site each morning over coffee and each night after dinner. They also awoke to its bells ringing every morning at seven.

The handful of crew who had trickled in early were pitching their tents and preparing the outdoor kitchen and dining space. One was seated at a pit full of blocks of raw flint, *clack, clack, clacking* and honing his flintknapping skills. Each time his hammer, a round river rock, hit the flint, it gave off a pleasing acoustic ping. We were in a parenthesis of pleasing acoustic experiences. A red-breasted European robin suddenly lit into his territorial song and the aural universe was complete.

Beyond the flint pile was a stand of bamboo that had grown vigorously because it stood next to the wash station, where all the sediment was wet-screened before being dried, sorted, catalogued, analyzed, and stored.

The backyard, the farmer's old field, was quite long and wide and seemed to lie in disuse because it was on the edge of an old swamp, but

Harold had effectively repurposed it for his camp in Carsac. Before the Dordogne River had been rerouted a few hundred meters farther away, this land always flooded. Now it only did if the rains were so heavy as to overflow the Enéa Creek that swept past at the farthest end of the field. I noticed a brown horse grazing there, a welcome visitor from the neighbors across the road. Their horse kept the grass low. In another three days, that part of the yard would become a tent city *avec cheval.*

Nearest the house, the crew were setting up the outdoor kitchen and covering it with tarps, that they tied and extended from the old tobacco barn's roof. Nearby two apple trees were beginning to swell with fruit and the promise of apple pie, applesauce, and Newtonian physics, depending on where you pitched your tent.

The brown horse wasn't the only four-legged resident courtesy of the neighbors. Gary the dog earned his keep by devouring the apples as they fell and clearing the paths from the risk of hominid ankles twisting when carrying heavy bags of sediment to the wash station. It was a self-sufficient setup, a peaceable kingdom. Soon, the red-breasted European robin would feed her newly hatched family here, too, picking off our crumbs to feed to the tweeting mouths, enchanting us.

Dennis and I retired to the front garden near the road and the open kitchen door as Harold began dinner. I peeked in to see him searing whole chicken breasts and giving chopping and cleaning orders to his excavation-crew-turned-sous-chefs.

Birdsong surrounded us.

To our right jutted a chalky cliff wall, the pan-regional landscape feature that attracted so many ancient inhabitants, from Neandertals to Celts to us. The more recent humans to make Carsac home, from the Middle Ages to the present, had built stately homes right up against the cliff wall, of the same yellow stone. I could just see the neighbor, the one with the horse and Gary, weeding her cliff-side garden, a white goat following her and nabbing morsels in her wake. Harold suddenly stuck his head out the kitchen door.

"Do you like snails?"

"I do." When I'd peeked into the kitchen, I'd seen his supply of *escargots à la Bordelaise* on the counter next to the Pecharmant and my mouth had watered.

"I don't," Dennis inserted quickly. "You can eat them. I won't. I mean, I like butter and garlic. I find snails are just a vehicle for the butter and the garlic. They're like erasers. I don't need to eat an eraser. But garlic bread is good."

He reminded me of what the evidence seems to indicate for early modern humans, who preferred hunting and eating the big game animals, such as bison and deer, and only began scavenging for shellfish and smaller fry when the herds declined due to climatic shifts. Maybe they too complained to each other around the evening fire that snails were a poor substitute for beefier tastes?

As Dennis gave his culinary rant, Harold pretended to ignore him and gave orders from the doorway to a nearby graduate student to get to work laying out the frozen herb butter–stuffed snails on a cookie sheet that he'd covered with a thick layer of sea salt. She executed his instructions as if she were still at the dig site and soon snails decorated the metal sheet in a grid pattern with scientific precision. He then went back inside and began preparing the sauce that would go on top of the now grilling chicken.

He sautéed mushrooms, caramelized onions, deglazed the pan with vermouth, and thickened the whole composition with cream. A pot of water boiled away and into it he threw fresh tagliatelle. Where had this man learned to cook? (And who cares if it's high fat? The Neandertals and early moderns never worried about fat and fat is good for the big brains we possess, I justified.) It seemed that in his backstory, cooking and archaeology—cutting-edge technology—were intertwined; one made the other possible.

Harold grew up in California and Arizona. He recalled being around seven years old when he devoured a book in his parents' collection, *The*

*March of Archaeology* by Kurt W. Marek, on the history of archaeology. Soon thereafter, as a Boy Scout, he tried to make flint tools and to make fire with flint, but he didn't know one could do this as a living until he attended the University of Arizona.

He took so many anthropology courses that the administration told him he had taken too many. That didn't stop him. After a time of working as a manager of a pizza parlor in California, Harold returned to Arizona for graduate school. He specialized in Paleolithic archaeology and wrote his dissertation on lithic industries at Tabun, a cave in northern Israel. He never stopped cooking. Moreover, his skills as pizza parlor manager translated well into running a dig, from balancing budgets to coordinating the feeding of a large group three times a day to making sure everyone pulled his or her weight.

Dennis also had childhood recollections rooted in his love for prehistory. He'd spent many of his childhood summers on his grandparents' southern Alberta ranch, near the Badlands, and fondly recalled looking for dinosaur bones and archaeological remains. That's when he knew archaeology was it for him, though he also made a living as a builder, another skill that translates well into running a dig. He focused his doctorate on the Levallois technique, a pan-Paleolithic stone-making technique most particularly associated with Neandertal stone tool industries from the Middle Paleolithic. It was only natural to ask the two men how they had met.

"Harold's one of the people you have to talk to if you want to do anything with Levallois," Dennis said. Ten years earlier Dennis had called Harold in Philadelphia from Vancouver and they hit it off so well talking about old stones that soon thereafter, "Harold invited me to join him for that year's dig season." In the short time I'd spent with them, I'd already noted that their dynamic was bizarrely smooth. They anticipated each other's concerns, issues, and, most strangely, jokes. Harold lowered the heat under the sauce and drained the pasta and then stood in the kitchen doorway and listed the reasons he liked Dennis so much.

"Dennis has a good sense of humor, he builds furniture, and he's mature and responsible." He paused and then exclaimed, "Oh my god, it's so easy when Dennis is around because he knows how to do a lot of things. You have to be able to do a lot of things to work on a dig."

At that moment Cécile Bordes walked into the garden. This was the first time I had set eyes on her and little did I know how happily bound up my life would become with hers in her own peaceable kingdom. I already liked her. It might have been because of the way she sassed Harold and treated him as her little brother—which essentially, he was.

Having grown up the daughter of two of the most famous French archaeologists of all time, she'd learned early that if she was going to be herself, beyond her parents' and grandparents' reputations—the latter being famous artists from Bordeaux—she'd have to be strong. She made her own life in the United States, Peru, and Australia. She pursued her interests in art and interiors, especially East Asian textiles, paintings, and sculptures, the aesthetic that attracted her the most. It was only recently that she had packed up her life abroad and returned to her own origins.

"I've always been strong willed," she confessed, and that helped. "I come from a family of strong-willed women, on both sides." Her own passions fell into the world of art and she was both an accomplished fine artist and a gifted interior decorator. She liked nothing more than to give Harold hell over his sense of, or really lack of, aesthetics and décor.

I wanted to hear everything she had to say. No one got away with anything when she was around, especially not Harold.

"Harold, when are you going to add anything other than beige to the dig house's interior?"

"I like beige," Harold defended cheerfully, pointing to his beige worker's shirt and beige work trousers. In Morocco, the local crew had nicknamed him al-Bahia, "the Radiant and Cheerful One." Not even attacks on his beloved beige were going to make him less *bahia*.

"But beige is so blah!" she retorted.

"Beige goes with everything. I match the house." Harold turned on his heels and quickly returned to the kitchen to check on the perfectly beige snails that were ready to be taken out of the oven for the first course.

Cécile declined dinner but in those first moments with her I pondered how she lived just down the road, and that down the other end of the same extended village street was the cemetery where her parents were buried, covered in flint stone tools made by admiring students. In the middle were Harold's dig house and the Delpeyrats' restaurant, and up the hill and a bit to the left, the original Chez les Neandertals, Pech de l'Azé.

Still, quietly and happily, I absorbed it all, overwhelmed by the reality that the village was an open-air prehistory museum and that Harold was adding the next living layer of legacy to it. And I got to be here and partake of it. And eat his snails and drink his scotch.

Little did I know at the time that I would return as a crew member and time-traveling journalist. Little could I imagine that a few years from now Cécile's stone barn would become my home away from home, that I would live at one end of her garden across from her family house, that I would fall as much in love with her as with prehistory, that each day I would enjoy crossing the garden and greeting three cats and two dogs to enter the main house in order to use the water closet and the shower. Little could I dream that even the loud bullfrog who lived in Cécile's garden would get to know me and come to greet me at the gate when I came home each night. It was truly a magical realm, including the frog of fairytales—only this time, the star prince was the Neandertal with his formidable brow ridge, larger brain, and charming wit.

HAROLD CALLED US all to the table in the garden. The sun had set and a camping light cast a soft glow upon the faces of the crew. Arrayed before us was what the hungry team declared normal daily fare: herb butter snails, braised chicken in mushroom cream sauce with tagliatelle, sautéed asparagus in Harold's secret cheese sauce, a garden-fresh salad with

Harold's secret dressing (all his sauces were "secret"—he refused to divulge), and a dessert of cassis sorbet and chocolate chip ice cream.

The conversation wove between archaeology, music, food, and humorous good cheer, often at the expense of one of the diners. A sole bird—that red-breasted European robin—sang a melody into the evening that soared across the cornfield and ricocheted back at us from the church's limestone walls.

After dinner, Dennis drove me back to Sarlat. That night, I began writing like a demon, inspired for an assigned magazine feature about Harold and his work on Neandertals, one that I had pitched and sold while Harold and Dennis were in Morocco. The whole spring season had been wrapped in the uncanny magic of cause and effect, of important and rare doors suddenly opening. In that late hour, in the back of my mind, I dared think to myself—and only myself—how very much I loved this topic, this life, and if only somehow, please, I could do more of it. It seemed so immense a pipe dream, so impossible, that I kept this thought there in my head, in that deep fold where our dreams get stored, for safekeeping, and quiet, earnest, crazy hoping without a clue as to how it could possibly ever happen. And there it stayed.

Until.

The dream slipped out from its quiet protective cave nearly three years later, in early January of 2013, unannounced, on a sleepy gray Sunday morning in southern New Jersey. I had sent Harold an email with a ranting op-ed piece I'd written, taking to task all the constant research on Neandertals that appeared weekly in the press, most of it published too soon. I wanted him to cast a quick eye over it to make sure I hadn't committed any grave errors. It being Sunday, I anticipated that sometime during the workweek I'd hear back from him. Instead, he wrote back immediately.

The op-ed piece was fine, he said, no errors. Moreover, "I've been thinking," he wrote. "Would you be interested in writing a book on the Neandertals?" He went on to explain that he'd been meaning to bring this up ever since the feature I'd written about him had come out. He liked both the way I handled the material and how it addressed an issue people constantly raised with him: Was he going to write a book about the Neandertals?

"I'm too busy," he explained, "but feel it's important. Would you be interested? If so, it would be a good idea to come to France for this summer's dig at La Ferrassie."

There's only one answer to that question. I sent my affirmative and from there began planning, arranging, squirreling away any extra income into my new Neandertal Fund to make it so.

A few months later, in late spring 2013, then the next year for the summer of 2014, and again the summer of 2015 during the post-dig assessments of all the data gathered in the five dig seasons, I found myself the upstairs–downstairs journalist-crew-anthropologist folded into this camp of some thirty quirky, very opinionated, very international, and very bright archaeologists and students as they worked into one of the great mysteries of the human journey on earth.

And only then, neck-deep in Neandertal dirt and all this business, did I truly begin to realize just how complicated this subject was going to be. The new advances in genetics were accelerating the rate at which new findings were coming to light and each week could rewrite or add new chapters to the story. And any given week you could find news in the press about Neandertals, not only from the geneticists but also from the paleoanthropologists who were finding more people interested in their work. And almost all of what was published was nevertheless uncertain, could change next week. Plus, this topic was rife with schisms, camps, and agendas. This wasn't limited to individuals, but also extended to the cultures where the research took place. Nations competed for being the first and oldest in just about anything exciting that defined being human: first for the emergence of *Homo sapiens*, first for the earliest Neandertals, last for the last Neandertals (a first of its own kind), first for symbolic art, and on and on.

What a weird and contentious field.

What had I gotten myself into?

The pendulum was in full swing and at times I had to dodge to miss its momentum. But I did, because I decided the interesting story was not the dramas driving the swing but the actual material that lay all around and beyond it.

As I worked as a member of the team at La Ferrassie, as I met specialists in the field, and as I gathered with locals in the cafés, their stories suspended the black-and-white pendulum and wove a tapestry of color and life that embraced all the possibilities and the single honest truth: that we're all human and all in this together, and it's messy. Welcome to the family.

FAST-FORWARDING THREE YEARS since that spring when I saw Harold while buying shallots, we were again sitting in the front garden at Camp Carsac shooting the Neandertal breeze. I was having another Harold-made scotch and soda on the rocks with him and Dennis, who stuck to red wine. There was the same calming birdsong, the deep green evening air, and the neighbor tilling her garden, this time keeping her three dogs in check, including Gary. I didn't see the goat. The Romanesque church of Carsac anchored us nearby as usual, giving time-depth to dinner as well as the conversation.

In a few days, the other team directors would arrive, Shannon and Vera from Germany, and Paul from Boston. Alain would join us almost daily at La Ferrassie, which was close to his office in Les Eyzies. The tent village in the garden was expanding into a tent town. True to tradition, Cécile walked down from her street at the other end, this time with one of her two dogs in tow, an eight-month-old puppy she'd just adopted.

"Her name is Hanoi," she said proudly, "but did you know, if she was going to be a boy, I was going to call him Harold *deux*."

It was a long legacy in a small place, but like a lot of promising archaeological sites, its small breadth hid a far greater depth below. All this, these people and their beloved Neandertals, were a strata of a chain of being and belonging that was as much a part of the story of the Neandertals as their bones, stones, and genes.

That evening in 2013, at the beginning of the second-to-last season of digging at La Ferrassie, the air was thick with anticipation. While finding another skeleton was unlikely (but unspoken and hoped for), there was so much being found—things the original excavators had no technology even to imagine—that would still help us re-create the world of 90,000 to 37,000 years ago, that it could very well take us closer to an answer to our mysteries and deeper into new and unexpected questions.

I soon found myself in my favorite place, that trench with my feet planted 90,000 years in the past. In that place I would fall into the most Zen-like state of mind, focused fully on the careful work in the earth and wanting to uncover the record without disturbing it. It always surprised me when Dennis would call from above that it was time for a break, that what felt like a few minutes had been a few hours.

I climbed out of the layers of the past and into the strata of the present and went and poured myself a cup of what Harold called his special cowboy coffee. The dark liquid flowed thick, like Turkish coffee, out of the saucepan set on a single gas burner. I took a moment to soak my surroundings in, my senses heightened due to the active meditation in the trench from which I'd just emerged. It was an irony to be so fully present in the now when also time-traveling thousands of years into the past.

The height of summer had arrived with a semi-humid heat that inundated the limestone cave, hills, and evergreen oak forest. The heat had also released the wild aromatic herbs growing low on the earth all around us. I picked out mint right away, then thyme, more quietly respiring its perfume. From above, that dark green forest looked smooth and unified, but once under leaf cover, it hid infinite micro-worlds where even villages a mere three to four kilometers away from each other spoke their own version of Occitan or Patois (a mix of French and Occitan). Micro-communities with their own words, phrases, and pronunciations. While cell phone reception remained impossible unless one climbed to the top of the hill and hunted for the right spot, we were an international hotspot and I heard Occitan from the local prehistory volunteers, plus French, Spanish, English, Dutch, Farsi, Portuguese, and Italian swirling in the air and mingling with the herbs in an aromatic United Nations of the Paleolithic.

In one corner, Alain, Harold, Dennis, Paul, Vera, and Shannon were staring at a section of the excavated wall that joined their excavation with that of Peyrony's decades earlier. They were puzzling out what the natural story was here, working with incomplete documentation from the earlier excavation and letting Paul, Vera, and Alain lead the way toward reading the earth's own history book in the nature of the soil and stone lying next to each other. I overheard Alain say, "La Ferrassie is like a sweater that someone keeps unraveling each time you think you have knit it correctly."

Earlier in the year, Paul had taken a closer look at the foot of the adult female, known as La Ferrassie 2 or LAF2 (but to me as Madame La Ferrassie, which I also kept to myself), because her foot was encased in its original sediment. It actually had been held together by the only remaining sediment that was clearly associated with the skeletons from Peyrony's excavation. The skeleton presented a mystery: it had been found on a slant; the pit that once held the body was lower, in Levels 2 and 3, while the foot was securely associated with sediment layers in Level 5, a leap of about 20,000 years in one footstep.

They wanted to learn with what level she was really associated to understand if she was contemporary with any of the others. They were also working out their exact levels. Partly it was to seek solid evidence for whether these Neandertals had been intentionally buried, but this was a piece of a bigger picture. They also wanted to see if there were fire hearths to address the fire questions. Most of all, they wanted to suspend all preconceptions about anything and dig well and gather good evidence and see what patterns emerged. At best, this also allowed them to reconstruct the past environment and the context of the lives of the people who once lived here.

When the huddle about the wall dispersed, I caught up with Dennis, who stood near where the second excavation, led by Delporte in the 1970s, had taken place.

"Can you show me where each of the skeletons were found?" I asked.

"Skeletons one and two," *Monsieur et Madame*, "were found over there," he cheerfully obliged as he swept his arm out and pointed toward the far corner of the open rock shelf near the road where it met the wall of the present excavation.

"Three, four, five, and six were around here," he indicated a sweep moving closer to us like a stream flow. "And eight is right about here," he pointed downward with both hands, "near where we're standing."

I fidgeted with my feet, not wanting to disturb the dead, even though they were now mostly in labs and safe storage. I felt a pleasant chill work its way up my spine and down my arms: It came not only from where we stood, but from listening to Dennis, an expert at this, re-creating the ancient landscape.

"But wait a minute," I suddenly did some math, asking, "what about seven?" I'd read there were eight skeletons and Dennis had skipped seven.

"We all thought so, too, but it turns out number seven was mislabeled and was really the child from Le Moustier." That was another nearby famous Neandertal site up the Vézère River from here. This too happens and it was lucky someone caught the error and reclassified seven to his own special cave. Another chill.

I was getting used to the frequency, though not the intensity, of these chills, for I had been getting them a lot these days. There were days in 2013 and 2014 when I rode a bike borrowed from Nadiya along the old railroad-turned-bike path that connected Carsac to Sarlat. Known as the *piste cyclable,* it was a narrow path on a ridge that cut through green, thick forest in an astounding Middle Earth landscape that alternated between sheer vertical limestone cliff faces covered in native oak and prehistoric-looking ferns, and sudden drops into thick deciduous forest and the Enéa Creek below.

At one point on the *piste* were standing rock formations covered in moss that made me think of frozen giants, stunned into their eternal mineral forms by some master sorcerer or the rising sun. But that wasn't the place that made the hairs on my arm stand up straight and goose bumps rush all across my skin. This happened nearly every time I passed the part of the path where it narrowed and both sides were steep, one side rising up into a vertical craggy hill with secret openings overhead pursing their lips at the passersby from behind their leafy camouflage. Up there was where Neandertals had once occupied the caves of Pech de l'Azé, in different periods, from around 50,000 to 180,000 years ago. Sometimes, I'd get the chills before I registered I was about to pass, as if they didn't want to be ignored. I could feel energetic fingers reach out and lightly stroke my skin. It was a puissant place. I was soon to find out that it wasn't the only place in those hills, or just beyond them, where Neandertals lived that was to have that effect.

# THE INTERNATIONAL NEANDERTAL

T WENTY-EIGHT DEAD BODIES tumbled into a deep vertical cavern like beans tossed into a jar. What looked like mudslides had moved and shifted their bodies in the pit below, cave bear bones mingling with the human as well as a few fox, wolves, and lions, but no deer or other plant-loving animals. A coconut-sized reddish quartz hand ax, a rare and beautiful stone with no use and wear patterns, was the only stone tool found among all the bodies. The investigating Spanish team called it Excalibur to emphasize its odd mythic pull.

Found in the Sierra de Atapuerca in north-central Spain, those twenty-eight were carefully reconstructed from some 6,500 human fossils found in the cavern called Sima de los Huesos, pit of bones. Included in the cache were seventeen surviving human craniums. The best science estimates they lived around 430,000 years ago. The archaeologists there think that Sima de los Huesos might have been a burial site, a pit into which the living threw the dead, along with Excalibur, giving the gesture more meaning.

From recent genetics and reexamining of their fossil morphology, these twenty-eight also appear to represent the earliest Neandertals found anywhere to date, pushing the timing of the emergence of our closest evolutionary relatives significantly back from the earlier 300,000-year-old estimates.

Genetics helped not only in this reassessment but also in the reclassification of the fossils, once called *Homo heidelbergensis*, to Neandertal. *Homo heidelbergensis* looks to have been a bit of over-labeling, as paleontology is wont to do with every precious fossil found, cradling it tenderly as unique and its own special entity (which it is).

One might as well get used to this, as well as to the fact that, especially with the added lens of paleogenetics, the stories and labels will shift overnight. Then there's another story with dating methods, which always provide the best possible ballpark figure. The best lesson in all this is that the story can change quickly with new and better methods, not only new finds, and that there is an urgent need to step away quickly from the outdated and simplistic images of family trees and single-line maps across the Old World of hominid migrations and minglings so popular in presenting human evolution.

Never before has it been so clear that there is no one neat trunk with finite branches. There are instead lots of breakout branches, lots of back-and-forth migrations at different times, lots and lots of minglings—because we are after all human, and all this while still retaining population uniqueness from genetic flow and genetic isolation and adaptation to unique geographical niches, not to mention the chaos of individual life stories and the choices people make every moment of their lives, which then drive what they eventually do and become.

Paleoanthropologist John Hawks recently penned in a column for *Aeon* magazine that "human evolution is more a muddy delta than a branching tree." A muddy delta is a helpful image. I would add that we must factor in the reality that the waters can shift direction and also go off on tributary tangents that may or may not return to the main waters, and may or may not continue to flow.

"*¿Dónde está la peregrina?*" Where is the pilgrim? The question broke me out of my effort to keep all of this straight, trying to stay on top of the breaking news while also taking in the public displays before me (that already needed updating). I was in northern Spain and it was 2015, the summer after the final dig season at La Ferrassie. I was doing double research, on the ancient pilgrimage road across northern Spain, the Camino de Santiago, also known as the Way of Saint James, while hitting Neandertal sites along the way. It was a telling confluence: While this was a road of very recent *Homo sapiens* with a special religious bent, it had much older roots than the Christian overlay. The landscape over the Pyrenees and across northern Spain has been a corridor of human movement since deep prehistory given the diverse terrain, microclimates, and wealth of places rich in resources. It remains rich today and the landscape is varied and stunning, something modern-day pilgrims will confirm and admit is an important draw to walk this long road.

And that was my name for the day, *la peregrina*. I had been reading a blurb about those twenty-eight from Atapuerca while I was standing in the Museum of Human Evolution in Burgos, in north-central Spain, and for some reason, everyone else in our group of thirteen waiting to go out to visit Atapuerca had real names on the roster. There were even two other pilgrims with us and they were known as Paula and Joanne. Maybe it was because I had signed on at the last minute.

I had just been in Atapuerca, the village neighboring the famous archaeological site and sierra of the same name, just twenty kilometers (twelve miles) east of Burgos. I had intended to sleep there and visit the local prehistory from there. But given the rising popularity of the pilgrimage route, and the village as a stopping point, there was no room at any of the inns or pilgrims' dorms.

It was May and I had been walking for just over two weeks, starting in southern France. Atapuerca proved archaic humans—European *Homo erectus,* Neandertals, and early moderns—had been here long, long ago, some 1.2 to 1.4 million years ago. Today it stands as the oldest hominid site in Europe, unless you count the Republic of Georgia, in the Caucasus just north of Iran, as a part of Europe, which some people do. There, another Lower Paleolithic-to-medieval convergence took place, uncovering five 1.5 to 1.8 million-year-old hominids (perhaps *Homo erectus*) under the ruins of the medieval village of Dmanisi.

"*Estoy aquí*," I answered, not wanting to be left behind, not after all this. I quickly rehuddled with the others—the two other pilgrims, two honeymooning couples from Madrid, an older married couple from Burgos, and a family with two small children, one in a stroller.

We three pilgrims looked the part, wearing the same trekking clothes and hiking boots we'd worn for the past weeks since starting. The others stood apart, too, chic in sockless calfskin loafers in the same colors as their tailored spring pants and form-fitting tops, all in the year's colors of yellow, peach, green, and rose pastels, men and women alike. They paired and partnered in a manner I'd long ago learned was a part of the tradition of coupling in Spain; it was as much an aesthetic as an emotional engagement. They were a shoo-in for the well-choreographed Paleo sex exhibit we'd see at the site's didactic center, complete with images from erotic cave art, so-called Venus figurines, and displays of carved-bone Stone Age dildos. All *Homo sapiens* stuff, I would add. Neandertals never considered leaving those things lying around for posterity. If they had them, they used perishable materials. Our closest cousins didn't kiss and tell, but apparently, we did, and we started early. I wonder if the difference in symbolic thought among us was that one group had no need to make it permanent and the other did. We *Homo sapiens* are a bunch of posterity- and memorabilia-addicted showoffs.

One of the three main archaeologists leading the work at Atapuerca, Eudald Carbonell, had coauthored a book on prehistoric sexuality. After flipping through it in the museum's bookstore, I began thinking of him as the Dr. Ruth of prehistory. He also coauthored a cookbook for those interested in the real Paleo diet, one based on meats, fish, vegetables, fruits, nuts, and seeds. (Best not mention the possibility of cannibalism, possible evidence of which occurs at Atapuerca, as well as elsewhere in the Paleo world, or that many times people ate their meat raw.)

Atapuerca is a very sexy and a very important site, and those in charge of it are rock stars and can write pretty much whatever they want. The international Paleo-public gobbled it up. I confess, I did too. Atapuerca is a mind-blowing site, chock-full of caverns unified like an octopus, with each arm containing human occupations from seemingly forever to the recent past.

I'd seen two of the three lead archaeologists already, not in person, but celebrated in two photographs in the café of the last place in Atapuerca where I'd inquired into available beds. It was trail magic for, true, I remained homeless, but I had landed in Spain's Café Neandertal.

Before I hightailed it to Burgos to find a place to sleep, I slipped off my backpack, sat at the hotel bar, ordered a beer, and asked the innkeeper about the photographs. I knew she was the *jefe*, for in both photos there she was with Eudald Carbonell, his arm around her shoulders as Jose María Bermudez de Castro held before them a 1.2 million-year-old tooth belonging to *Homo antecessor* (a new name designation for European *Homo erectus*). The two men possessed very virile mustaches.

"They are regulars and very important." She beamed, pleased I had asked. "Do you know them?"

"Only from reputation," I said. Along with Juan Luis Arsuaga, these three formed the holy trinity of prehistoric studies at Atapuerca.

"Being right next door to the archaeological site," she said, "they often come here for meals and during breaks."

I detected pride and a slight French accent. "Are you French?" I asked.

"*Mais oui*," she switched from Castilian to French. "I married a local and love it here, but I'm from Bordeaux. It's similar to where I grew up, the prehistory, but it's not as green. My grandparents are from Sarlat in the Dordogne. Talk about green! Talk about an even more imbedded place for prehistory! Do you know it?"

Trail magic, I tell you.

I was very excited for this small-world connection but took a second to answer. Even though I'd grown up in a bilingual context, with language switching par for the course, when it happened, I still felt a moment of pause where my brain, as if a record player with needle, was lifting off one record, dropping in another, and resetting the needle to play in new grooves. It was a strange feeling and, it occurred to me, it was yet one more unfathomable thing about being human that would never leave signs of itself in the archaeological record. The brain remains a mystery, and along with it, language and culture and all that symbolic and abstract jazz. The debates about this prove the point: nothing is more contentious and unsettled than the issues of language, art, burial, and other symbolic acts, largely because, how do you find clear expressions of these things left for posterity? Before 40,000 years ago, if you do, there's not too much of it, maybe due to preservation issues or a more recent obsession among humans to document things more permanently.

The needle took purchase on the new track. I could speak again. I told the Bordelaise how right she was, in my humble opinion, and that I knew Sarlat really well, and that with Carsac and Les Eyzies, I considered it the heart of Café Neandertal for France.

Between prehistory fetishists like ourselves, we hardly needed to spill more words over this established fact, but she added that no one was as attuned to their prehistory as locals from the Dordogne. She said that, more and more, the Spanish were joining those ranks, but in spite of parallel histories, with remarkable prehistoric discoveries in both countries and in the same recent decades, the French public still exceeded any other national public for passion about the early human past. I nodded a lot in agreement.

Then we came back around to the holy trinity of prehistory.

"What are they like?" I had to ask.

"Very charming and very warm," she said, "and they are doing such important work. When you get to Burgos, just go to the museum and sign up for a tour. It's actually easier to get to the site from there than from here." Trail magic.

I was glad for this seeming derailment from trying to see the site directly from the village, for had it happened I would not have met the innkeeper from Aquitaine who confirmed the rock star status of those three and the rock star status of both the Dordogne and the Sierra de Atapuerca.

And besides, I had already fulfilled the main ambition, which was to arrive in this ancient place walking—the oldest hominid mode of transport, exactly the way the ancestors had come here. It was remarkable, too, that after two weeks of walking, my brain and body had actually rewired to see the world in more detail and depth. I also curiously craved protein and vegetables, nuts and seeds, sometimes fruit, and shunned bread, didn't want to touch the stuff. I hadn't read the Paleo diet books or even the gluten-free ones. I simply didn't crave cereals.

THIS DAY HAD begun in a large native oak and pine forest. All morning I walked through it as I descended into a valley with a huddle of more trees and medieval buildings at its center. It was the twelfth-century monastery and church of San Juan de Ortega, an engineer and monk turned saint who was celebrated for how much he made this route hospitable to pilgrims in the Middle Ages, especially his bridges over dangerous waters, his roadworks, and his churches. By the twelfth century, people were already geographically linear: to get to the holy city of Santiago de Compostela (where the purported tomb of Saint James the Greater lay, another contested burial but for different reasons), they forged a relatively straight line across the peninsula and crossed many rivers, thanks to the likes of San Juan and his bridges.

But these northern Spanish regions, like the south of France, had been highways long before medieval pilgrims traversed them, for many archaic humans. Their highways were the natural contours, probably following the rivers and enjoying the fertility of the valleys that the waterways forged. The prehistoric sites all along the north, as well as elsewhere, attested to this closeness of life-giving fresh waters. In southwestern France, it was the Garonne, the Dordogne, and the Vézère Rivers (among others); in northern Spain, it was the Ebro, the Duero, and the Arlanzón Rivers (among others).

Soon after climbing out of San Juan's valley, the forest ended and I entered the landscape of the proper *meseta*, the high plateau of central Spain. The remainder of my day, on approaching Atapuerca, had been in this rolling hill country—this tableland ripples a lot on its climb up to its eventual high flat top—all of it under a strong direct sun.

Millions of years had formed a system of limestone caverns and tunnels as underground water carved its way to join tributaries and rivers nearby. So while on the surface all was smooth and hilly, I walked over a subterranean world of Swiss cheese. Occasionally, something only locals knew, one of those tunnels emerged at the surface here and there, offering an entry. These places had been occupied by all the peoples who passed through, from the Lower Paleolithic's first migrants, some 1.4 million years ago, to Middle and Upper Paleolithic peoples, to the first farmers of the Neolithic, to the Bronze and Iron Age peoples, to the Middle Ages, and on, to today's large-scale industrial agriculturalists and all their bread.

Many of these caverns had been sealed long ago by collapsing cavern roofs, but a mining company, between 1896 and 1900, cut a deep trench into the sierra with the intention of building a rail line to transport minerals from farther east to Burgos farther west. The trench did not reveal much mineral wealth, and the rail works seem to have been suspended, but it exposed those long-ago collapsed and sealed caverns full of animal and human fossils. It was a wealth of a different magnitude that took a little longer to be uncovered.

Excavations began in earnest in the 1970s and have continued steadily to the present. Atapuerca alone has challenged a lot of prior ideas about human evolution, and will likely continue to do so, from as nearby as Iberia to as far away as China.

While other pilgrims on this road were destined for the holy medieval city of Santiago de Compostela, I was making my way to places holy to me, Neandertal sites. I had already been to some in Catalonia, farther east, a region rich in Neandertal occupations as well. While there, I had met with João Zilhão, a rising star from Lisbon in paleoanthropology now teaching in Barcelona and doing research at sites intersecting in time with the presence of both Neandertals and *Homo sapiens*, from Portugal to Romania.

His view of human evolution was more in sync with the one-species view, an assimilation model that proposed that all humans of the genus *Homo* who ever existed from some 2.6 million years or earlier to now are really one species, that there is no division between different hominids, all just flow in from the other, intermixing and absorbing and evolving as one. To him, at any given time, there was and only ever has been one species of *Homo* on earth.

It's a philosophical difference more than a scientific one, revealing a field that is both science and humanities. His view differs from prehistorians who see Neandertals as a different variation of being human that deserves its own distinct designation to tease out their own unique walk on earth.

Harold takes that latter view and so does paleoanthropologist Ian Tattersall at the American Museum of Natural History in New York. This view seeks to know what made Neandertals unique and perhaps, as a mirror, to reflect back to us why we made different choices with our similar capacities.

When I asked João more about this, he said, rhetorically, in charming shorthand and with the rounded full sounds rich in the Portuguese language, "It's tomato, potAto, you know?"

Or human, humAn, you know?

I asked this same question of pretty much all the prehistorians I spoke with. Alan Mann from Princeton, who with João is more a proponent of the outlook of influential paleoanthropologist Milford Wolpoff, emphasizes that these names and labels are arbitrary ways to refer to what is in truth a dynamic process of gene flow and geographical variation. Names are arbitrary; species are dynamic. And he sees a whole lot more flow and unity than not.

The way biologists, geneticists, and paleontologists handle the concept of species was a bit confusing to me, so I asked Jean-Jacques Hublin to clarify this when I met up with him in Paris. He said that he was radical in this field by actually holding a moderate position. He really didn't care what way people wanted to go, with lots of labels or just one, but he emphasized that everyone still needed a common language through which to speak to each other.

"You have many definitions of species—more than twenty. Some are extremely strict. The strictest definition is this notion that species are defined by the total lack of interbreeding between members of two different species. But basically, for paleontologists, as soon as you have phenotypes [physical appearance] that you can separate easily, you give it a name and you call it a paleontological species. But when we compare that with extant species, we know that there are cases where phenotype is not that different but there is no interbreeding, and on the other hand, we also have examples where the phenotype is very different but there is still the possibility of interbreeding. So we know that the paleontological species are sort of a proxy for biological species."

He painted for me a scenario in which a species is separated maybe for ecological or geographical reasons, the gene flow between the species stops, and over time there are genetic changes—mutations accumulating on both sides and resulting phenotypic changes also occurring on both sides. Then at some point, fertility is harder and at some point, they grow more and more separate. We were seated in his office at the Collège de France, a stone's throw from the Cluny Museum in the Latin Quarter on the Left Bank. What a setting to contemplate this. His rooftop window looked out over a sea of humanity, an ocean of potentials, changes, and fertilities. Notre Dame held the central focus, on the Seine, as the pale palette of gray, silver, and blue defined the rest of the City of Light, nuances of shade weaving an exquisite and complex tapestry that somehow hung together as one.

"The different definitions of species that we have right now, you can sort of organize them as strata along this process." He continued: "So probably one of the first stratum is the stratum where you see a difference in the phenotype. But still, these two populations are able to interbreed. Then, the more you go along in time," and the groups in question are more isolated from each other, geographically for instance, "the more this interbreeding is going to become difficult, and at some point, it will stop. For geneticists, they would say, at this point, they have a real species." He paused and we looked out that magnificent window again. The sun was beginning to lower and the palette was changing. The pale, cooler colors took on an early evening cloak of darker blue and gold. It all depended on the angle of light one shined on things, how they would appear.

"In other words," he resumed, "what paleontologists identify as species are biological species in the making. They are not yet fully separate from a reproductive point of view. Does it mean we should drop inside one species everything that is related for the last three to five million years and say, 'It's one species'? Call it *Homo sapiens* and *voilà*?"

I found this idea of a *species in the making* very helpful. It applied to paleontology as much as to life forms of the present. We are all species in the making, every life form on earth.

"We know that Neandertals and modern humans could interbreed," Jean-Jacques elaborated. "We also know that the difference between Neandertals and modern humans is much bigger than anything we know between recent humans. We are talking about something that is another order of magnitude. Personally I don't care if you call them species or subspecies. It's a complex thing. It's a process."

Surely we see this with other animals but for very obvious reasons, about othering others, we get caught up in the labels when it applies to humans. We don't get up in arms over wolves or bears. He was reading my mind, or had explained things in such a clear way that my mind went to the next logical idea.

"To me, the best analog to this is what we have with polar bears and brown bears. Polar bears and brown bears divided one from the other in the middle of the Middle Pleistocene, at the same time that Neandertals diverged from the ancestors of modern humans, and we have two, maybe it's a bad word to say it, but we have two sort-of species in nature today that we call 'brown bears' and 'polar bears.' Maybe some people would be happy to decide that we should not see a difference between polar bears and brown bears. But the fact is, there are many differences; not just the color, but also the ecology, the way they reproduce, their diet, even the shape of their feet. I would say we're facing the biological species in the making. They are not fully isolated, but they are already sufficiently isolated for us to recognize them."

I liked the bear analogy. In fact, it made things click. We're all bears, modern humans and Neandertals, and can embrace our unified beardom while also celebrating our diversity.

I also had the added good luck to speak with Paleolithic archaeologist Ofer Bar-Yosef, one of the era's grand synthesizers. Thanks to all the people I had spoken with who knew him—Harold, Jean-Jacques, João, Paul, and Alan, among many others, of whom he said for each, "I knew him when he was a young man"—we arranged to speak via Skype. He was in Brooklyn en route to Jerusalem and I was in southern New Jersey, back from the Dordogne. From our shared time zone, we traversed across Western Europe to East Asia with some rich stops in the Levant along the way.

One of my first questions was how he maneuvered all these pitfalls of labels and species.

"The Neandertals emerged as a special population about four hundred thousand years ago," he said. "Some think earlier, some suggest a bit later. But let's say four hundred thousand."

"Okay," I agreed. This new, older date was largely thanks to the new findings at Atapuerca.

"In human evolution there are successful mutations and there are unsuccessful mutations. So just imagine that the Neandertals were at their time a very successful human mutation. Their daily cultural attributes, generally the artifacts and so on, as well as some of their social structure, allowed them to grow and expand successfully. If you look at their situation in Europe four hundred thousand to two hundred thousand years ago, you can see Neandertals everywhere."

Right. Atapuerca may be the oldest but they were already in Wales and the Channel Islands at Jersey—thanks to low sea levels, with water locked up in glaciers forming land bridges to such places—as well as across continental Europe.

"Then these people, because they were successful, they were expanding. All successful populations expand until someone blocks them." He took a sip of coffee and confessed he was addicted to the stuff.

"This is the reason you have the genome from the Neandertals in the Altai Mountains in Siberia, which is far from Eastern Europe as well as Western Europe." He was citing the most recent findings from Siberia, especially the cave of Denisova, but there were others nearby that also showed Neandertal occupations. "I would not be surprised if somebody in northern Korea will find a Neandertal," he added with a sort of told-you-so knowing smile. "For sure in northern China, it's a possibility. This is an idea that is catching up. Everyone who is intelligent enough to see that population expands. That's all. There is nothing magic about it."

We zoomed ahead, from 400,000 to 200,000 years ago to 50,000 years ago.

"When modern humans were coming out of Africa . . ." He paused and had to back up. "Right now all this is in turmoil because there is a trend to understand that maybe modern humans came out of Africa not only fifty thousand years ago but also perhaps two hundred thousand or two hundred fifty thousand years ago. Not all migrations succeeded. Not all migrations went one way. Maybe some came back. Though I suspect that coming back, the people were already different from the ones who expanded in one direction."

The muddy—all-directions, sometimes flowing, sometimes going extinct—delta blues.

"They were an expanding population and there were some other populations, locally, like the Denisovans in East Asia, and the coming of modern humans, the *really* modern humans of fifty thousand years ago, moving into the Levant and then into Europe and the result of it is it's not a full mixing with the Neandertals. We have some percentage of the Neandertal genes. If you take the beginning of the Upper Paleolithic, so somewhere around forty thousand years ago, by twenty thousand years ago the percentage decreases in the genome, which means the Neandertals are gone somehow." We mixed in several places, most likely and especially in the Levant and in Russia.

Before they completely disappeared, he felt, their smaller populations moved into areas that were more marginal but less inhabited by us. "Some of the Neandertals moved farther north, but they could not deal with the glacial maximum, the cold period between twenty-four thousand to eighteen thousand years ago, and probably they became extinct. You have this kind of Neandertals at the sixtieth latitude in Russia [farther north and deeper into central Siberia]. It is like all this science, short-lived and they are no more." I loved his turn of phrase and sense of humor. He took a sip of coffee and I was sorry I had finished mine. Talk of extinction made one thirst for a jolt of caffeine.

"Of course," he added, "leaders of hunters and gatherers were making mistakes, even in better places, so people became extinct. Once too many groups became extinct, the whole interbreeding system became so small it was no longer viable."

I came to see that he smartly avoided the species closed loop. He never referred to Neandertals as anything but human, but a different "successful mutation," just as we now are a "successful mutation." At times he also used the term *meta-population* to refer to the collective populations of Neandertals and of modern humans, each. Within meta-populations are the individual populations, all related more closely to each other than to anyone else but also taking on their own histories and geographies and stories. Neandertals are a unique meta-population of humans and modern humans are another unique meta-population, each with extinctions and successes and failures and mutations original to each while also being related; they by and large could interbreed. Polar bears and brown bears. Bears.

We talked for a long time and I gained many new ways to regard this material that would journey with me deeper into this pilgrimage of a different kind. One thing he said as we signed off seemed to capture the best posture of all toward the field, especially when entrenched in its labels as if they were real, not arbitrary signs given by the science and not by the species. "You can't remain a worm in your own turnip."

Though he was referring to how he decided to expand his own area of studies, I loved this phrase so much I decided to use it more broadly to apply occasional chiropractic to a field that bunched itself into knots over both philosophical and scientific issues. *You can't remain a worm in your own turnip.* Get out, see other turnips, meet other worms, don't get so entrenched and comfortable in one way of thinking and seeing.

The deeper I went into Café Neandertal, the more I also discovered a paradox in all this swinging of the so-called pendulum. Among the many prehistorians, no one—not a one—was saying that Neandertals were anything but smart, but how the different camps were saying it was where things differed. Some were saying Neandertals were smart by way of saying they were like us, and others were saying they were smart and *not* like us.

Most fell in between a range of smart both like us and unlike us. Most saw themselves as moderate in their views, even the extremists. But I also wondered about the unexamined multicultural overlay that seemed to think smartness was a desired feature simply because we all are trained to see it as a valued quality, schooling ourselves, getting degrees, taking tests, on a pendulum of a different order that left the craftsperson, artist, or manual laborer earning lower wages in the modern world but not necessarily in the earlier world of humans. Were we applying yet another modern and recent cultural concept to our past kin, not only early modern humans but also all the other archaic humans? All these labels and phrases said more about us, and the competitive nature of academia, science, and even religion, than they did about who we really were and who Neandertals really were. Yes, they were smart. So are we. But so what? So are bears and wolves and, my goodness, have you watched birds lately, or dolphins? As Harold would say, show me what they were *doing.* That is indeed a deeper and more honest insight.

"We are the pinnacle of nothing," Ian Tattersall wrote in his book *The Case of the Rickety Cossack and Other Cautionary Tales from Human Evolution.* "Instead," he concluded, "we are simply a twig on what was until very recently a luxuriant evolutionary tree." Or a tributary on a very muddy delta.

You can't remain a worm in your own turnip. It seemed time to get out from the confining *sapiens*-centric turnip and into another root.

BACK DURING MY final hour of walking to the village of Atapuerca, before I knew I would have to continue on to Burgos for access to the nearby archaeological site, a very sexy Iberian kept me company. All along that last stretch of the Camino to the village I could see his distant billboard grow slightly larger every few hundred meters. A huge poster portrait of *Homo antecessor* grinned quietly at me with a thoughtful and intelligent over-the-shoulder glance that seemed to say, *Welcome home, we've been waiting for you.*

That he was handsome with soulful Spanish features in that Javier Bardem way made that last hour very pleasant in spite of my fatigue and the hot sun. I let my mind go with the association and felt an extra shot of energy by the time I arrived in the village after the long day of walking. *Homo antecessor bardem* I called him, and his story awaited me, once I boarded the bus in Burgos back to the site.

I was beginning to notice a curiosity. Each national group seemed to artistically reconstruct their archaic humans with their own most common features. It was something akin to how painters of different cultures depicted Mary and Jesus, running the gamut from Europeans to Africans to Asians. (The sacred art bubble was sort of popped, and deepened, by African-American artist Henry Ossawa Tanner, who went to Palestine and painted the Annunciation with a Palestinian model for Mary, garbed and surrounded by Levantine textiles and returning her to her most likely look and culture. Rather than take away from the story, it added to it.) Similarly, the Neandertals in northern European depictions looked rather Viking and those farther south, rather Mediterranean. I had also glimpsed East Asia joining the bandwagon and though they say there were no known Neandertals there, some of their models of *Homo erectus* look rather East Asian.

Now at last in Burgos, with my group of pilgrims and prehistory day-trippers, we boarded a bus from the human evolution museum and made our way (back) to Atapuerca, disembarked, donned hard hats for protection, and entered the narrow corridor of the old railway cut. To stand in that old railroad trench was potent, like being in a small canyon with rust red striations, only this canyon was a layer cake of humanity, a *millefeuille* of the Pleistocene towering far overhead with its many older ways of life.

We entered and walked to the excavated cavern where my buddy Bardem was unearthed, dating to some 800,000 years ago. Here at La Gran Dolina, the big sinkhole, they had uncovered thirty-six fragments of human fossils and these looked like people who were sort of *Homo erectus*-like but different. Perhaps, they asked, this was what *Homo erectus* had come to look like in his and her gene flow, isolation, and unique adaptation to the unique geography of Europe? To make this distinction, they called the new fossils *Homo antecessor* (the explorer). This led others (but not everyone) working on *Homo erectus* in Africa to call those fossils *Homo ergaster* (the worker) for clarity, and those in Asia to hold to the prior more all-encompassing name, *Homo erectus* (the upright), to refer now more particularly to the Asian adaptations and characteristics of this pretty much same species on all three continents.

We next visited a nearby cavern called Sima del Elefante, elephant pit, where they found fossil remains some 1.2 to 1.4 million years old, potentially earlier forms of *Homo antecessor*. Factoring the long stretch of dates and the new Latin name for an ancient relative, the common one to us moderns and Neandertals, we next turned our attention to the twenty-eight Neandertal individuals of Sima de los Huesos.

Our guide indicated the location of the cavern that held their bones, just over the slope far to our right and beyond the rail trench, but public access to it was impossible. Excavators themselves had to walk one kilometer underground to get to the site. But it was at that locale where they detected the original, now collapsed, opening above to the surface that must have been what made this the pit of bones that it is, the place where the dead were thrown in or arrived here by other means.

"Raise your hands," our guide directed, shifting topics. "How many of you are left-handed?" She asked this while cheerfully pulling out a replica of a skull and holding it. It was one of the most complete skulls found in Sima de los Huesos, affectionately named Miguelón to honor Spain's five-time Tour de France champion, Miguel Indurain.

I felt vindicated. Between Excalibur and Miguelón—and many other names they were giving to fossils, such as one of the most complete pelvises ever found in the fossil record called Elvis—I could go on and call my favorite *Homo antecessor* Javi. Miguelón even had the forward lean and intensity of a professional cyclist. I raised my hand and looked around. No one else raised his or her hand.

"Well, *la peregrina*," our guide said to me, "there were no left-handed people in Sima de los Huesos." She then turned and spoke to the others. "They were all right-handed."

The researchers had arrived at this conclusion by studying the dental microwear patterns, because many Neandertals appear to have used their teeth as tools in unison with their two hands, the dominant hand leaving definable marks on the teeth if it hit them with a stone tool, such as when cutting meat held in the mouth.

Others have done experiments on handedness. Some have looked at asymmetry in arm bones, finding more robust right sides, with more worked muscle attachments, as signs that the right was favored over the left. Others have experimented with toolmaking patterns, recruiting modern master flintknappers who are both right- and left-handed and watching for how tools made by each differed in clear patterned ways. From that, they could interpret handedness in patterns found in the archaeological record. This helped determine that by the time of early Neandertals, right-handedness was a dominant pattern.

"So the rest of you are more like the Sima group than she is." The guide pointed back at me. I put my hand down and continued taking notes, trying to shake off being used as an exhibit and also, the big question mark, What then did that mean about us lefties? No one seems to have an answer for that, except that we are the element of surprise, such as in a swordfight. *Ha ha, but I am not really right-handed!* Switch and thrust.

Today, about every nine out of ten people are right-handed. It is a tendency that begins to appear in the fossil record with the genus *Homo*, from the *erectuses* to the Neandertals to us. Chimpanzees seem to be pretty ambidextrous, favoring neither side more. So handedness in *Homo* speaks about a relationship with brain lateralization—the two hemispheres that began to specialize to perform different functions on each side. The biggest deal in all this is language, which is largely based in our left hemisphere. A complex theory says that the evolution of language drove our brains to lateralize more and one accidental result was handedness. As our hemispheres specialized, the left hemisphere, which controls the right side of the body (and vice versa for the right hemisphere and the left side of the body), added mostly right-handed toolmakers to the repertoire of the speech-making monkey.

I'm still not sure where that leaves us left-handed folks, except that there is still more to-ing and fro-ing between the hemispheres and the brain is more complex than these theories. Maybe being left-handed made me furrow my brow more, not seeing it all straight, rationally, as a right-hander might?

I had been writing and contemplating this so deeply that I hadn't noticed that the guide had stopped talking and everyone was very still. That was when I noticed that the whole group was watching me, bemused expressions on their faces. They were entertained by the way that I wrote.

Very funny.

Taught by a right-handed teacher to write in cursive, I had to hook my hand in order to slant my letters the right-handed way—just like President Obama, I would like to add—to get a good grade. It suddenly occurred to me, if I had adapted to a right-handed person's world to survive, and could leave a material record that looked right-handed, couldn't the rare lefties from ancient Atapuerca have done the same? Maybe the only way to learn to make a stone tool was to mimic exactly a right-handed teacher?

Thankfully, our guide next talked about how Miguelón, the fellow in her hand, had died, and attention was back on her. "He made it to thirty-five, a good old age compared to the others." Two-thirds of others from the pit were between the ages of eleven and twenty. "But then he succumbed to a bad tooth infection," she said. "It eventually spread and went to his brain and killed him."

Miguelón's infection had been discovered from the scarring in his nasal cavities caused by the infection's inflammation. It had been a very painful last existence on earth and then a gruesome end. Another story followed, of a young man who had two punctures in his skull that had never had a chance to heal and were directly related to his death. Had it been violence or a really bad hunting accident or fall? No one knows, but the punctures looked as if they could have been made with a stone tool and if so, this could be a first case for interpersonal violence. In this scenario, for the record, the weapon wielder was right-handed.

The final story left the dark end of the spectrum toward the light. It was gleaned from another skull, that of a girl whose cranium had fused and could not expand with her growing brain, severely handicapping her and necessitating others to take care of her. And they had, for she died much later, at age twelve, than such a person possible would have if left unaided. "Obviously," our guide concluded, "she was cared for and loved." She looked at the two children, the older one appearing ready to cry, and so she stopped the forensics tales there.

The Sima de los Huesos fossils and site continue to alter the current shape of what we thought we knew about Neandertals. From genetics the Sima fossils offered up another mystery, a relatedness to a group of humans called the Denisovans, a group known until now only in Asia.

This new species was related to Neandertals and to us. They branched off from Neandertals sometime soon after we all branched off from our common ancestor (*Homo erectus/ergaster/antecessor*), perhaps around 700,000 years ago. Denisovans were identified entirely via their different genetic signature, not any fossils. The fossils to date are very few, some teeth and a tiny finger bone from the pinky of a young girl.

They were found in the Altai Mountains of southern Siberia, near the intersection of the Russian, Kazakh, Chinese, and Mongolian borders. Located in one of the layers of Denisova Cave, named after Denis, an eighteenth-century hermit who had lived there, the site was occupied many times, perhaps around twenty-two unique occupations over a 280,000-year period. Among the occupants were Neandertals, in a different and later layer. Neandertals were the better-known Middle Paleolithic occupants of these mountains and their fossils have been found in other neighboring caves, Okladnikov and Chagyrskaya being the most famous. (In the latter, researchers also analyzed the teeth and learned that these Neandertals enjoyed a diet of a lot of meat, fish, and various plants, including the Siberian pea shrub.)

It appears that this newly discovered Asian sister group lived at the same time as Neandertals, around 400,000 to 50,000 years ago and mostly in Asia. Genetics shows that they interbred with Neandertals and also with us. The largest surviving DNA from the Denisovans in modern humans occurs among Australians and populations in the South Pacific.

Earlier, there was probably a dance with Neandertals, soon after they diverged from each other, perhaps somewhere farther west, for the mitochondrial DNA extracted and sequenced from the Altai Denisovan turned out to be a match with the mitochondrial DNA of one of the early Sima de los Huesos Neandertals. Perhaps it was a far-flung love affair, but it was one that speaks of us all as species in the making and that the terrain for all human variations was wider and that intermingling, again, was (and is) a habitual human affair. But the nuclear DNA of the Sima de los Huesos fossils showed a firm signature of the Sima crowd already being Neandertals, in fact, the earliest Neandertals found to date.

Almost all the famous Neandertals, the ones we hear a lot about in the news, are from a later period and are considered "classic" Neandertals with classic and very distinct Neandertal morphologies: brains larger than ours, a thick and wide build and heavy musculature, strong faces with prominent brow ridges, and strong jaws with large faces and receding chins.

Among the most famous and well-studied are the Feldhofer skeletons at the Neander Valley in Germany; the Spy Neandertals in Belgium; those in France at Roc de Marsal, Regourdou, La Ferrassie, Le Moustier, La Chapelle-aux-Saints, Pech de l'Azé, La Quina, St-Césaire, and Arcy-sur-Cure; and those at El Sidrón in Spain; Krapina and Vindija in Croatia; Kebara, Tabun, Amud, and Zuttiyeh in Israel; Dederiyeh in Syria; Shanidar in Iraq; Kiik-Koba and Zaskalnaya in Crimea; Mezmaiskaya in the northern Caucasus of Russia just north of Georgia; Teshik Tash in Uzbekistan; Grotta Guattari in Italy; and Denisova in southern Siberia in Russia. All of these Neandertals lived between 40,000 and 180,000 years ago. The North Sea, after being dredged by a fishing trawl, offered up a 60,000-year-old Neandertal skull fragment not far from Holland, from a time when it had been above sea level and another Neandertal habitat in northern Europe.

Other even earlier sites for Neandertals occur in places north and south. One is La Cotte de St-Brelade on the island of Jersey, first occupied by Neandertals around 250,000 years ago, and they continued to visit the area until about 60,000 years ago. It was accessible due to lowering sea levels from water locked in the icecaps during glaciation. It was a massive mammoth kill site, and hundreds of these daunting creatures were driven with coordinated effort on the Neandertals' part to stampede over the cliff into a crest and to fall to their deaths, as attested by the huge numbers of whole butchered mammoth skeletons, stone tools associated with Neandertals, and some Neandertal bones to boot.

Another older site is in northern Wales, at Pontnewydd, not far from Liverpool. It's considered the most northwesterly region in Eurasia that Neandertals inhabited, some 230,000 years ago.

Just east of Rome, the site of Saccopastore in Italy dates to a 250,000-year-old Neandertal presence. There, two skulls that are considered Italy's first Neandertals were unearthed. Southern Italy has a younger Neandertal, around 150,000 years old, at Altamura.

And France, too, is not only the homestead of the middle years of classic Neandertals but has some older sites as well; one, Levallois, giving its name to the whole Mousterian technological tradition, dates to around 200,000 years ago.

After seeking the oldest Neandertals, peoples and nations also seem to be clamoring to be in possession of the last Neandertals, those who lived and overlapped with migrating *Homo sapiens*, usually around the pivotal date of 40,000 years ago and located mostly across the more southerly sites, from Iberia, France, Italy, Croatia, Romania, and Georgia; or the more northerly ones, such as the Altai, but even farther into the Arctic edge of the Ural Mountains in Russia.

And at Atapuerca, the early Neandertals showed an earlier maternal line related to Denisovans, while they were already established firmly as Neandertals in the making. Bears.

I took one more long look at that old railroad trench in a cut of earth in the bowels of a hill that revealed so much about human prehistory. Not only had archaic humans lived here, but so had bears, lynx, wolves, deer, bison, mammoth, horses, rhinoceroses, and many other animals. We then left and took a break for lunch at another village, Ibeas de Juarros, which like Atapuerca neighbored the archaeological site but on the opposite side.

Everyone enjoyed shifting gears to focus entirely on the pleasures of twenty-first-century food, including tapas, and good wine from the Ribera Duero, the river just south that offered conditions for winemaking so remarkable that many Spaniards I spoke with were torn between which was better, Rioja or Ribera. What a delightful conflict. No one talked about the Neandertals, though it was clear from the villagers also gathered there, just in how they interacted with us, that they were proud of their ancient site and felt a kindred spirit with the depth of humanity here.

In the afternoon we returned to the site, but now to a large indoor and outdoor didactic center. A beautiful day outside made most pass up Paleo titillation at the prehistoric sex exhibit inside, opting instead for spear-throwing in a nearby field. We aimed our stone-tipped spears near a huge model of a true-to-size rhinoceros that once lived here in the Paleolithic. Not far away was another reconstruction, a Neandertal burial, complete with a mourning friend reaching over the pit toward his dead friend, where he had scattered some wildflowers. The contested flower pollens of Shanidar were not contested here. No wind, bees, or gerbils had dragged these in, but rather a friend.

I was taking this in when the two children of the group came and stood next to me with their mother. The youngest just stared, but the older, about six years of age, wrinkled her brow in exactly the way I had been doing a lot these days, trying to put everything together.

She knelt and studied the deceased closely, his fetal position, that he lay on his left side, the nature of the flowers offered by the living. She even made me see that there were more items in the pit, a large stone and an animal horn. Offerings.

*"¿Qué pasa aquí, mamá?"* she finally asked after her close investigation.

"A friend is sad," her mother answered, "because his friend is dead and is honoring him and showing his *tristeza* with the flowers." She said this without pause, her most natural and quick response. I also was reminded about another thing I enjoyed so much about the Spanish. The friend is *dead*. Not *passed away*. They go direct, deal with it, even with a small child.

Her little sister suddenly found it more interesting and craned her head over the railing of the baby stroller as I heard a sudden exhale from the older girl. It sounded like a compassionate sigh and one that said, oh, okay, now I get it. It was very human and very primate, as we all are, for chimpanzees also mourn their dead and show emotion over loss.

As the family wandered over to the rhinoceros, it occurred to me that neither mother nor child said or implied anything about anything symbolic, nothing about the afterlife or helping the spirit of the deceased on his journey beyond or any existential issue for the living of dealing with their own mortality. That was interesting, because that is exactly what fills the tomes of spirited archaeological debates about prehistoric burial, that it is very human to make it into a symbolic and abstract act, stretching it to cover existential issues that might have gone on in the minds of the living as they confronted death. This reasoning is extended to the Neandertals, as some argue that this is proof that they were just like us.

Yet here, in the early twenty-first century—in the secular but culturally Catholic country of Spain, where even if you don't believe in god and the angels or heaven and hell, many people still believe in an afterlife— the first instinct of a mother and child was simply to feel sadness and see it as an act of honor and beauty of a friend who is now gone. Gone. *Y nada más.*

# 5

## A DIFFERENT SORT OF PILGRIMAGE

**M**Y TIME IN Atapuerca and Burgos complete, I continued to walk a little longer on the Camino de Santiago to Frómista and then turned north as my fellow pilgrims continued west to Compostela. I followed an older route, up the Ebro River—a mythic river for all Spain that gave its name to Iberia—to its source at Reinosa in the Cantabrian Mountains, another area rich with prehistoric occupations for reasons similar to the Dordogne and the Sierra de Atapuerca—good food, water, shelter, and climate.

My destination was farther west from there to the mountain village of Villamayor in Asturias, along the banks of the Piloña River, a waterway that wound from the mountains to the Atlantic Ocean, where it joined the Sella River and decanted at Ribadesella. In Villamayor, it passed near El Sidrón, Spain's most famous Neandertal site, and at Ribadesella, it skirted Tito Bustillo, one of Spain's most famous Upper Paleolithic painted and engraved caves. Just by following the water highways, you walked in the footsteps of ancient humanity.

For fourteen years, beginning in 2000, a core group of paleoanthropologists, Antonio Rosas from Madrid, Marco de la Rasilla from

Oviedo, and paleogeneticist Carles Lalueza-Fox from Barcelona, excavated at El Sidrón. In all, Rosas's group uncovered thirteen Neandertals who all appeared to be a part of a single event that left their bodies together in the cave. They all showed cut marks on their bones. Ritual defleshing was a possibility, a mortuary practice also known to us modern humans, but the researchers also found evidence for cannibalism (also known among us).

They noticed that some of the long bones had been banged with a sharp stone point to crack them open and get at the marrow. Marrow is the most nutritious and coveted part of an animal, human or otherwise, and other carnivores don't use stone hammers to get at it.

Paleogenetic analysis of the remarkably well-preserved bones, dating to around 49,000 years ago, revealed that the three adult males in the bunch were all related. By interesting contrast, the four adult females were not. The men, it seemed, stayed together, and adult women from outside came in to join the group.

El Sidrón has opened a rare window into a whole group, not just individuals, and their social organization and behavior—at least as populations living in the Cantabrian Mountains 49,000 years ago expressed it.

In Villamayor, the closest year-round settlement where it was possible to stay and visit El Sidrón, I landed in another Café Neandertal. It was also Corpus Christi weekend, which meant my hike to El Sidrón was punctuated by a village fair complete with games, fire pit–grilled foods in the open air, fly fishermen in the Piloña, free-flowing golden hard cider poured like a fountain stream from above one's head into a glass waiting near one's hip, and bagpipe processions harkening to the Celtic culture the North celebrates from its own Iron Age.

I went with the flow and followed a procession of people into the center of the village of sixty-three inhabitants. We went past the twelfth-century Romanesque church with several expressive medieval dragons carved into its capitals. When we arrived at the fairgrounds, they stopped and settled into games, tapas, and flying cider, engulfed in the primordial smells of grilling meat over an open fire, but I pushed on. I passed the fly fishermen, oblivious to the racket all around them in their Zen zone (the same one I felt when excavating at La Ferrassie), and went up and over a medieval bridge and into the hills, where I was assured by a local that in a few kilometers I would encounter my pilgrim's goal, the famous cave. It was so near, according to them and to my topographical map, that I had brought only a small bottle of water and looked forward to the return reward of fire-seared flesh and sparkling cider in the festivities I could now spy just below through the trees.

As if to punctuate the gaiety I left and the morbidity I approached, soon, the higher and deeper in I went, all sound but wind and occasional birdsong disappeared. A sinister feeling of isolation and foreboding overcame me. I was walking away from people, into remote mountains, toward a site known most for one thing, ancient cannibalism. As if to animate my mood, the sun slipped behind heavy dark clouds and spent the rest of my ascent coming and going, lighting then obscuring my way as if I'd stepped into a black–and–white Hitchcock film.

I passed one homestead. No one was at home. I passed a village, and still, no one around. I climbed more and arrived at last at the village where, according to my topographical map, I could reach the cave via a little jaunt through someone's backyard and field. No one was at home. I backtracked. As I reached the village center, a couple about my age came out of their house. Life. They did look a bit worn, as if they'd overindulged at the festival in the valley below, so I hesitated to disturb them. But it was now or never, so I stepped forward and asked how I could get to the cave.

"You're near, as the bird flies, but that map is wrong," the woman said. "There's no direct path from here to there." She pointed at the errant line. "You have another six or eight kilometers that way." She pointed with the same line-eradicating finger toward a sinuous road leaving the village to circumvent the valley, moving away, not toward the cave. Seeing my doubt, she added, "It goes up and down through two other valleys *y al fin*, at last, turns to head back to *near* the entrance to the valley where the cave is nestled at the foot of that hill." She pointed as the crow flies to the painfully near but far hill before me. *Mierda*. People in Villamayor, so nearby down below, seemed to have different local knowledge than people up here a few mere kilometers away.

I had already walked twelve kilometers (due to some backtracking and a wrong turn) and realized that by the time the day was done, which, judging from the sunlight, was sooner than I cared to admit, I would need to walk a total of forty kilometers, most of it still ahead of me. My small bottle of water was now almost finished; I had no food. The sun menaced more, lowering in the sky. I must have looked pathetic because she took pity upon me.

"My husband is about to head up to our pasture to feed the horses. He's going that way and can drop you off at the beginning of the path that leads directly to the cave." I took the offer, even though the husband's lack of enthusiasm over being volunteered and his grizzled appearance would inspire anyone to decline.

But one thing I knew from many years of trekking in these hills was that they were generally safe and that no matter how remote things got, someone still lived just over the bend, even when they appeared not to. I checked my phone. I had reception. *Not quite as remote as La Ferrassie,* I thought and smiled. But then, there had been no sign of cannibalism at La Ferrassie. My smile evaporated. Over hill and dale we went.

The husband was a decent person, even if worn and terribly laconic. The whole ride was a conversation in monosyllables. He thought I was a nut job: a woman on her own hiking to visit a grim Neandertal site when this was a family holiday. That was rich, I thought but did not say, because the holiday in question was celebrating the eating and drinking of the body and blood of Christ during the Eucharist, ritual cannibalism at its best. But by the time he pulled over to drop me off at the path for my final descent into possible prehistoric cannibalism, he loosened up a bit and told me that the village was really proud of this site because of the work Rosas and his team were doing and the contribution these hills were making to our knowledge of the deep human past.

"They were Asturianos, like us, but," he paused and never finished the sentence. He didn't have to. *But we don't eat each other.*

I thanked him and waited for his car to disappear before I turned my attention to the path. I wished I'd brought my machete. The path was dark and descended into overgrown forest with crisscrossing vines. I looked more and finally located a partially hidden sign behind overgrown stinging nettles that told me this was indeed the way to El Sidrón. It also informed me that it was a rare site, where DNA had successfully been sequenced from the Neandertal bones and firmly proved that we all had Neandertal great-great-great-great-grandparents. It concluded with an arrow, pointing directly into the forest, affirming that four hundred meters from where I stood, I would come upon it. It said nothing about the possible legacy of being munched.


A FEW MONTHS later, Antonio Rosas gave a lecture in Paris at the Collège de France on "Cannibalism, the Case of El Sidrón." By then, I was back in the Dordogne and learned that the video of the talk was streaming on the internet. I made myself a bowl of popcorn and settled in to watch.

Rosas wanted first to dissociate the listeners from biases they might have about cannibalism. It is not as much of an anomaly as you might think. My hand, endowed with popcorn, happily supplied my mouth without a thought but this: I certainly knew of a more recent, fully modern, case of cannibalism from my Colorado childhood.

In 1874, a mountain man, Alfred Packer, was hired by five mining prospectors to lead them through the mountains. An unusually severe winter ensued and when Packer reappeared alone near the town of Saguache weeks later, he claimed he'd had to eat the others to survive and that they'd already been dead due to exposure, except for one, who tried to kill and eat him, so in self-defense, he successfully returned the favor.

He was found guilty of murder but the truth was never clear. In 1989, a forensic scientist examined the bones of the five and found that all had died violently and also been cannibalized.

Rosas also reminded the audience that evidence for cannibalism, cut marks from defleshing the bones of humans that look like the same marks made when defleshing the bones of deer, for instance, appeared among *Homo antecessor* at Atapuerca some 800,000 years ago.

While it didn't appear that many Neandertal fossils found in the Dordogne had cut marks, nearby in the Charente, to the west near the Atlantic, the site of Les Pradelles in southwestern France was bringing up a rich cache of animal and Neandertal bones mixed in the same deposits, all bearing a similar style of cut marks.

Paleoanthropologists Bruno Maureille from Bordeaux and Alan Mann from Princeton had been excavating there together for many years. It appears to have been a Neandertal hunting camp, once a cave but long ago collapsed, full of butchered deer and horse bones and also a healthy handful of butchered Neandertal bones mixed in. Dating to between 40,000 and 80,000 years ago, the human fossils seemed to represent around eight Neandertal individuals. With cut marks no different than those found on known game, one reading of the evidence was cannibalism.

But perhaps the largest case of such material is in Croatia, mostly at Krapina, but also at Vindija. The two sites are separated by almost 90,000 years, with Krapina dating to around 130,000 years ago and Vindija at around 38,000. I asked for information about this theme from paleoanthropologist James Ahern, who works in central Europe, especially in Croatia.

"We have no compelling evidence of any Neandertal burials in Croatia. The oldest and largest sample from the site of Krapina is an amazing amount of fossils, mostly fragmented. It seems there was a very high concentration of Neandertal remains in a couple of the segments and some have interpreted that as burial, but then a lot of work in the 1980s showed that there was a lot of processing of the bodies—a lot of cut marks and purposeful breaking of the bone—either because of cannibalism or because of secondary burial practices or something." The most correct idea of all this might be "or something."

But El Sidrón's case is a different window into this sort of evidence because it comes with a group that seemed to have lived together and died together. The Krapina Neandertals could be from separate times or even individuals from different groups who visited that site separately.

Rosas and his team speculated that maybe El Sidrón had been the site of some sort of final act of warfare, maybe a way of taking over another group. Everyone in the cave looked as if they had been eaten in one great feast. My mind returned to Homer's *Iliad* and the battlefield of the Trojan War when Hector's mother said of Achilles, who had just killed her son, that she wanted to sink her teeth into Achilles's liver and eat it in vengeance. The Bible, too, holds classic tales on cannibalism. It's been with us a long time.

I had stopped eating popcorn by now.

A lot of the context for the butchering and possible feast at El Sidrón was lost because the final resting place of the bones was the result of collapse through a sinkhole from above, perhaps through the action of a flood. The bones, and the stone tools that had butchered the bones, were all washed into a deeper cavern and covered over, a lucky thing for preservation and why these bones have more ancient DNA intact for extraction and analysis.

If this sounds like grim circumstances, consider also that when spelunkers accidentally discovered the cache in 1994, the first thought investigating authorities had was that these were victims of the Spanish Civil War in the 1930s. Asturias was a largely left-wing Republican region and many locals had used the caves to hide in and to resist Franco's right-wing fascists. It was a sad legacy and the find of human bones in a cave was too commonly attributed to this period in recent history. It was with relief that the bones were soon identified as so old that they were beyond some of the worst atrocities committed by modern humans in Europe.

The excavated bones from El Sidrón added up to around 2,500 fossils representing nearly every part of the skeleton, and lots of teeth, making it possible to determine the thirteen unique individuals in the jumble. Three were the grown men whose genetics showed they were related. Four were the grown women whose genes indicated they had come in from other groups, probably as mates. Another three, two boys and a girl, were adolescents, and the remaining three were infants, also two boys and a girl. There seemed to be no difference in how any of these thirteen were defleshed or smashed, a sort of equal opportunity rite of death and dinner across age and gender.

I WAS GRATEFUL that, from my high school track days, when my main race had been the four-hundred-meter dash, I knew exactly how far that was, though not precisely when translated onto forested and rocky terrain. But in I went to the cave at El Sidrón. It was a dark native oak forest and no matter where I looked, and how I felt, I saw beauty. I had left the modern human-altered world behind. I memorized stones and trees on the path for backtracking and even took photos of them in case my mind played tricks on me. I checked through the leaves for the height of the sun and the location of the hillside with the cave. I was glad I had my compass. I was disappointed I had but one gulp of water left.

I had two options for a reasonable 400-meter run. I took the first one and it opened into a pasture with grazing cows and no cave. I backtracked and took the other. When I had twenty-five meters left and could see I was very close to the foot of the hill, I had to stop. This was where that machete would have come in handy. Thick forest undergrowth and strong vines wove across the path, barring any passage. The sun lowered more. I drank my water, and just stood there, studying the surroundings, the contours, and the mood.

It was a valley floor easily hiding many secrets, as if I entered the disorienting labyrinth of the medieval old city in Fez, a perfect place if one were trying to survive and hide from danger. It seemed also a place that would be wealthy in plant and animal foods, but in this case, a cold and grim winter 49,000 years ago had left thirteen Neandertals as the best possible dinner option.

I shivered and turned and made my way up and out, and then up and down, and up and down, and then down and down and down and, exhausted, famished, and thirsty, wandered into Villamayor as the populace was revving up for the evening round of more festivities. I lingered a moment, long enough to take in the festive community, but I no longer wanted grilled meat, not tonight, even though I was hungry.

As I walked toward the center of the village, I stopped to speak with a man and his daughter who were curious about my solo arrival, looking pretty worn out in hiking clothes and boots when everyone else was there with family and friends and dressed for a party. He was pleased when I told him my mission, my little pilgrimage into the deep past.

"We're thinking of making a visitors' museum," he said, "but we also wonder how interested the public would be." His daughter went off to join up with friends she just saw.

"Pretty interested," I offered, "considering how popular Neandertals are these days. And the genetics is really fanning the flames of their interest."

He smiled and nodded. "I think you're right, but we still wonder about . . ."

". . . the whole cannibalism thing?" I ventured.

"*Exactamente,*" he answered.

"I think that's a draw," I said. "Imagine all these kids coming here with their families. Wouldn't that be the selling point for a family vacation?" I told him about Alfred Packer and how my alma mater, the University of Colorado in Boulder, used to host Have a Friend for Dinner and Give a Friend a Helping Hand events to honor the annual recognition of his marching down the mountain and reporting what had happened. "Maybe here it could be Have a Family for Dinner," I suggested.

Thankfully, he laughed. "It probably would be the highlight. The Spanish love doing everything as a family."

We wished each other well and I made my way to the central café in the village and ordered a warming bowl of vegetable soup and a big bottle of mineral water.

As the edge of hunger softened and the Hitchcock noir of the day burned off in my mind, I realized I had just logged a few hundred kilometers on foot in search of Neandertals—from the earliest known in Europe, some 430,000 years ago at Atapuerca, to more recent times at 49,000 years at El Sidrón. Most of the famous sites in southwestern France were somewhere in between, from 180,000 to around 40,000. One, La Micoque, edged into the earlier register, around 300,000 years ago, possibly earlier. Soon enough, I would be back in the heart of things there, back to that place in the middle. What a very long stretch of time Neandertals had been on the earth. We were still youngsters by comparison and had already left deep cut marks and broken bones on the planet's flesh on a scale they never had.

SOON AFTER MY pilgrimage across northern Spain, I was back in southwestern France. I arrived at the national prehistory museum in Les Eyzies and was efficiently directed to the side, private entry door. It, as with the public entrance, was like walking into a cave, which it was; the museum was built straight into the rock shelf high above the town. *What a great place to work and what a great commute,* I thought as I went in to speak with Alain Turq one mid-autumn morning.

Several prehistorians and their staff welcomed me and ushered me through to the entrance, up the stairwell and to Alain's floor, where he invited me to take a seat in his office. I was catching him just before he needed to head off to give a private tour to a visiting group at one of the nearby prehistoric caves.

I think he enjoyed all the moving parts of his work, from prehistorian and field archaeologist to guide to synthesizer and scholar. He came to archaeology through his love of nature, geology, and paleontology. When he first had worked in medieval archaeology, all the extra textual and archival research was unappealing compared to the potential of piecing together the past by reading the earth as text—as was the case with pre-history—and he never looked back, pushing deeper into time. Something all these people I was meeting and speaking to had in common was their love of leaving the modern world and its issues for a past so far away that the slate was cleared for something else. Jean-Jacques had even con-fessed, in the context that we needed to tell stories, that this was in fact the appeal of the story of origins: going back to a different place, before the modern world existed with all its woes, its huge populations, its pol-lution, and its violence on a scale unimaginable before the Neolithic. Harold had begun in ancient Mesopotamia and found it was too modern and kept going back too, and like Alain and Jean-Jacques and all the others, he found his people. My people were these people and the people of this place, the Dordogne. Alain was from both tribes.

He hailed from a town just south of Carsac and like Didier grew up with the region's forests, rivers, and valleys as his childhood playground. As a young archaeologist he also excavated at prehistoric sites in Catalo-nia, Spain, which gave him a broadening perspective on the whole re-gion. When he regarded the Dordogne now, I could detect that he was also fitting it into a larger cognitive map on both sides of the Pyrenees, from the Atlantic to the Mediterranean and all of southern France and northern Spain.

Likewise, he liked to step back topically and take in the bigger picture, very much a synthesizer and a generalist as much as a specialist. I had noticed he listened carefully to others and also read diverse sources. Not wanting to waste the time I had with him, I decided to begin with a big-picture generalist's sort of question.

"How do you explain who the Neandertals were and what our rela-tionship with them might have been?"

As I asked, he settled in at his desk, wearing a striped hand-knit sweater against the soft morning chill, and rested his elbows on the surface with his hands clasped, listening. Stacks of different papers and articles took up the rest of the surface and his office looked like a busy magazine editor's workplace with thousands of different projects in progress.

"They were human, like us," he began, unclasping his hands and facing his palms toward the ceiling. "But also different from us, and there's the fascination, that, and they were the closest to us of all other humans, and then," he moved his elbows and set his two palms facedown onto the desk, "they disappeared. It's dramatic.

"But the challenge of Neandertals is chronology," he continued, "because you have well over two hundred thousand years to cover for them and less for us. Then, we have to be careful because our evidence is partial. I'm not a pessimist when I say this. I just understand the limits of this field. I'm a realist."

"Tell me more of what you think we can say, then," I asked.

"Well, the DNA studies are interesting because they are showing these facts, that we were both similar and different." He relaxed back into his seat and for most of the remainder of our talk stayed in that more kicked-back posture, his hands free to animate and talk with him to make his points.

"Language is clear; the genes are there and so is the morphology. The capacity is there. Language is a no-brainer. But what sorts of language? We have no idea. Furthermore, tool-making shows future thinking and future planning. Such as executing the idea in your mind, step by step, to get the form and symmetry you envisioned. This shows that they had complex ways of thinking, that they had past and future thinking while in the present, to plan and execute." It's essentially stone-bound syntax in a way, language's time-bound grammar of conjugated verbs, as seen in action through tool-making. "It's evidence of abstractions," he continued, "say, to make a biface," a hand ax, "because of what you have to think about to project an image from your mind onto the stone and then to make a planned and symmetrical object like that. It's a fundamental development in our common cognitive evolution as humans."

At that moment his phone rang and he paused to take the call. It was a tour group leader wanting to arrange a visit to one of the caves. He cheerfully arranged the time and logistics with her, hung up, and turned back to me, waiting for the next question. I loved where he was going with this one so asked for more.

"So, how you see these sorts of thought processes or choices is by looking at something like how a tool was made?"

"There was no technological revolution; it was just different," he said without hesitation. "Neandertals made generalists' tools and modern humans made specialists' tools. Neandertals made lissoirs," bone tools for smoothing animal hides, "but they never specialized in particular bone tools. It's a clear difference: Neandertals were flexible and modern humans were [and remain] very rigid."

In that moment, I felt my mind expand as if a tight band popped off and fell away. What a different way of seeing different approaches to intellect and adaptation: generalist versus specialist and flexible versus rigid. Oh my god, we moderns are such a bunch of rigid apes! I was so excited by what he had just said that I struggled not to interrupt and lose this delicious stream of thought. To my delight, he riffed on.

"It was a way of thinking that was more *à la mode, tu sais,* a part of their particular culture. Neandertals were more adaptive." *C'est tout.* He clasped and unclasped his hands again.

They were more laid-back and less OCD.

"For example?" I asked.

"Here in the Dordogne, *silex,* flint, is everywhere, so that changes the formula. It's here so they used it. But in Quercy," the historic region to our south and east that also encompassed the Lot, "flint is rare but quartz is available. So Neandertals used more quartz there and more flint here. But modern humans went farther away to bring flint back to Quercy."

Harold had said something similar, and I could see that the two saw things in similar ways, including being realists and admirers of the Neandertals.

Alain next leaned forward, resting his elbows and arms on the desk, and moving his head into a huddle. I leaned in to join him, knowing he was about to place the final capstone for this idea.

"Knowing the natural environment and living with it was key."

I suddenly looked at our modern human need to materially express symbols as a convention serving the rigid mind that insisted everyone have and know the rules and operate by them, into whatever environment they went. I asked him if that was a plausible read on our documented symbols.

"Sure," he said.

I couldn't stop from going one step further. "Do you think our need for a creator and religious beliefs and spiritual ideas is because of our rigid minds, too? A way to control the world and even facilitate or justify altering it?"

"Yes," he said without hesitation. "We're anxious because of it. We're structured and controlling because of it."

"So maybe we just don't see engraved and painted caves or tons of body adornments with Neandertals, at least that survive, because they didn't need to leave a heavy impression on how things were, with bound rules, or to let others know what the rules were, now and in future generations."

"Yes. I think that Neandertals adapted to each environment," he said, "and we adapted each environment to ourselves."

*Kaboom.*

Alain had no idea how much what he just told me had altered everything. It was the secret ingredient, the special key that unlocked a lot of mysteries while deepening others, the more interesting ones. I thanked him profusely and left his office walking on air. The pendulum lost steam and stopped swinging. Anyhow, it was a clichéd picture of how these modern humans think—making visible symbolic thinking, such as en-graved images and evidence for grammatical language, the pinnacle of symbolic thought. What if the visible symbols are just control mecha-nisms and the ones left invisible have a deeper, different story to tell but no less complex? What if evident symbols are not the apex of symbolic thinking but instead, the pinnacle of rigidity?

I went back to the place I was staying, typed up my notes from the morning, and then returned to the museum to take in its collections with new eyes, array after array of stone tool types from the Lower to the Up-per Paleolithic, trying to see in them what Alain saw. By midafternoon I was so consumed and fully taxed by this wonderful new conceptual shift that all I could think of was, I have to walk and get out of my head.

I took off along the Vézère River, a natural highway since its begin-ning; followed its flow through Les Eyzies, a village built entirely on its banks; and I went with its northeast exit along a dirt footpath that could eventually take me to La Ferrassie. But I wasn't going there today.

I took instead the circuit to La Micoque, the site that gave the regional tourist board the right to call the Dordogne a "vacation destination for 400,000 years." It seemed fitting to go there after having been to Atapuerca.

The late afternoon in this sinuous geography was magical and attested to the good life, past and present. Flashes of turquoise and rust orange that occasionally careened across my path accentuated the electric fresh air of approaching dusk and birdsong. I followed the flashes and saw *les guêpiers*, European bee-eater birds, in flight as they beefed up on flying insects to prepare for their migration south back to Africa using the Vézère as a highway with great roadside diners. They strafed past me and then flew across the river's silky surface and disappeared at the bend where I was heading.

La Micoque was rich in strata from many independent occupations over many separate times, the earliest level dating to around 350,000 to

380,000 years ago and considered Lower Paleolithic, with Acheulean tools that are often associated with *Homo erectus* or perhaps now I should say *Homo antecessor*. But here also, as at Atapuerca, the current thinking was that perhaps the first people who used this campsite were Neandertals. My heart skipped a beat and I quickened my pace. As they were La Ferrassie's neighbors, even if some 300,000 years earlier, it only seemed right to pay them a visit.

Approaching *l'heure bleue*, the blue hour, the sky was turning dark orange to fuchsia and soon would be deep lavender, then that rich cobalt blue before things darkened to black. I passed Laugerie Haute (one of the first places Alain dug) and then Laugerie Basse, both occupied by Cro-Magnons and containing beautiful, much later, Upper Paleolithic art.

I reached a farmer's field and a bridge and the footpath went around the bridge and through the cornfields as the road disappeared to my left and the river also departed, bending away to the right. I soon found myself climbing a cluster of low hills that huddled beyond the more formidable and towering cliff walls forged by the river behind me, where so many past humans had resided in the Gruyere cheese–like limestone caverns.

This mid-autumn had unusually warm days, so much so that when exploring another cave, I was half an inch away from setting my hand on a confused, trying-to-hibernate viper, an asp. Known for biting first and thinking later, in his groggy, half-asleep state he stirred slowly enough for me to remove my hand before I earned a Darwin Award. I was lucky. This Indian summer was also making it more intense to feel the old land, to delve more deeply into the fertile natural landscape with all the senses. The day was tinged with moist air saturated with mineral scents from damp limestone and decaying topsoil, cut grass, and wood fires from a nearby hamlet, which I discovered was tucked just beneath La Micoque.

I still had a little over half a mile to go to arrive, taking another sinuous path around, then up that hill, passing six little stone cottages that seemed to make up the whole settlement. A woman coming home from work pulled into her dirt driveway and I wondered what it was like to stoke one's fire, to sleep, and to awaken and head off to work every day at the foot of the oldest human residence in the Dordogne.

I thought about filmmakers Sophie and Vincent, with whom I'd recently enjoyed a dinner near La Ferrassie. After eating we took in the sky and there was the Milky Way, so easily visible in a night sky free from cell phone reception and city lights. As we watched the swirling galaxies overhead, I felt my feet tunnel in and reconnect to my Cro-Beebe not far away in La Ferrassie, connecting the stars to the sediments of iron-colored soil, from my eyes to my feet, and feeling fully physically, not abstractly, the sacred meaning in spiritual traditions of the joining of heaven and earth.

Deep down the final serpentine road from the hamlet, I climbed and snaked up to the site. La Micoque was still a remote place in a terrain that was unsuitable for industrialization or large-scale agriculture. Instead, it preserved the older ways of living on the land and benefited from all the micro-ecologies of diverse flora and fauna that the cliffs, stone, and river forged still. I thought at this juncture about what I had just learned from a visit with Randall White.

I'd had the chance to visit him at his home near the Vézère. A Canadian archaeologist teaching at New York University, he has excavated and worked on material in the Dordogne all his professional life. For his doctorate he did a survey on all the known Upper Paleolithic sites in the region, documenting many forgotten places, relocating them and remapping them, often knocking on villagers' doors to get the lore and lay of the land, learning to comprehend Occitan because this is the first language of the people here—not French. He came away with such intimate knowledge of the prehistoric landscape that sometimes locals now call him in New York to ask him about an obscure local site. He has spent the last twenty years excavating two Aurignacian sites at Castel Merle, Abri Blanchard and Abri Castanet. He is well-known for his contributions to Upper Paleolithic studies in the Dordogne, as Harold is for his to the Middle Paleolithic.

I had arrived midmorning on a pleasantly warm and sunny day and we settled outside on his terrace, where we could gaze out across the Beune and Vézère Valleys and the many layers of their dark green forests and undulating, tributary-forged golden-toned hills.

"Is there something about the Dordogne that made it different, more attractive, to humans in the past as in the present?" I had asked him. "Or is this just my bias because I love it here so much or because of the luck of preservation, given the many caves with more stable environments? Or is something else at work, some je ne sais quoi?"

"There *is* something special about the Dordogne," he said, "that attracts humans from a long time ago to now." He laid out an imaginary map on the table at which we sat. "The Dordogne is transitional, between the Massif Central and the Atlantic coastal plain." The Massif Central encompassed the south-central volcanic mountains to the east of the Dordogne and the Atlantic Ocean's coastal plain was to our west.

"It's transitional," he continued, "between the Pyrenees to the south and the Mediterranean to the south and the European plain to the north. What does that actually mean in concrete, day-to-day existence?" He smiled enthusiastically and I could see the younger man who had walked practically every inch of this landscape.

"Well, go into any of these side valleys—for geological reasons most of them have a north-facing, south-facing, east-facing, or west-facing slope." He gestured out beyond us, toward the valley in the middle horizon and at our feet that like all the region's valleys and cliffs had been cut out that way by a river or stream, such as the Vézère before us.

"The south-facing slope has Mediterranean species—animals and plants—and the north-facing slope has northern European species." And the east-facing slope has mountain species from the Massif Central and the west-facing slope has Atlantic species: each slope was as a mirror for the region it faced, the influences that came to it. "This area is a complete transition zone. That doesn't just translate into hybridization. That translates into enormous variability, habitat diversity that's related to relief."

That reality, on the ground, was mind-blowing: there is a crazy amount of variability in the Dordogne for such a small geographical territory. A ten-minute walk from your cave or valley encampment *in any direction* and you can gather plants and animals to eat from four different geographical zones—and not just on one level, but given the slopes, on several altitudes that added more variety depending on the part of the slope. Randy added that once he walked with a botanist from a location on the Vézère, beginning at the valley bottom and climbing up to its plateau. In the 3.5 kilometers that this covered, they identified seven distinct botanical zones just on one slope. It was the prehistoric equivalent of having a Whole Foods *and* a Trader Joe's right next door when other regions offered only 7-Eleven options. This simple fact of geography and climate drew animals and plants and humans to the region and continues to do so today.

I saw this everywhere I now looked in the landscape around me at La Micoque, with slopes nearby facing nearly all the directions, and very different plants and trees growing on either side. The sun was just kissing the limestone clifftops behind me and casting a red-orange hue onto the striations of the enclosed site. I could look through the fencing and see all the strata and see that this had been an ancient highway, a crisscrossing from the east into the west with a natural watery highway, like the *guêpiers* used, taking one into the variegated wealth of Whole Foods and Trader Joe's flora and fauna.

The blue hour was now firmly upon me and I took one more glance at the site and then turned back to the small road while I still had enough light to see. Once I was past the farmer's field, the rest of the way was along the river, with the limestone cliffs ethereally lit by a light that seemed to emanate from within them. I needed no headlamp to find my way and was intoxicated by the air, the colors, and the soft sound of frogs burbling their night song from the riverside.

By the time I got back to Les Eyzies, the whole village was in the velvet black of night but the citizens had invested in night-lights that illuminated the cliffs, with the museum and the Neandertal Man limestone sculpture standing at a ledge near it acting as a sentinel for the town. I crossed the bridge to reach the other side of the river, seeing the cliff reflected in its slow-moving and thick waters. It was sheer enchantment, and I was all the more elated because I had left my turnip for other fields. My turnip was in the generalist's field now, not the specialist's. I recalled a day not too long before when Harold had initiated me to the same way of thinking as Alain, and I realized it had taken a few passes before I really got it.

"I LIKE HOW Harold says, 'Why do they have to be like us to be smart?'" Vera said as we drove back late one afternoon from the dig during the last excavation season in 2014. Not long after that, during a lunch break at La Ferrassie, I asked Harold to elaborate how he saw behavior in the technological traditions he studied—the modus operandi of lithics specialists.

"My view of Neandertal behavior versus modern human is this," he said as he kicked back with his cowboy coffee and began to expound on it with a dreamy look on his face, so very much in his happy place. "Neandertals, basically in any situation that they found themselves, figured out a solution. You find yourself here, you've got these kinds of resources, you make do with these resources, and you make it work. It's why you go over to the Lot," the region just south of the Dordogne, a part of the Quercy, which Alain had also mentioned in a similar way, "and you've got quartz. Okay. You make do with that."

You see what you've got in your attic to solve a construction issue rather than running off to Home Depot to buy the exact piece of wood or fitted part. You don't go looking far and wide to find flint when quartz is right here and is good. Harold took a sip, the happy face went deeper into the happy place. He so completely and wholeheartedly loves and admires Neandertals, prefers them, I think, to us.

"So there," he gestured toward the Lot south of us with his free hand, "they're doing these kinds of animals. And here, they're doing this kind of animal, and so on. With modern humans, as I see it," I could almost detect a bit of disgust in his tone, "there's a certain way to act. We've got these rules and the rules say you use this kind of stuff, you do this kind of thing. It's a little bit like 'mad dogs and Englishmen.' You do it the same way no matter where you are all the time."

Flint, flint, flint, always flint, and flint for this and another style of flint for that, carving more deeply into the earth's flesh until we have urban landscapes and have forgotten what the earth looked like. Now we'll pollute the earth to have tomatoes shipped to us all year-round. We've bent our technology to alter the earth, rather than remain tomato eaters only in summer and move on to squash in autumn.

"The difference," Harold continued, interrupting my own private rant, "is the Neandertal way requires a lot of smarts. If you're going to be successful, you've got to figure out how to make do with the resources that you've got. The modern human way of doing things, you don't need to have as much smarts. Anybody who can learn the rules can get along and behave appropriately." And the rules belong to what we call modern human culture. Rules require symbols written or etched in stone, things that can be carried to other groups you've never met, to tell them also what the rules are. Rigid intellect, Alain might say, not flexible, like Neandertals.

It was time again to get back to the trenches but every now and then I peeked up out of my hole to cast a glance at Harold measuring lithic dimensions with Aylar, a lithics specialist in training from Iran. The two looked like peas in a pod, hunched over their beloved stone tools, measuring, refitting, and contemplating the hands that had made them. I could also tell that Harold was ruminating the rest of the afternoon on the theme we'd opened at the coffee break. He confirmed it when we wrapped up for the day and headed back to Carsac and he said to me in passing, to complete the conversation with a good conclusion, "I just think it's an insult to Neandertals to make them like us. We're not so great."

# 6

## A Moveable Neandertal Feast

ARLAT'S SATURDAY MARKET was bustling around us at midmorning when I joined Aurelie and Nadiya at a café. Soon, a friend of Aurelie's joined us as well. I could smell old books, Moroccan leather, chickens rubbed with lemon and rosemary roasting on a spit, coffee grounds, and the juicy perfume from cuts of fresh green apple for fritters, all stands nearby melding their activities of smells, sounds, and textures into our little round-tabled vortex. We ordered our drinks and Aurelie told her friend that I was interested in local prehistory. An administrator for the local secondary school, she grew animated and sat forward.

"I found a stone tool in my garden when I was planting my squash. It was so exciting. It was as if I were transported to somewhere back in the past, communing with the person who had left it there. In my garden!"

Though by now dozens of locals had told me something like this, because people are always doing something with the land—the field, garden, or forest (especially looking for mushrooms)—it never got old. That giddy childhood excitement would erupt in someone's face as they shared the magic of discovering something that was capable of eliciting a sensation of time travel as well as a heady communion with both the earth and humanity.

"It made the past immediate and real and present," she added.

"What did you do with it?" I asked.

"I wrapped it in a cloth and put it in a box," she said, "and took it to a specialist who identified it as Solutrean." She now knew who had lived at her spot on earth. Most of us like to know the prior owners and the history of a house before we buy it, but few can go back this far. The Solutreans had been early modern humans who had lived here between 17,000 and 22,000 years ago. She said she connected with them and that time period, each time she was in her yard. "I love my garden even more now."

"Had it been a Neandertal tool, identified as Mousterian, what would you have thought?" I had to ask. I could feel Monsieur La Ferrassie leaning over my shoulder, waiting to hear as well.

"That would have been *trop chouette*, too cool." I'm pretty sure I heard a dreamy tinge to her breathy answer.

It was the theme among those of us drawn to this time period. Most recently joining our crew was a young woman who had come from Paris, where she was working on her master's in prehistory. Originally from Languedoc, she first began excavating at medieval sites and then the Neolithic. As interesting as these periods were, she couldn't resist, as so many prehistorians before her, going back deeper in time. I had asked her why she found the Middle Paleolithic of greater interest than the Upper Paleolithic or the more recent time periods she'd studied. In a very Jacques Cousteau, understated way, with that shrug–pucker gesture the French delight us with, she had said, "*Beh, c'est la mystère.*" I then asked for her to push into the mystery; what exactly was in it?

"I'm fascinated by our roots and origins and Neandertals get me closest to that while still feeling like a period I can still understand, that I can relate to as a human, as closely related to us." There it was, origins again—not the deepest origins, but origins of where we felt it hit us at what was still identifiably this version of human.

Neandertals were like a pivotal meta-population that sat on the rim, relating to the more ancient ancestors but also to us in ways we could identify. Before and after them, it seemed things were more different. They are our link, as we seem to make them, to our own humanity. You'd think the Australopithecines would be poster children for the vegetarians and *Homo erectus* for manly men who love to hunt, but no, it was Neandertals or bust.

At one point in my time in Carsac, I was also writing a feature on Michael Chazan. This archaeologist at the University of Toronto works on that rare deeper time way back, the Lower Paleolithic, between 2.5 and about half a million years ago—when much of our evidence comes from *Homo erectus* across Africa and Eurasia. As I was immersed in both worlds, Carsac and the Neandertals and Chazan in South Africa, I asked Shannon McPherron about the difference between those who studied the Lower versus the Middle Paleolithic and then the transition into the Upper Paleolithic. He had done his doctorate on the earlier transition, Lower to Middle Paleolithic, and the pattern in Acheulean tools being expanded upon with new industries broadly called Mousterian for their technical style and similarities.

"It's often called the 'muddle in the middle,'" he said. "For some time now, two of the more intensely researched areas have been the origins of stone tool technology (the Oldowan) and the origins of modern humans/replacement of Neandertals. Between these two is a huge expanse of time that is covered by very few sites and relatively little research. One reason for this is that origins and replacements are more attractive topics than what happens in between."

We humans like drama. Look at our movies and novels and who makes it most into the esteemed pages of *Science* and *Nature*: people doing research in time periods with drama. But that muddle in the middle, not always the page-turning novel, is very important even if we the public or we the students don't gravitate toward it. But still, the Neandertals remained the most preferred poster child for human prehistory.

IT WAS THE full swing of the dig season and Saturday was our day off. My ritual was to spend it at the market, reconnecting with friends in Sarlat, sometimes walking the *piste cyclable* in both directions for the simple pleasure of being in forest, reliant on my feet, and passing Pech de l'Azé both ways, still feeling the goose bump–raising chill each time.

Sometimes I would take an alternate route and follow a small tributary that came off the Enéa Creek and cut back into Carsac on the bike path at the last minute. That triangle was like wandering into the land that time forgot. It was another way to time travel, in addition to finding a Stone Age tool in your garden.

I learned only later that I was also walking past another important Paleolithic site, Abri Caminade, which happened to be where Cécile's mother, Denise de Sonneville-Bordes, led her own excavation, mostly in Aurignacian material but with a solid Mousterian and Neandertal foundation that seemed related to the folks in Pech de l'Azé, where her husband dug.

Once back in Carsac, I loved standing at the fork in the road where one side led to the new dig house and the other to the old. First to Chez Bordes I went and did some wash and hung it to dry in the garden, as I caught up on writing and sleep in "the barn," and when the stars were aligned, I ran into Cécile in the garden or the kitchen and heard more stories of growing up here.

Come evening, I would stroll over to Harold's dig house and join the directors for Saturday night dinner. Most of the crew would go out to a local restaurant while others relished cooking for themselves and then retiring with a good book. Cécile was often busy with several art projects and staying in touch with her four children in other parts of the world.

"How is the barn?" she often asked as I passed through, concerned that I was comfortable. I loved how she called it the barn, dressing up a rustic word in her classy English that was intertwined with many accents: French, Australian, American, and British. Calling it *la grange* in French, which it was, might have made it sound more elegant, but she wanted to call it a barn to remind me of its simplicity, its lack of plumbing and heating. Of its two levels, the lower was a storage area and the upper, where the roof angled in sharply with its thick beams, was the sleeping nook. She had set her childhood bed into it, over which she had hung mosquito netting. Nearby was an elegant small writing desk, a family heirloom. She wanted to be sure that I had a solid place to write daily and without interruption. Her grandparents' paintings decorated the walls that did not angle. Her childhood hand-embroidered teddy bear sat on the bed.

"Splendid," I answered honestly.

The other days of the week had a well-regimented schedule. Each morning, I awoke extra early to write. When it was time to head to the camp, I would cross the garden, pass through the front gate, watching for frogs still slumbering in leaves and morning dew underfoot, make my way down the street along the Enéa Creek, cross the park, and pass the twelfth-century church—where I would intersect either with the two or three crew members who had gone up the hill to the bakery to fetch the day's bread, or one of the neighbors who unlocked the church precisely at 7:30 and then walked her big black dog.

It's not that three people are required to carry that much bread, even for a team of thirty, for two people could easily do it as well. It's just that it was so warm and smelled so good and the early morning fog still hovered over the green village and the skirts of the church nestled in its little crook-armed valley that it was a sublime time of day to simply be alive and present. And moreover, *c'est la belle vie en France,* and we knew it and we all pinched ourselves regularly to be sure this wasn't a dream. To dig in France. To fetch and eat fresh bread every morning.

We also felt the sore muscles in our arms from our hard labor. The rest of the day offered a view of *la belle France* that was not what the tourists motoring about the countryside or heading to the market in Sarlat saw. It was an intimate, old, gritty, striated France, the real dirt of the place, layers and layers of it.

The bread crew would leave a few loaves for the dig directors in the dig house upstairs, and take the rest downstairs to the outdoor kitchen in the backyard. The dig directors first held a pre-meeting meeting and I joined them to listen in. Then, at 8:00 AM, the dig directors and I went down to join the rest of the crew as they finished breakfast and went over duties, chores, strategies, and goals for the day.

I loved all of this ritual: The frogs. The soft fog on Cécile's garden. The sound of snoring animals—Nelson sounded like an old sailor, remarkable for his small size, while Hanoi, larger and stouter, snored like a dainty lady. The fluttering greeting on a low branch from the red-breasted European robin and his territorial song. The soft burble of the Enéa and little metallic blue dragonflies skimming the water's surface. The golden limestone of the cliffs that gave their stones to build the medieval church at their foot. The quiet and peace of this little fold in the earth. All of it reminded me each early morning why ancient humans came here, why Neandertals and later we were all so splendidly happy here. Each morning was a fresh primordial reminder of the stunning beauty of this geography that energized me and carried me through the day.

MIDWAY INTO THE final dig season at La Ferrassie in 2014, everything intensified, with a lot happening but no comforting sense of clarity or closure. What were we finding at this famous Neandertal cemetery and what were the experts beginning to see as they added the new data to the puzzle left by Peyrony's less well-documented digs? What could and could not be said about La Ferrassie and its relationship to the even bigger picture of who the people who had camped here were, as well as their possible relationship to the whole, the meta-population?

What was clear was that most days that I worked at the site, I dug in levels that were rich in animal bones and stone tools. Once, that human tooth was found; another time, a finger bone. The immense amount of animal bones, though, made it clear that I was standing in the midst of a lot of butchering, blood, and eating. Bison, deer, horse, and rhino. Precisely where I kneeled and worked could have been a pretty messy place.

Given Paul's initial reconstructions, we were near the cave opening of the larger, lower cave that had collapsed, leaving the rock shelf looking like what we had today. I imagined that access to open air was a good thing, given all the raw meat and infrequent baths in the nearby stream.

On the days that I worked at the lab in Carsac, I followed Virginie's meticulous instructions on washing, sorting, and labeling the animal bones, flint, and minerals that came back with the buckets so as to keep them all with their unique scan code numbers identifying them in the database.

From both efforts, at the dig and the lab, one thing was certain: Neandertals ate a lot of animal meat. Just the massive quantities of broken bones found at Neandertal butchery and campsites made this apparent, but an even more pinpointed way that proved this was a chemical procedure to measure nitrogen and carbon isotope levels in the bones and teeth of the human fossils. These levels proved that Neandertals, more than even us meat-loving hominids, were top predators and that a good portion of their diet was meat.

Recently, a team including Shannon, Jean-Jacques, and Teresa Steele—a zooarchaeologist from UC Davis in California who worked on several projects with both Harold and Shannon—had worked together at Jonzac, a Neandertal site in the Charentes-Maritime west of La Ferrassie toward the Atlantic that dated to somewhere between 55,000 and 40,000 years ago. (Jonzac is just south of Cognac and just east of the Medoc and Blaye wine-growing regions, so you see how one suffers and how very smart our archaic cousins were.) They quantified the carbon and nitrogen isotopes found in the collagen of a Neandertal tooth and several animal bones from the site, including horse, bison, deer, reindeer, *Megaloceros* (a huge extinct elk), and bear. The tooth results showed high reliance on large herbivore proteins, mostly horse and bison.

They also compared the isotopic results with other sites in France, Belgium, and Croatia that had done similar analyses and fell within the same general age ranges, such as Les Pradelles, Spy, and Vindija. They also analyzed the isotopes of a hyena and found that he or she ate mostly reindeer, so perhaps they weren't competing as much as some have thought, or perhaps there is another story there, about migration, seasonality, and who used the site when.

More recently, extensive work on isotopes and diet led by Hervé Bocherens from Tübingen University in Germany has come out with the results that about 80 percent of the Neandertal diet was large game meat and 20 percent was from plants. They based most of their study on two sites in Belgium where the isotope signature in Neandertal bones was for mammoth and woolly rhinoceros, even larger game animals compared to farther south at Jonzac. But it all speaks of a very real human fact, of variation and diversity and adapting to one's geography, going for the tastiest of what that geography offers, if it is that plentiful to pick and choose. Farther south into Spain, the dietary patterns shifted more, where rabbits, birds, seals, and perhaps more plant foods also factored in.

So while a big feature on the Neandertal menu, meat is not the whole picture. Animal remains also preserve better and longer in the earth after dying and being consumed. The chance of a 70,000-year-old plant making its way to the present to be found in one of the levels or buckets was far slimmer. But researchers are developing new ways to extract more plant-rich information from the fossils as well as the soil that surrounds them, and that long-ago idea of "man the hunter" is growing more moot by the minute. (For one, both genders could easily have done the hunting. Indeed, adolescent female bonobos—our closest kin among the living primates, who are also closely related to the common chimpanzee—have the habit of being the hunters of the group. *Voilà*. And for another, too much protein in the human diet can lead to dangerous forms of toxicity.)

One thing that preserves plants better for posterity is if they have been cooked or burned in fire. The charred remains survive better in the record. At Kebara in Israel, there were "a million and one" hearths in the Mousterian level, as Paul told me once while looking at some of the (far fewer) hearths at Pech de l'Azé near Carsac. He exaggerated to make the point of just how remarkable Kebara's hearths were. And thanks to all those hearths, archaeologists found charred acorns, pistachios, pea seeds, and legumes, rounding out a diet that also included a range of animals, including small game, more common in Mediterranean Neandertal sites than farther north.

At Gorham's Cave in Gibraltar, Clive and Geraldine Finlayson and their team work at one of the last sites Neandertals inhabited before they disappeared entirely. There, along with rabbit, ibex, red deer, all sorts of shellfish (mussels, limpets, cockles), tortoise, monk seal, dolphin, and roasted pigeon, the team discovered that they also ate a good deal of plants, including pine nuts.

Both Kebara and Gorham's Cave reveal an ancient version of the Mediterranean diet. But the ancient diet of the Dordogne—a place now known for its wealth of delicacies, from truffles to walnuts to foie gras and cured duck breast—was more a diet of deer, bison, and reindeer, as far as evidence currently tells us. Southern diets may have been richer in plant foods because the southern areas were more temperate and rich in plant-based nutrition—and perhaps less populated with large herding game animals.

Moving from one rich patch of plant foods to another, which were spaced closer together in more southern ecologies, people could consume more plants and get enough nourishment compared to northern ecologies. There's also the possibility that in warmer territories, where natural fires were a more frequent occurrence, fire was more available for cooking hard-shelled seeds and wild grains to make them more edible.

This position—that fire-making and fire use are two separate issues that don't always occur in the same place—is more contested. But how many people living today, if deprived of their matches, lighters, and gas torches, would know how to make a fire? I would wager if it came down to this for cooking dinner, most of us would be eating our food raw.

Another way to find plants in the archaeological record is through phytoliths—microscopic fossils of plants in the soil, an area where Paul and Vera contributed a lot because these little fossils can be seen in the thin sections, slides made from super-thin slices of soil samples—in context with other naturally occurring materials, such as flint, bone, small animal remains, fossilized fecal matter (called coprolites), ash, and other contents of the sediment at that slice of place and time.

Sometimes ancient pollens can also be sussed out from the soil, but as seen at Shanidar in Iraq, pollen studies are tough and have to come from sections of a dig that were so undisturbed that no recent pollens could have made their way in. Then, investigators have to be sure the pollen got there by human actions, not naturally such as through gerbils, insects, or the wind.

Climate can inform us about food sources during warm versus cold periods. I knew whom to ask about this. One of Dennis's specialties was reconstructing the Paleolithic environment during different climatic conditions and speculating about these sorts of things.

"During warm periods," he told me, "when much of Eurasia was dominated by deciduous forests, animal biomass [density or population] was actually relatively low because it was composed of more solitary-living animal species (roe deer, fallow deer, wild pigs, and even red deer to some extent) and fewer that lived in large herds. Getting enough to eat may have been particularly difficult then." That's exactly the opposite of what I would have thought.

"During cold periods," he continued, "depending on the specific region, the environment shifted between steppe and tundra. Tundra environments have the lowest animal biomass, but steppe actually tends to have quite a high biomass (grasslands supporting large herds of reindeer, bison, and perhaps horse). During glacial periods some populations may have undergone serious food shortages and others may have been doing quite well."

As with everything, we can't overgeneralize, but still we need to take in all the factors and look at each context as a unique window into a wider past way of life.

"GOT ONE," I said to Matt from my sea of animal bones and flint. He was manning the survey tool called a total station, which was connected to a computer running site data entry and organizing software. A total station is electronic surveying equipment that can accurately measure objects at near and far distances, making measurements with its laser beam more accurate than usual in more standard recording methods in archaeology. The software, New Plot, was one of several software programs that Shannon and Harold wrote to make data recording and entry more accurate and also available for comparative analysis. It began by shooting in at its level and square each designated artifact that we found in the site, naming it for what it was—bone, flint, or other mineral—and automatically giving it its own unique bar code, which I also had on hand, printed out on sticker labels, to place on the bag into which I placed the object once its location was shot in and recorded.

This method was one of Harold and Shannon's biggest contributions to the field. Ever dedicated to bringing objective scientific practices—systematic and standardized, offering clear data sets that then could be compared with other clear data sets—and tapping into both of their interests in math and computers, the two collaborated to create innovative software and site-mapping techniques that more accurately mapped the objects and performed spatial analysis with the resulting maps, including in three dimensions.

Moreover, this method was inspired to eliminate excavator bias, setting standards that everyone followed so that each excavator at each square wasn't making their own choice about what was important or not important to document.

At all the Paleolithic sites where Harold and Shannon and their extended teams worked together and apart on other projects, this method and software were used, making for incredibly powerful comparisons given the unified units of comparison. Moreover, all their software was available for free download on their website, OldStoneAge.com, where they shared their data and results with everyone. They really wanted archaeology to be more a science than a humanity, more deductive than inductive. Archaeology had largely been a discipline where each dig and its head director had his methods, learned from his mentor, and dug the site in that chain of transmission, picking his own units and measurements and often leaving excavator bias as a major player in how the data from the ground up made its way to being recorded, analyzed, and with luck published.

Publications were another hair-pulling matter. Many excavated sites have yet to be published; people all over the world are just sitting on unpublished information about one-of-a-kind sites, so all that data is not available for the future. There are in fact many more unpublished Neandertal sites than there are published, which also skews the data, not to mention the interpretations people have. Harold and his team have strived to publish as soon as possible to get the data out to others. How else can we have well-informed ideas of who the Neandertals were?

Back at the dig, Harold, Shannon, and Dennis make sure everyone is trained from the beginning not to make their own judgments in their own excavation squares. At the Middle Paleolithic levels, everything that is 2.5 centimeters or larger gets shot in, whether a person thinks it's a pretty tool or bone or not. If it is smaller it goes into the bucket, which also receives its own unique bar code identifying it with the levels at opening and closing the bucketful of sediment. If a person is working in the Upper Paleolithic levels, where there is simply more stuff and where many of the flint flakes are small blades, a more common style in the Upper Paleolithic, the standard is that anything 1 centimeter or larger gets shot in.

Two-euro coins are exactly 2.5 centimeters in diameter and ten-centime coins are exactly 1 centimeter. So at the site, at the respective levels, nearly every square had a coin lying to the side to act as a reference for the excavator. Each morning it was a bit like climbing into a treasure trove, the sun glinting off the modern bling in the ancient pits.

Now that Harold and Shannon had been digging together for over twenty years, in France, Morocco, and Egypt, dedicated to the unifying theme of understanding late Neandertals and early modern humans, they had a growing set of sites from similar time periods that could be compared with things that were actually measureable and consistent.

"*Os* or *silex*?" Matt asked me, keeping with dig protocol to call things in French since France was the native site.

"*Os*," I said. It was a broken piece of bone the shape of an oblique triangle, the length of my index finger and the width of my big toe. It was probably from a bison or a deer. There were thousands of these faunal remains at La Ferrassie but I had eyes only for this sweet 70,000-year-old ungulate, last touched by a Neandertal and now touched by me. It was three times larger than a two-euro coin and a no-brainer that it needed to be shot in. I was so happy to be in the Middle Paleolithic and at the Neandertal levels.

As one of the crew, Anna from Boston, said casually, giving voice to what most of us thought, "Studying the Middle Paleolithic and Neandertals feels extra important because they're an extinct species." She then paused and added as an afterthought, "And studying us, even early us, is a bit like navel-gazing."

The bone was likely the ancient remains of someone's dinner, and my hands trembled as I strove to hold the pointer still for Matt to fix the laser and click its exact position. Right next to it was a gleaming piece of flint that looked like a scraper emerging from the earth. It wasn't yet ready to be released from the dirt, but soon. I reminded myself of Dennis's mantra, to carefully and evenly ease the soil encasing the artifacts, "like a bathtub full of toys draining its water." It was key to keep everything level as one worked down, never to dig holes and get so obsessed with one object that the others on the same level were left behind. Levels were crucial to the data set. With Dennis's bathtub water mantra in my head, I took a deep breath and waited.

My feet again stood in 90,000 years ago as I worked 20,000 years later on a terrace above it. The breadth of time was still an overwhelming prospect. My knees quivered as I thought of this. A friend back home had recently sent an email asking, "How does one process that kind of time?"

I thought about it, trying to give it words, and realized that you don't process it at all; *it* processes *you*. My mere fifty years of age—the magical marker of half a lifetime for twenty-first-century *Homo sapiens*, when we begin to fret in earnest over wrinkles, gray hairs, bucket lists, and having enough savings—suddenly seemed so small, so banal. *It* processed *me*; it folded me into the long strata of human existence that went on long before I came along with my concerns, and will long persist in a beautiful striated pattern well after I am laid down and decomposed into the stripes. There were great big wondrous things in life and some were long lived, and others brief, and both made their way into these layers. It overrides total death, I thought, thinking of Jean-Jacques's words. It cheated death of its full sting.

I carefully picked up the bone fragment and set my marker at the base of where it had been and Matt fixed a red laser point on the spot. A few seconds passed.

"Got it," he announced. The position and type were documented and shot into place for that level. I took a breath and placed the bone in a small zip-lock bag and then stuck on a unique scan-coded sticker with the number Matt had just given me. It would forever identify this bone, this place, this level, this day. Death stood at bay. I set the bagged and tagged bone into a bucket and continued to work my imaginary bathtub water level in soil, slowly removing sediment to see what new piece would come to the surface.

With the gray scraper arrived more bones. Each time I uncovered a stone tool, I placed an inconspicuous black dot with a special marker on the side that faced up. Shannon had asked us to mark them this way and I was curious why.

"We want to interpret Neandertal behavior from the lithics," he answered, "so we need to know where they dropped the lithics and it's important to know if they've been altered by post-depositional processes." Once everything was shot in, they would look at the patterns and percentages of tools found at different orientations and this was a part of adding details to how best to read what had happened. Was the tool just dropped by a Neandertal or had shifting earth and water moved it? If a natural process was responsible, many of the tools would be found lying in a similar formation compared to the more random nature of tools being dropped by humans.

I also tuned my ears to listen in when Dennis talked about overall site formation processes and speculated that Neandertals might have used La Ferrassie briefly each time that they came here, perhaps for two weeks, before moving somewhere else in the neighborhood.

Also, to date, we had not found any fire hearths, which surprised the team. So if they ate here, and it seemed that they did, given the cut marks and severely broken animal bones scattered all around, it looked as if food had been consumed raw. All these deer, bison, horse, and sometimes rhinoceros bones made me hunger to learn more about the plants that might also have been eaten. What else had they foraged from the surrounding forest, hills, and streams?

As luck would have it, one morning at midseason, when I stepped into the dig house for the pre-meeting meeting, Amanda Henry from the Max Planck Institute for Evolutionary Anthropology was sitting with the dig directors. She led her own research group called Plant Foods in Hominin Dietary Ecology. Among many projects, she has also looked closely at the Neandertal diet using a special technique of investigating fossilized tartar—dental calculus—on ancient teeth for signs of plant matter (phytoliths and starch grains). Dental calculus contains microfossils that one can see under a microscope. She, with colleagues Alison Brooks from George Washington University and Dolores Piperno at the Smithsonian Institution, analyzed the tartar from three individuals, two Neandertals from Spy in Belgium and one from Shanidar in Iraq. The selection of a northern European and a Levantine site was intended to cover the wide range of habitats in which Neandertals had lived, for the purpose of gaining a wider and more diverse view of their diet.

I was excited to ask her about the edible plants she was finding in ancient people's teeth. Suddenly the plate before me that had held deer, bison, horse, and rhino had some greens, seeds, and roots to round it out. So when the pre-meeting meeting was over and we all walked down the hill to the backyard, Gary in tow, licking my hand, then moving on to hers, I asked her, "What did Neandertals eat?"

"Plants!" She enthused, patting Gary on the head. "We found water lily roots and various grass seeds . . ."

". . . Water lily roots?" I asked. That one surprised me.

"Sure, and date palms, barley, and lots of legumes."

I later looked up the water lilies and learned that not only are the roots edible, and also starchy and potato-like, but so are the flower buds and seeds.

While Amanda's research doesn't contradict the fact that Neandertals seemed to have eaten more meat than a rancher in Texas or Argentina, it did add more nuance to their diet as omnivores. Other research with dental calculus, led by Karen Hardy at the University of Barcelona, extracted plant fossils from five of the individuals from El Sidrón. They discovered quite a few carbohydrate-rich foods in the form of starch granules; plus wood smoke that suggested a fire and potential cooking; and most surprising to some, two herbs, yarrow and chamomile, known for medicinal use but without nutritional value.

One day soon after Amanda's visit, another young scientist arrived, Ainara Sistiaga, who was affiliated both with MIT and the University of Laguna in Tenerife—one of Spain's Canary Islands in the Atlantic. Where Amanda looked at teeth, Ainara looked at coprolites, the scientific word for old poop. She was here to gather soil samples from different levels in La Ferrassie, hoping to land some that contained the passage of someone's meal back into the earth.

*Coprolites*, fossilized feces, is a term from the Greek meaning stone dung. (Similarly, phytoliths are stone plants, plant fossils.) I was delighted that I met these two women in the right order, first in with the teeth, next out at the other digestive end.

Paul and Vera often found coprolites in their work in micromorphology, appearing in their thin sections. They were from hyena at times, from herbivores and ungulates at others, and on some rare occasions, from a human. Their ability was limited by studying these things physically and being able to say these animals had been there because they shat there. But Ainara was working with a cutting-edge technique that ultrasonically and chemically extracted dietary information from the ancient poop.

She had recently applied the technique to soil samples from El Salt, a Neandertal site near Alicante on Spain's Mediterranean coast. Her method extracted cholesterol, old, old cholesterol, from the ancient fecal matter she'd collected in the field, and that could tell her how much plant food in comparison to animal protein the person had eaten that day (or day before, depending on how regular they were). From this effort she learned that Neandertals in eastern Spain were eating tubers, berries, and nuts, which showed up as phytosterol. Animal-based foods also showed up, in the form of cholesterol.

When we eat plants and animal meats, gut bacteria in our bodies metabolize the phytosterol (from plants) and the cholesterol (from meat) found in these foods into $5\beta$-stigmastanol and coprostanol, respectively. Both are metabolized forms of ingested foods that then are excreted in fecal matter for posterity. Ainara also looked for biomarkers in the fecal matter to establish it as being from a human and not another animal such as a deer or hyena. The result was a quantification of that person's meal, preserved in the ancient poop, of how much plant and animal matter had been consumed.

High proportions of coprostanol told a story of a big meat meal. But significant proportions of 5β-stigmastanol showed that the person also munched on a good helping of plants. This was the image that began to emerge for Ainara, that, yes, Neandertals were eating a pretty meat-heavy diet, but that there were significant and measurable quantities of plant foods too.

All this new research from the likes of Amanda and Ainara was inspiring me to write a new Paleo cookbook. Harold had already written one, *The Human Evolution Cookbook*, showcasing his favorite recipes at the dig house; including at the dinner table the whole human family and lessons on human evolution, from Australopithecus to all the rest of us in the genus *Homo*; and also riffing on place names in the Dordogne (Pech Peach Melba, for instance). It really was not Paleo in the sense that there were a whole lot of carbs, but very Paleo in the sense that there was a whole lot of meat and fat, including butter, cream, pig, and duck fat. "Which is why Harold's cooking is so good," Shannon chimed in.

And my cookbook would also be different from Eudald Carbonell's, I think, where I would dream up regional Neandertal menus and their famous eateries, such as charred Kebara acorn hummus with toasted pistachios, La Ferrassie stir-fry with bison and water lily root, and while we're at it, since naturally fermenting fruits do occur in nature, Feldhofer Neander Valley berry wine with wild boar and berry sauce.

That day at La Ferrassie, Ainara selected places in each level of the site and at different spots to take soil samples, which she gathered, sealed, and marked to take back to her lab, where she would carry out the complex extraction of phytosterols and cholesterols.

"Does your family give you grief when you tell them you're a fecal specialist?" I asked as we took a coffee break. She laughed. "I always explain what I do from the start with scientific procedures and explanations so that it's hard for people to joke about my life being all about the poop."

Along this moveable feast I passed, from one end to the other, and soon found myself with another scientist on the food chain when I got back to Carsac in the early evening. There, I joined Kate Britton, an archaeologist from the University of Aberdeen in Scotland, to gather dead snails in the forest above the cemetery. She'd been gathering snails all over the place near prehistoric sites.

"Make sure they're dead snails," she emphasized. This was not a foraging exercise—Harold had gone off food shopping again—but a scientific one. "That way," she said cheerfully, "we can publish that no animals were hurt in the making of this study." Dead snails served the study well, so why accrue karma?

As we climbed up the hill, we gathered not only dead snails, but also leaves, tree and shrub bits, and grasses. With this environmental sampling, Kate was charting a map of the strontium isotope's absorption and decay in living things and the soil of this region, toward the goal of making a baseline to help re-create the surrounding Paleolithic environment. Snails, dead or alive, but better dead, offered a good average reading of locally available strontium, which is in the soil and plants. They ingested it and offered their reference average for what was available in that environment and its absorption by other living things. In this way geology could reflect back on biology, re-creating the past environment.

Next, by measuring the strontium absorbed and remaining in the teeth of reindeer and bison from local Paleolithic hunting sites in the Dordogne, Kate could compare the levels and see if they were local levels—as shown by the snails (she also tested snails found at the archaeological sites)—or fluctuating with other values that indicated the animals had visited other environments with their own strontium levels. So these snails could lead to helping tell a story about local migratory patterns among larger game animals and seasonal activities.

That then offered patterns about the habits of humans, how they exploited food sources around them, and in what seasons. Kate had already done a study at the nearby site of Jonzac, where Teresa and Shannon also worked, in the Charentes region to the west. She found that the strontium of a bison tooth at the site was of local levels, implying the animals stayed around, but that the reindeer teeth measured had fluctuating levels, showing they were migrants. So bison steaks were year-round, but reindeer steaks were seasonal, probably in the early spring.

At a lunch break at La Ferrassie, as we ate leftover spaghetti with red sauce (olive oil, sautéed onion, garlic, fennel; then tomatoes, herbes de Provence, and red wine left to cook down and concentrate the flavors), salad, and garlic bread from at least a thousand garlic cloves, Harold began to worry about the next few dinners ahead of us. As the daily meal planner and food shopper, he seemed to spend more of his time on food and sustenance than on any other aspect of the dig.

"We have to do the fire-baked camembert," he began. I liked how he worried.

"Definitely," affirmed Shannon.

"But I'm so tired of food shopping. I noticed, if I buy food, they eat it. So maybe I should stop buying food." He laughed at his own joke but no one else did.

"They can forage like the Neandertals and Cro-Magnons in the forest for food," I offered. The rest of the crew stared at me, not happy I was fanning the fires of a flaming bad joke.

"Yeah, let them learn," he said, leaning back in his chair, which we all feared would snap at any moment, and slipped his hands behind his head with a self-satisfied smirk on his face. "Let them learn to live the way of Neandertals."

But he's too much of a foodie and one of the things about foodies is, as much as they love to cook and to eat, they love more to cook and watch others eat their creations. "Nah," he said a few moments later, "we definitely need to do the fire-baked camembert."

Everyone else smiled and returned to eating.

"And don't forget," chimed in Anna, "we're going to do potato latkes, too."

"Right," Harold affirmed. "Plus, there's the lemon meringue tart to make, and we need to use all those apples that are falling on our heads in the backyard. You all need to eat more fruit," he added almost sarcastically. A third of the crew were vegetarians and all of us, vegetarians and omnivores alike, were concerned about staying regular and healthy and constantly asked him to buy more fruit. No one said why, but it was understood; life was a chain of action, from dental calculus to coprolite formation, but while alive, no one wanted stone poop. Leave that for the scientists of the future.

"And we can make applesauce," added Jonathan.

"And apple pie," added Anna.

"And apple cider," chimed in Dennis, adding the most popular suggestion into the mix.

"We still need good cheese," Harold repeated, going back to the idea of baked camembert a third time—which told me it had to be really good and obviously a tradition, whether the way of Neandertals or not. But apparently, everyone else was already dreaming their own dreams and hadn't quite heard him.


JONATHAN WAS ALSO one of the vegetarians in the crew and, maybe related or not, his research focused on the ancient human relationship with plants. Normally a vegan, he worked his way around the meat on the table, although he accommodated cheese and eggs. He knew that to exist as an excavator he needed to adapt to somewhere in the middle—a very Neandertal approach, I might add, adjusting to the local environ-ment rather than trying to change it to suit his diet, as *Homo sapiens* seem to do.

One day at our break, as Jonathan snacked on apples and cheese, I asked him why he was interested in the Paleolithic and plants.

"I study the Paleolithic because it is separate enough from us to be different," he said. "Later periods, even the Iron or Bronze Ages, are still too close to our reality. But the world before agriculture is rich with ideas of who we were before we became this." He swept his arm over the col-lective of *us*, humans alive today living as we do, the team, the road, the tourists to the Dordogne and their quest for foie gras. "Plants tell us a lot about social relationships, not only nutrition."

At that moment, the wind blew and the oak branches overhead lifted gently, as if to say they were a part of the conversation. Two electric green-and-blue dragonflies flitted past and right after them, more lan-guidly, followed four orange-and-black butterflies. That afternoon, as I walked toward the forest to use the facilities, I crossed paths with Sophie and Vincent, arriving to film us working for the afternoon. "Look for the chanterelles," Vincent said to me, "they're coming up everywhere."

Jonathan now asked me to consider how everything really changed in our social relationships with agriculture and using plant foods as surplus and class-building. Or consider, he added, even how hunters and gather-ers divide their world into plant and animal foods and who gathers what; it said a lot about the social order of the group.

"Plant foods are also a more reliable food source," he said, "so those who know how to get edible plants from the environment can keep the group alive more readily than those who hunt." That's what Jonathan wanted to know above all else: what was the world like before agriculture?

"It's unknown because there are no more true hunters and gatherers and even the traditional ones left who survive today have too much influence from us—except maybe the Australian Aboriginals and the people deep in the Amazon."

True to pattern, Jonathan discovered his passion for archaeology early in life, first stimulated by seeing Phoenician salt mines on a visit to Crete when he was thirteen. But like all the others gathered in this field, he pushed further back in time into the Paleolithic, where he could study a way of human existence different from all the commoditized and property-owning modern reality that risked the very balance of life on earth.

He got me thinking more about how archaeologists can read the past for indications of past social dynamics based on relationships to food sources. As for all things about reconstructing the ancient Paleolithic environment, I turned to Dennis. All caveats about our biases of being part of modern mind-sets understood, he said, "Among recent hunter-gatherer groups we can see that when faced with very patchy distribution of resources—food distributed across the landscape in small packages (a deer here, a pig there, a patch of ripe berries there)—groups will tend to remain very small and move very frequently, perhaps even daily. They will move the whole group to the food location."

But, "When resources occur as large packages (a herd of reindeer) that are perhaps unpredictable in where and when they will occur, groups tend to be a bit larger and stay a little longer in any one location. These groups will tend to send out a smaller group who bring the food back to the camp."

"How does that reflect on what you're seeing in the Middle Paleolithic with Neandertals?" I asked, intrigued. What was going on, for instance, at La Ferrassie?

"We can generally assume that Neandertals were, overall, subject to the same general factors, considerations, and constraints on group size and mobility as modern humans. We expect they followed the same general patterns in response to the nature of their resources. However, there is no doubt that there were some important differences between Neandertals and modern humans that might have affected how they would respond to changes in their resources. This is difficult to guess at, but for example, we think that Neandertals had a higher metabolism, which, coupled with poor clothing and limited use of fire and shelter, would mean that they would require more fat and protein in their diet and just more to eat. We could imagine that this could have a major impact on how they had to respond to changes in access to prey animals."

Not only that, but it appears that Neandertals often endured food scarcity. "At many sites, the degree of fragmentation of the bones is so intense that it has been difficult to explain. If all one is doing is eating the meat and perhaps getting the marrow out of the larger bones, the degree of fragmentation should be limited. At Roc de Marsal and Pech IV, all the bones are smashed into very small pieces; this often includes very small toe bones."

Toe bones. Such a funny phrase when you hear someone say it, a bit shocking. But then it also reminded me of crab cookouts, my friends and I sitting around with our wooden mallets smashing every appendage, no matter how small, to eke out the little bits of precious, and very expensive, crabmeat. It was the equivalent of toe bones on herbivores.

"I think that is what was going on," Dennis said, "that Neandertals were smashing up all the bones into small enough pieces so they could suck all the available bone grease out." As in marrow.

Bone grease. Okay, that is even more shocking sounding out loud than toe bones.

"There are a few ethnographic examples of such behavior," he concluded, "but it's not that common and is associated with serious food stress. I am not the only person to suggest this, but it's not a widespread or common idea."


ONE OF THE most comprehensive studies to date, combining a comparative view of Neandertal diets and ecologies from all their ranges of occupation within a period of 120,000 to 30,000 years ago, came from Luca

Fiorenza from the University of New England in Australia and seven other colleagues, including Amanda Henry, (The study bore the punning title, "To meat or not to meat.") While they looked to expand the wider understanding of the Neandertal diet in time and place, they also concluded that the view of Neandertals as top predators—consuming a lot of meat, akin to lions, hyenas, and wolves—was close to the mark. But they added that the picture of plants was also complex.

Fiorenza and his colleagues also reconstructed the climate and landscape between three climatic fluctuations and discovered that even with changes in terrain, game, and opportunities, Neandertals did not change their diet much. They adapted well to the changes but still went for medium to large game and then filled in the rest with plants and smaller animals found locally.

What I found especially interesting was that in the climatic fluctuations, the southwest of France proved to be the rich transition zone Randall White had spoken of, being between one kind of environment and another. Around 120,000 years ago, during a warming trend, northern Spain, southwestern France, the British Isles, and the lower reaches of northern and central Europe were mostly deciduous forest.

At the same time, the Mediterranean area was mostly evergreen forests. During a colder more recent time, between 75,000 and 59,000 years ago, southwestern France became a mix of tundra and cold steppe, with edges of emerging Atlantic coastal plains and cold steppe near the Pyrenees. The Mediterranean was also mostly an arid cold steppe, while the Levant was a plains ecology.

Another warming trend occurred after 59,000 years ago to about 24,000 years ago, though not as warm as the prior one. Southwestern France again was richly diverse compared to other geographies. It was dominantly a mix of conifer forests and mixed conifer and deciduous woodlands, the latter also defining the Mediterranean from Iberia to the Levant.

These last two climatic periods combined, from 75,000 to 24,000 years ago, encompassed the times and places of the Neandertals we know best. They showed not only diversity but also solidity in knowing each environment and subsisting as they had all along. This stable diet didn't change too much but adjusted to shifts in the types of game animals and plants, still apparently showing the same preferences and percentages. Put another way, one band wasn't opting to be only meat and potatoes while another went vegan. They were pretty much heavy meat-eating omnivores with about the 80/20 helping of meats/plants that Hervé Bocherens had found in his study.

If I were to apply these numbers to our crews' dietary habits alone, of the thirty regulars, about one is 100 percent a plant eater (vegan, and he adapted), and about five are 5 percent animal protein eaters by way of eggs and dairy and 95 percent plant eaters. The range for the remaining twenty-four of us would be anywhere from 20/80 to 30/70 to 50/50 meat/plant consumption. No one, not even Harold who loves meat, came anywhere close to the 80/20 level of meat-eating. We also seemed, from the general picture, to be more varied than perhaps Neandertals could be. Maybe this was a part of our more rigid adaptation, as we changed the world around us to suit each of our preferences rather than hanging as a group. Ironically, Neandertals kept eating as they were accustomed to but they were adapting to what was available in their environment and learning far more about what their environment had to offer than we ever bother with. We'll go farther to keep eating reindeer while they shifted from reindeer, which had migrated in and out, and went back to deer, horse, and bison.

ONE LATE AFTERNOON, back from the dig and covered in dark red dirt from La Ferrassie, I made a detour to pick up local strawberries, one of five varieties grown here, to take back to Cécile. Entering the garden Chez Bordes, I found Cécile watering her flowerbeds, very much the contrast to me, elegant and fresh in one of her Japanese kimonos she'd collected when she lived in Australia. She saw the strawberries and began telling me about the traditional subsistence of the Dordogne before tourism altered the local economy in recent decades. Ironically, the popularity of the region with tourists was due to its land and its traditional life. Before it became a vacation destination, the Dordogne was an economically poor region and most people lived on subsistence agriculture, growing and producing enough to live on and that was pretty much it. They were economically poor but wealthy in independence and self-sufficiency.

"It was a patriarchal society on the outside," she added with a curious note, "but on the inside it was matriarchal. Men owned the animals, the wheat, the tobacco, and the vines. Women owned the vegetable gardens, the poultry, the nut trees, and the geese." She emphasized geese so that I would fully understand what that meant. Geese, more than walnuts and truffles, drive the local food economy and now all of France and Europe flock here for the various goose products.

"By the way," she added, "the 'sisters of Carsac' ask for your and my presence for *un apéro dinatoire*. Are you free Sunday night?"

But of course. I loved the sisters of Carsac, the name of dear childhood friends of Cécile's who had her sense of adventure and mischief. They also called Cécile their "little sister," because she was the youngest and had been with them since early childhood. "I'll be there," I said, "but, what's *un apéro dinatoire*?"

"A wonderful French invention," explained Cécile. "It is a light dinner, just some nice aperitifs, and then a really good lusty dessert."

I went and took my shower, the water running rust red, then orange, then at last clear, feeling so happy with this amazing life, this endless Neandertal feast.

A few days later, Cécile and I made our way to the home of the sisters with a view of the entire Enéa Valley below, including the church nearby and the cliffs of Pech de l'Azé farther away. Above us was a huge hidden cave, an idyllic place to play as a child. They explained that, along with

Cécile's little brother, they would go to that cave and pretend to be pre-historic cave people. Usually Cécile's little brother wound up being tied and bound and the others pretended to roast him for dinner. He went along with it just to bask in the aura of all these older sisters.

We feasted on five courses of hors d'oeuvres and aperitifs and then they brought out *un gâteau Saint Tropez*, "the whole point of our light little dinner," said one of the sisters. It was composed of tiny brioches dripping in caramel and forming a ring around a thick vanilla cream. We continued to sip Champagne and cut in. As we ate cake, I learned that the sisters' father had excavated the cave behind us with Cécile's father, and that he had found a lot of Neolithic remains, as well as those from the Bronze Age, but nothing Neandertal. But that was okay, we con-cluded, gazing across the valley toward the cliffs of Pech de l'Azé, raising our glasses, for there they were, permanent neighbors with secrets still left to uncover. We helped ourselves to seconds and sipped some more.

Somehow, Cécile and I successfully walked home after such splendid indulgence. She told me that the next evening she was making boeuf bourguignon for the whole crew. She had been lassoed into doing it when Harold heard her critique *his* boeuf bourguignon and he chal-lenged her to make a better one. She loved the dare and the next morning rose early and was already in the kitchen when I went to make my morn-ing coffee. Everyone was there: Ming, the dignified self-governing cat she'd had the longest, three other mischief-maker cats, and the two dogs, all waiting and sniffing and hoping. It smelled divine. I thought about it all day as I unearthed more ancient bones and stones. That evening, after second helpings, we declared it the best boeuf bourguignon we'd ever tasted. Harold did well to say nothing, but instead asked Cécile to reveal her secrets.

Well, in a heavy cast-iron pot she'd sautéed the onions and garlic in butter, she said, then the bacon and then carrots and celery. She added the beef to all this and when it browned and seared to seal in the juices, she'd added a lot of red wine. "Good red wine, mind you. And as much as the dish is from Burgundy, it is better to use local red wine," she advised, "along with all the other local ingredients, the meat and the vegetables." She then added mushrooms. After that, she made a roux with butter and flour. She added this and let it all meld and release its flavors and then she set it in the oven in the cast-iron pot and let it slow-cook.

We all listened and our mouths watered, the way of all of us, Neandertals and Cro-Magnons, and were the better for it. Thankfully, we were also living in a time of abundance, where we didn't need to smash toe bones to suck out bone grease.

# 7

## GATHERED AROUND THE
## HEARTH FIRE

IT WAS A perfect summer night in the southwest of France. Cicadas were rattling in the trees, an errant owl was hooting in the nearby forest, and a blazing campfire was roaring in the center of the camp. The evenings were cool, but this night I needed only a light sweater against the cold. Everyone was gathered about the fire, crew and directors, golden light flickering off their vibrant faces, eyes dancing in the light. We had already enjoyed a dinner of grilled red and green peppers, zucchini, eggplant, sausages, thick slabs of French-style bacon, burgers, and veggie burgers, all cooked on the open flame. I'm not sure what aspect of it had been more sensory-satisfying, the smell of the meat and the peppers hitting the grill, or eating them afterwards. The smell seemed deeply wired in my body, an old memory, and one we all know when neighbors heat up their grills on summer weekends, when the steaks hit the fire.

Cécile was with us, looking as content as I felt. She had joined us for dinner and was now enjoying a glass of wine with Harold, Dennis, Paul, Vera, and me. Shannon had taken off early to turn in at his own digs, where he and his wife were staying nearby with their young son. Everyone was still enjoying the high of being around their little boy, for it was through his exuberance that we re-experienced the wonders of life in the Dordogne afresh: The just-harvested fields with their bales of hay spotting the green and yellow dappled field. The creek and its murmuring frogs and electric blue dragonflies. The moon rising and the stars clear in the velvet black sky of village life. And the blasted apple trees in the backyard that bombarded us and made us dodge, but made this little boy cheer with delight as he and Gary the dog bounded to investigate another unique green orb from the sky. They intuited something there, that each act of procreation was unique, evolution in action with unknown effects. Each apple, each seed in each apple, was a whole new potential direction. A fruit that had originated in Kazakhstan and had through sheer chutzpah made its way all over the world; each seed defied domestication and honored evolution's riotous creativity.

So, in all this contentment and poetry, it was suddenly halting to hear the growing sounds of grunts and moans of a particular kind of exertion that made even made Cécile turn toward it with raised eyebrows and say, "Oh my." All conversation ceased. The source of the seemingly illicit effort did not come from a nearby tent but instead from the center of the gathering around the campfire.

A circle had formed around two graduate students. I peeked around someone's shoulders and found nothing amorous whatsoever. Instead, two people were trying to make fire of a very different kind.

Dennis, Paul, and Harold had spent their day off visiting other Neandertal sites in the southwest, the highlight being La Chapelle-aux-Saints just northeast of us in the Corrèze. Given its claim to fame as the site of one of the most famous Neandertal burials, it had parallel issues (and concerns) with La Ferrassie.

On their return, they had purchased a kit for kids, a fire-making apparatus with two types of wood, one soft in the shape of a plank that had been cut into a zigzag shape, and the other one a hard, simple rod. Also in the kit was a strip of leather. To make fire, one inserted the rod into a crook of the zigzagged wood, wrapped the leather around the rod, and pulled back and forth with each end of the leather, quickly and smoothly, to generate rotating friction, then heat, then smoke, and with luck, fire.

Matt and Kris took up the challenge when Dennis brought out the kit. They disparaged it as a toy, a kid thing, no problem. They took it to show the dig directors, backed by the crew, how swiftly they could make it flame. Matt held the zigzag wood, and Kris manned the rod and leather.

Nothing happened, except a lot of heavy breathing. And sweat. The less there was any sign—was that the faint smell of wood sap given off from a bit of heat?—the more violently and vigorously Kris worked. Some minutes into the exercise, we saw ever so briefly a small waft of smoke that appeared like the tiniest gas leak and then was gone. The two continued the effort for many more long minutes and never arrived at the sparking moment we all needed to see to believe that fire was ever-present with our ancestors.

It is small wonder that almost every world mythology has a great origin story involving the first fire. It's a magical act to get it and to keep it, and the two are separate skill sets.

In Iran, the national poet, Ferdowsi—who wrote in the tenth and eleventh centuries in as pure a Persian as he could muster, pruning from the language the invading Arabic words as much as possible—wrote all the stories of ancestral memory of the Iranian peoples as pertained to their origins and their kings. This probably was also inspired by the threat of successful Arab invasion from the west, with the goal of safeguarding Persian culture against deeper alien incursions.

Called the Book of Kings, the *Shahnameh* remains as much a sacred text to Iranians today as the holy texts of the many religions of Iran. Children to this day grow up reading the *Shahnameh*; adults have memorized the stories and poetry and will recite these at the drop of a rose petal. Though called the Book of Kings, it's really the stories of the Persian culture's mythic heroes. It's the old stories that come from ancestral memory boiled down and rendered to a concentrate.

My mother can recite all the classical texts and mystical poets from memory with the smallest provocation. And so when I asked her when she first heard anything about Neandertals as she was growing up in Iran, and what it might have been—she, to my surprise, told me Ferdowsi's story of Hushang. He was Iran's second king from the mythic period, when Iran was the culture that existed forever, and Arabs and any other invaders and interlopers did not exist. Hers was not a biblical creationist tale, but one where mythology aligned with evolution.

"Growing up," she said, before giving me the story *à la Ferdowsi*, "I knew from our stories that prehistoric people lived in the surrounding mountains." The Zagros to the west and the Elborz and the Caucasus to the north. "The signs were always there. People would find stone tools and animal bones in the caves. It was from Ferdowsi that we knew there were ancient people who wore animal skins, hunted with spears, and who did not have fire." She said she imagined that these first peoples were the Neandertals and also the early modern humans arriving later. The differences between the two were fairly nonexistent for Iranians, who seem to have missed the whole nineteenth-century Victorian-era bias on that front.

One day, Ferdowsi wrote, Hushang went out hunting, but as luck would have it, instead of flushing out game, he encountered a dragon that began to hunt him. As he ran to escape, he turned and threw his flint-tipped spear at the dragon as hard as he could. But it missed and instead struck a rock with such velocity that a spark shot out and ignited into fire. The dragon dispersed and Hushang took this chance occurrence and replicated it and was able to make fire, which he showed to others. People began to cook their food and stay warm. Thereafter, new adaptations arose: The story goes on to celebrate Hushang as the king who, after fire, also introduced new technologies, such as making clothes from animal hides (bone needles and hide smoothers, or lissoirs, perhaps being implied) as well as from woven flax and hemp. He also led the way to domesticate animals and cultivate plants and even introduce irrigation techniques that channeled river water to cultivated areas. It was the

GATHERED AROUND THE HEARTH FIRE

whole Paleolithic and Neolithic rolled into one long chain reaction, thanks to discovering fire.

The Western world has the dominant story of Prometheus, thanks to the Greeks, and how fire was such a thing of the gods that when he stole it, he incurred gruesome and eternal wrath. Fire does so much for us that these stories have high drama and high consequences.

Blisters and burns formed on their hands but not the wood, so Kris and Matt finally gave up. As Kris blew wisps of hair off her forehead, Dennis grinned his Cheshire Cat smile and said, "We just wanted you to have firsthand exposure to how hard making fire is."

The temptation to throw the fire-making kit into the campfire was strong but someone had grabbed Harold's beat-up guitar and was strumming some chords to a favorite song, so Kris handed it to Dennis, filled her wineglass, and went back to the gathering around the existing fire, grateful for matches and their little tips mixed with phosphorous and potassium chlorate, an igniting mix when heat from striking friction churns up the phosphorous. Paul blew a couple smoke rings and listened to Cécile. He was a fire master in many ways.

Paul is not only the cave whisperer and the soil CSI guy, but also a world expert in identifying, among other things, fire—combustion events as they are called in the biz. Vera trained for her doctorate with him and with Harold, and now, a top geoarchaeologist in her own right, was working with Paul at La Ferrassie to closely analyze and discuss the fabric of the soil samples they took from different levels at the site. She had come to this specialization from her training as an archaeologist in Portugal, where, after her university studies, she directed salvage archaeology projects across the country, working with construction teams to excavate areas where they intended to build and to first make sure they weren't going to destroy or cover over important history or prehistory. Her skills as a field archaeologist were already phenomenal by the time she took on geoarchaeology.

I had watched several times as Vera and Paul worked at La Ferrassie, carefully selecting and removing brick-sized and -shaped cuts of earth from different layers and carefully wrapping them in special plaster-treated fabric strips they moistened before applying. When the plaster dried, they transported the cut of earth to the lab and injected it with a special resin. (*Impregnate*, not *inject*, is the technical term, and the fertile connection with the earth is strong.)

The impregnating resin renders the block of earth solid and permanent so that it next can be sliced into very thin sections and mounted onto clear slides. The geoarchaeologists then study each slide closely under a microscope. The slides looked like tissue samples writ large to me, as if taken from biopsied flesh, and had a pretty similar power to reveal what was going on in the fabric of that section of tissue from, in this case, the earth's body. This was essentially what micromorphology was about, a specialty within geoarchaeology that looked at the microscopic level. They were also trained in the macroscopic stuff, reading the earth's body as a whole, seeing what the story of the place told.

I had no idea how sexy rocks and dirt could be, how much they could dish, until I spent time with these two. I also understood how crucial their presence was. Others could easily read a formation as something made by humans, but Paul or Vera often pointed out how frost action, for instance, could create the same geometry as hands.

And if a thin section from their impregnated soil slides showed a combustion event, there would be telltale signs, such as ash, burnt plant material, burnt bone, burnt stones, or heat-altered soil.

From his extensive years of work since the 1960s, applying this fairly new technique for which he was world renowned, Paul knew fire was a sketchy affair, so he took his time and looked extra hard. Fire was hard to generalize, from site to site, region to region, season to season, or different time periods to different time periods. He would exhaust all possibilities before he declared something was a fire, and then, if that fire was anthropomorphic, forged by humans.

Ancient fire that was handled by humans, especially any dating before

400,000 years ago, is a big deal for a lot of reasons. The two most important reasons are that early evidence for fire is hard to find because most ancient sites are open-air and naturally occurring wildfires cannot be eliminated as a cause, and because fire has mind-boggling implications for human evolution.

This latter reason was recently a huge debate when Harvard primatologist Richard Wrangham penned "The Cooking Hypothesis." In his book *Catching Fire: How Cooking Made Us Human*, he laid out a detailed case for how hominid use of fire most likely altered the course of our evolution on many levels. He speculated that hominid fire use went back further than our present archaeological evidence and that our use of it may have helped select for the evolution of larger and larger brains—a trend whose trailhead appears between 1.8 and 1 million years ago with *Homo erectus*, who is most likely the common ancestor of both Neandertals and us. Big brains required a lot of calories to fuel. Cooking hard-to-digest raw foods made those foods more easily edible. With cooking we could eat more calories, more quickly, all in one sitting, and take the heavy processing burden off our digestive tracts and send the surplus energy to manage bigger and bigger brains.

Wrangham also added that fire offered our ancestors warmth, protection from predators, and maybe even stimulated greater sociability among hominids, given the appeal of gathering around a campfire. But this is all speculative and still needs more solid evidence in many ways, for first fires, for the more frequent use of fires, for the ability to make fire at will, and then that the fires were really human-made and not wildfires. I even learned that caves with a lot of accumulated bat poop (I can attest to a lot of this in the caves in the Dordogne) can actually spontaneously combust; so these sorts of causes also have to be investigated.

But one thing that seems certain is that the appearance of habitual fire is not something that will conform to simple stories or seductive Edenic moments. It didn't start somewhere and steadily grow. It's pretty patchy, actually, with appearances here and there, more frequent appearances as we get closer to the present, but still not the same everywhere or even the same in the same place. Fire seems to have been pretty opportunistic, based on each situation, so that even when we had the power to make fire, not just control it, we may not always have done so. Consider when you come home after a long day of work and decide whether or not to heat your food or just eat it cold. That's opportunistic, weighing and balancing the effort versus the end result you'll be fine with in order to feed yourself.

Before matches, lighters, and electric and gas stoves, there were only a few ways to make fire. One was to rub together two pieces of different-density wood, as demonstrated by Kris and Matt. Another was striking flint against a form of iron ore held over a pile of dry leaves or grass, which once lit is inserted into a pile of dry leaves that are set within twigs. Once this takes, more wood is added. Another is not to make it at all, but to steal it, as it were, Prometheus-like, from lightning or volcanic fires or from Zeus.

In the Dordogne, I hiked a lot with local prehistory buffs, who sometimes would show me how to make stone tools, spears, and sure fire; they became a sort of impromptu Boy Scouts for befriended Paleo-passionate adults like me. Nicolas was one. My outdoor-trekking professional guide friends, Béa and Bruno, had asked him to join us in the forest near Les Eyzies and Le Bugue to initiate me to prehistory's basic survival skills.

He settled himself in a cavern opening in the hillside where we met and pulled out a huge piece of raw flint he'd acquired near Bergerac, known for fine flint that was coveted by flintknappers across the region. He then rapidly set to banging out a dessert plate–sized hand ax from the Acheulean tradition (aka *Homo erectus*, meaning, these beauties have been made since 1.8 million years ago) in less than five minutes. That bit of tool-making was a result that would have taken me a few hundred hours of practice before I could knock out such a beautiful piece in so little time.

Next, he set to making fire. He had with him flint and the iron pyrite, kindling, and dry grass, but he then added one more special secret ingredient, known by all those native-born to the Dordogne, that assured the fire would really catch. It was shavings from a specially foraged and super-dry tree mushroom that grew on trunks like a half saucer pushing out from the tree's bark.

There was a tree in Carsac, now that I learned how to identify the mushroom, that had tons of these growing on it, right in the center of the park through which the Enéa Creek flowed and I did too each morning to go from Cécile's to Camp Dibble. On another hike with Béa and Bruno, I'd noticed Bruno would just casually walk past a tree with one of these saucer mushrooms and give a soft backward blow with his elbow and knock it off. He'd then tuck it into his pack or coat pocket.

"Is that edible?" I asked, always wanting to know what I could and could not eat.

"Oh, heavens, no," he said gently to my naïveté, "but it's magic with fire."

Even at Bruno's over-six-foot stature, those mushrooms grew low compared to those on the tree in question in Carsac. One morning, as I was standing and coveting the mushrooms on high yet again, working out if a rope or stone would do the trick, a local walked by with his black-and-white pug, who, in that endearing puggish manner, stopped for me to give him a good ear-rubbing.

"I know. I know," the man stated simply, looking at the mushrooms on high where my eye had been before his dog had charmed me into submission. "Everyone knows they're there, but no one can reach them. We all covet them. They sure would make a good fire."

Few of us know how to forage anymore, let alone make fire. For our ancestors, foraging was a no-brainer, but fire? A mystery. More often than not, they ate their food raw.

The team's collective results, from Roc de Marsal and Pech de l'Azé IV, had unsettled the world of certainty about fire by revealing that fire was present only during warm, lightning-rich periods, not the colder periods when a fire sure would have felt good.

Around the same time that Dennis, as the lead author, and the team published their findings on fire and climate at Roc de Marsal and Pech IV, Wil Roebroeks from the University of Leiden in Holland, and Paola Villa from the University of Colorado Museum in Boulder, came out with a comprehensive survey of evidence for fire from Europe, from the earliest claims at around 1.6 million years ago, right up to the eve of agriculture around 10,000 years ago. Assessing it all in one effort, they surprised themselves by uncovering that habitual fire use was not common until about 400,000 years ago, when it appeared more often and in the hands of Neandertals.

The firmest and earliest evidence for fire use dates to around 1 million years ago and comes from a stable sediment layer inside Wonderwerk Cave in South Africa, a place I learned about from talking to Michael Chazan, an archaeologist from the University of Toronto who worked with Paul to identify the fire. It's a single site and associated with Homo erectus and, while holding as a true fire hearth, it doesn't show any habitual activity. Almost all other evidence for early hominid fire use has come from open-air sites, making wildfires—sparked by nature, not humans—a hard possibility to eliminate. One very early site, Gesher Benot Ya'akov, in northern Israel near the Dead Sea, has fire evidence that dates to around 800,000 years ago. But it is an open-air site.

The firmest evidence for hominid fire use comes much later—from Beeches Pit, England, and Schöningen, Germany—from around 400,000 years ago, and with Neandertals. But such examples are few and far between. As much as fire is seen more and more in the record after 400,000 years ago, these few sites are still used to make a broad statement.

Habitual fire use has to show high concentration and frequency. That's a hard thing to prove with a record that is so patchy. Even the work at Roc de Marsal and Pech de l'Azé IV is a beginning, a foundation for further inquiry to build on the data and test the observations there for wider application.

In some places, fire control had to mean fire-making, in Roebroeks's and Villa's interpretation, because a few sites in Germany and Italy had contained Neandertal spear tips bearing the residue of a strong adhesive glue made from birch bark, which had been used to attach the stone spear tips to wooden spear handles. At the same site of Schöningen, archaeologists also unearthed eight such wooden spears, a rare trove of well-preserved wood in airtight sediment that dated to earlier than 300,000 years ago. These confirmed that there was hafted spear-making among Neandertals.

Making birch bark pitch is a multi-stepped, highly technical procedure, one that shows complex technological knowledge of the materials involved. Applying fire at certain times and a specific range of temperatures, and not allowing oxygen to enter the sealed area where the birch bark burned, were all a part of the argument for the Neandertals who made this resin to be in full control over both making and controlling fire.

Dennis and the team were elated that Roebroeks and Villa confirmed habitual fire use as a more recent phenomenon, but they disagreed that it began as early as 400,000 years ago. They think habitual fire use—the ability to make it at will—happened closer to the end of the Neandertals' era.

Everyone agrees, though, from all sides of the debate, that the habitual use of fire is also sketchy in the Upper Paleolithic. Places that have fire seem to have a lot of it, but there are many early modern occupation sites with no fire whatsoever or with infrequent use of it. This is all just evidence of fire use. It is even harder to find evidence of fire-making.

Archaeology is as much about fieldwork as it is about filling in the gaps between the theories and what archaeologists find on the ground. To do this, they need a lot of well-excavated sites to look at individually and comparatively, but they also need good experiments that can bridge theories to help accurately read what they find in the record.

Fire is a good candidate for experiments. There are a lot of theories, but not a lot of experimental data that help interpret the evidence accurately. Experimental archaeology (as it sounds) and ethnoarchaeology (looking at documented cases of traditional cultures and how they forage, use the environment, make and use fire, and the like) are two areas that archaeologists developed in the field to test their reading of sites, artifacts, and evidence.

Vera was beginning a series of fire experiments to do just this, build observed data for how controlled fires at different temperatures affected not only the matter they directly contacted, but also outlying matter, plus material underneath the fires measured at different depths to see how the effects changed with distance from the combustion events. She was conducting it in a safe setting in the nearby forest with soil sediment similar to that found at La Ferrassie. These days, she was often out somewhere in the forest, keeping the conditions controlled and the fire burning at constant temperatures.

"We need more standardized data on a lot of things, not just lithics, but also fire," she said, not too many days before she began the fire experiments. She had been scouting for a place to set up her experiment.

"We also need way more data on Upper Paleolithic fires," Dennis added. "Upper Paleolithic research is just like Middle Paleolithic research. Everyone just assumes that fire was a part of the repertoire and nobody ever looks at it."

Harold perked up; the word *fire* was all it took. He told us about one of his colleagues in the U.S. who had argued with him when their paper came out on Roc de Marsal.

"She said that, if our conclusion was correct, that Neandertals didn't have fire at will, then early modern humans also didn't have fire [at will] in the Upper Paleolithic where she worked in the Middle East. If she applied our findings there then maybe it meant they didn't know how to make fire, either."

Which seemed an utterly preposterous thing to say about the Upper Paleolithic because everyone assumed fire at will was common by then. But the problem was that everyone made assumptions without fully substantiating them. Another problem was that everyone wanted one broad story to apply to the human story, rather than seeing that each time, place, and particular group of people was making unique choices that day.

I thought of what Ofer Bar-Yosef had told me when we spoke, about the idea of continuity—looking for a smooth flowing relatedness to everything in human evolution—when it might be one of the worst preconceived ideas people brought into the field. The reality might be more upheavals and discontinuities than most care to admit. This could apply as well to fire.

"Well, maybe," Dennis offered to the projected virtual colleague who stood as if a hologram before us at La Ferrassie.

"That's what I said, maybe," Harold replied. "But the thing is, fire may be a bad example, too, because it may be such a low thing on Neandertals' adaptation that it really doesn't become important until you're cooking vegetables, with domestication."

Maybe, Ofer might reply. He had also reminded me that plants were always a part of the diet, whether we were nomadic or agricultural; they didn't suddenly appear with agriculture. But maybe the domesticated cereals needed more processing, too. And maybe we ate more plants once settled. And maybe Neandertals ate slightly fewer plants. And maybe these plants were edible raw, not hard cereal seeds, but soft leafy greens? And maybe there are a lot of maybes in this business.

"And the preservation is always an issue . . ." Vera added. Right. How well did fires preserve and how good were archaeologists at identifying them in the earlier record? She was already working to narrow that gap.

I loved when this happened: There was a lull, then the dig directors and anyone else who wanted jumped in to chew on the issues and dynamics of the world they loved. Café Neandertal.

"But you can always look for . . ." Harold said to Vera's prompt.

". . . burnt flints . . . and burned bone," finished Dennis.

"But even at Kebara . . ." Paul joined in, pausing for a second to light up his *après dejeuner* cigarillo and then explaining that the Upper Paleolithic there had a pretty dense presence of human occupations but had very few fire hearths compared to the Middle Paleolithic layers just underneath, which had so many it was the difference between a handful versus truckloads.

"So, what was your colleague's solution to our data?" Dennis asked Harold, returning to the hologram.

"Nothing," Harold answered. "She just felt it was wrong to characterize Neandertals as being without fire when the Upper Paleolithic went without fire too."

"But even in the Upper Paleolithic," Shannon joined in, "there were about four thousand years without fire, versus the tens of thousands of years in our sites, or Atapuerca, at one million years, with no fire. I don't think those two things are comparable." Besides, Shannon added, based on comprehensive studies among modern hunters and gatherers, "some modern humans just don't want to make fire, or forget how to make it."

"Right," Harold agreed. "It's a technological thing, not an . . ."

". . . intelligence thing," Dennis finished.

"Exactly," Harold said. "It's not genetic. It's not a species thing." He rolled his eyes as he said this, tired of the way people made the issue into a biological difference when all he ever claimed to look at was technology; and technology varied wildly between living peoples today, so why not in the past? It had very little to do with biology. Performance, not capacity.

It was refreshing, too. Only recently, Jesse Prinz had come out with his book *Beyond Human Nature*, which eloquently got at the root of this issue, often called nature (biology) and nurture (culture). Many are inclined toward biological explanations because they seem more fixed, clear, and logical. I think it is also because people are lazy, and biology gives simpler but more easily distorted explanations. These explanations are also dangerous, not only in creating false ideas of difference as fixed and in the genes but also in derailing us from the truth about human reality: that we are born with a very flexible brain that can create all sorts of variation in human existence without huge changes in our biology.

And everyone gets one of these, in all cultures, and has for a very long time, and the flexible brain has the capacity to express a range of variation far beyond anything biology can dream up.

This wildly adaptable mind has allowed humans, both Neandertal and us, to come up with all sorts of solutions to problems without a lot of changes to our biology. Among the most significant problem-solving is seen in how many different environments we all inhabited and figured out how to live in. Few other mammals show that range of flexibility. Prinz was turning the gaze back to this pliability, this nurture aspect, pointing to the very biological brain and exposing it for its brilliant pen stroke of evolution: to be so flexible and malleable as to be capable of creating all sorts of possibilities to which we can adapt, just by changing our ideas and actions, not our bodies. Since our brains are very much like Neandertal brains in size and hemispheric activities, examining actions and performance—cultural expression, behavior—makes a lot more sense than looking for capacity. Capacity is already there and it is flexible, like a yogi.

"And don't forget the cost thing, too," Shannon added. "Early modern humans may have gone to the damp sites, and said, 'You know what, you want to make a fire? No.' They might say, 'We have to go get all this firewood over here, so, let's not make a fire.' You make a decision at any one point, 'Do I want to make a fire or not?'"

The cost thing. We do this weighing and balancing all the time. How often have you eaten your food cold because you could not even be bothered with heating it on the stovetop, or, for goodness' sake, in the microwave? Making fire is more work than all that, and hunters and gatherers past and present made these choices one at a time, under daily circumstances and moods, just as we do constantly.

"It shows that you're not dependent on fire," Harold said, "or, that it's a major part of your adaptation."

This was what Roebroeks and Villa concluded in their comprehensive study of the time periods up to around 400,000 years ago. Harold and his team, based on what they saw in the record for southwestern France, felt it made more sense to push the beginnings of habitual fire far later, perhaps to around 50,000 years ago and later.

"Which is why I like the word *obligate*," Shannon replied. "Some Neandertals, at some times, were using fire, but they weren't *obligate* fire users. Their adaptation did not depend on it."

The cicadas joined the conversation as if a Greek chorus had launched into full swing in the forest above and around us. *Even when Prometheus stole fire from the gods, incurring eternal torment out on the rocks, it was a bloody choice, not a necessity. Voilà.*

"I LOVE MY life," I heard Vera's voice ricochet back toward me as we passed through the cave tunnel—the salami, as Paul liked to call it—connecting the cave of Pech I to the cave of Pech II, both excavated by François Bordes between 1948 and 1951. Another team, affiliated with the University of Bordeaux and the Max Planck, led by Marie Soressi, had dug at Pech I more recently, in 2004–2005.

We were here for a closer chronological consideration of Pech II and Pech IV. The only way to Pech II was through Pech I, a sort of cool reality. Like beads on a string, the many efforts of all the different teams were being strung into some semblance of reconstructing the whole cave system, itself like beads on a string, where at different times and for different reasons, Neandertals had chosen to live. Here I was now visiting intimately, like the camera probe of a colonoscopy in fact, the place that gave me perpetual chills each time I passed from below on the *piste cyclable*, the bike path.

Pech IV, where Harold first dug with François Bordes in 1976–1977, and then later led his own team with Shannon from 2000 to 2003, was a few meters behind us on about the same level on the cliff. Collectively, the caves had been occupied from 180,000 to 50,000 years ago. Pech IV also had medieval layers but was occupied by Neandertals between

90,000 and 50,000 years ago. Pech I, where Peyrony had found a Neandertal child's skull and partial mandible, dated to around 50,000 years
ago. Pech II was the oldest, from 180,000 to possibly 50,000.

This day allowed me to be a fly on the wall shadowing two great geoarchaeologists, Paul and Vera, and the geochronologist Zenobia Jacobs,
whom I'd just met. She was a dating specialist—something Harold and
Dennis loved to kid her about, that even Neandertals needed matchmak-
ers. From South Africa, she worked at the University of Wollongong in
Australia and traveled all over the world to help different researchers
arrive at the most accurate dates, as in chronology, for their prehistoric
sites. She specialized in many things, but the relationship between late
Neandertals and early modern humans, before, during, and after they
came into contact, was one of her top interests. Nothing was more crucial
toward understanding this dynamic than having accurate dates for when
each moved around different environments and then intersected and
therefore influenced one another.

Zenobia was also refining and developing techniques for more accurate readings taken from soil and artifacts, working particularly with a
method called optically stimulated luminescence (OSL). OSL, which
uses light to stimulate the release of trapped electrons in the crystalline
structure of in situ minerals being tested, can be measured and corre-
sponded to a chronological band.

There are many different dating methods, each with areas and age
ranges best suited to them. The team most often used these four: OSL,
thermoluminescence (TL), radiocarbon (carbon-14) dating, and elec-
tron spin resonance (ESR), along with the classic relative and contextual
investigation, again and again, of stratigraphy.

Dating can change the whole story. Just recently, a team led by Thomas
Higham from the University of Oxford in the United Kingdom, redated
forty Middle Paleolithic sites in Western Europe with better methods.
They discovered that all came out being 10,000 years older than previously believed. The youngest of these places, which also claimed to have

the "last Neandertals" and the populations that most likely encountered and lived with early modern humans coming into the area, also dated to 10,000 years earlier. Instead of the last Neandertals disappearing from the record around 30,000 to 25,000 years ago, Higham's team's new dates made it appear more like 40,000 to 35,000 years ago. That narrowed the overlap of when Neandertals and early modern humans coexisted in Europe.

(The story is different in Asia, where contact was much earlier and potentially much longer. At cave sites such as Skhul and Qafzeh in Israel, early modern humans arrived from Africa around 100,000 years ago, perhaps earlier. Neandertals were already there, as indicated by sites such as Zuttiyeh, where they may have lived as early as between 300,000 and 200,000 years ago. This is why the Levant is viewed as the most likely place where the two groups of humans first met, interbred, and potentially influenced each other in areas such as fire-making, burial, and social organization. But that first, earliest early modern human presence in Asia, outside of Africa, seems to have been a dead end. Those early moderns seem to have gone extinct. We're not related to them as much as the later ones who spread across Africa and then the rest of the world from 60,000 years ago and on and on.)

Paul, Zenobia, and Paul's student Kris were already through the tunnel on the other side waiting for us, an incarnate near-death experience in a sense, considering the drama of the place: I followed the light, it was wonderful, and passed through the tunnel to find kind people waiting for me on the other side. Paul actually said, "Welcome to Pech II," as I stepped in just after Vera, completing the mystical journey. The four then engaged in a poetic give and take about soil, stratigraphy, micromorphological features, integrity, fabric, and all manner of highly specialized ways to see what I could not see; the way software engineers might discuss code. They were putting their heads together to review everything and refine the chronologies for the different sediment layers.

This tunnel had been walked through many times by François Bordes when he first began his work here. He had woven his family into this history of prehistory. Added to the near-death spin, it also felt like the sort of tunnel you would go through to reach the land that time forgot.

My first foray into Pech IV happened two days before the one to Pech I and II. I was again with Paul, Zenobia, Vera, and Kris. Kris was there to begin gathering around a hundred soil samples from different levels including the medieval one (to see what it would show in comparison), to analyze the samples for phytoliths, fossilized plants. This would flesh out the faunal data with more on the lesser-known and more perishable flora.

"Did you know that Pech de l'Azé means hill of the donkey in the local patois?" Paul asked me as we stepped into Pech IV.

"No. Really? Why donkey?"

"No idea." He smiled. Probably some colorful local kept his donkey on this hill, we agreed. According to François Bordes's report, the cave system along this hill and cliff had been used by pastoralists to shelter their sheep, so why not a donkey? It had to have been one so notable as to get the hill named after him. When Bordes began here, he still had to remove a heck of a lot of modern animal debris—lots of dung—plus modern to medieval human refuse and artifacts, with a view toward clearing the surface and finding intact prehistoric levels.

Is not the difference between "refuse" and "artifact" really a value judgment of time? The medieval trash was refuse, interesting junk, but the prehistoric trash was now the highly valued artifact, making poetry out of the fact that we worked through bones from a Neandertal dinner and brushed past 60,000-year-old hyena poop evident from the white phosphate layer in the soil at that chronology. Indeed, they used to share these caves with other carnivores; fox, hyena, wolf, lion, and bear being common residents.

Standing before Pech IV with Paul, he was clear that it all began for him here, this hill of the donkey. He had come here in 1976 to try out his freshly minted innovative methods from the then-new field of geomicromorphology, and now well over three decades later I was in the sublime position of standing next to him before the pivotal cave site.

"It's like imprinting, you know?" His tone was reverent.

Yeah. I know. I looked about the old collapsed cave mouth behind me, the piles of car-sized stone that had to be hauled or climbed over to get at the occupied zones, and saw myself standing in what felt like the vacant hole left after some giant cut out a healthy wedge of three-story-high chocolate layer cake. Like those little ceramic baby Jesuses one found in Epiphany cakes, we were the baby Jesus and this cake was potentially far larger than the baker had originally intended.

I left Paul and Zenobia to finish their dating efforts and stepped to the edge of the mouth, trying to imagine what this place had been like had I lived here as a Neandertal. Around 90,000 years ago, as attested to in Layer 8 behind me, there were many fire hearths and it was a warm climatic period. Fires that had most likely been gathered from thunder and lightning storms. Then later it grew colder, around the same time when no fire hearths were found in Roc de Marsal; here too, none were uncovered. But the density of animal bones and used flint tools was still there, in both warm and cold periods. That density showed that people were still coming here, hunting, gathering, and eating, but in the cold periods, oddly, without fire.

When Marie Soressi and her team recently excavated Pech I, set between Pech II and Pech IV, they uncovered many human-altered pieces of magnesium dioxide, several smooth and shaped, as if used to color things, but also some with scratch marks on them as if scraped with a flint edge.

At first the team thought these were a part of an emerging trend to use magnesium oxides and ochre as pigment, something many now think Neandertals did. But for black color, charcoal is a lot easier to use as a pigment and magnesium dioxide, a harder mineral, not as easy. But it did do one thing with ease. Soressi's team showed that along with wood chips and kindling, adding in shaved magnesium dioxide helped a spark from flint struck against iron pyrite ignite more quickly and at lower temperatures. So this is a possibility, and one that still has to be aligned with the fire hearths and checked against climatic fluctuations. But it exemplifies (and boggles the mind with) the complexities of working out our relationship with fire.

I decided to go back to 90,000 years ago, with a nice certain fire flickering at my back, and continued looking out and imagining away the bike path so that all that was left was the steep slope to the valley floor where the Enéa Creek flowed softly. It was a narrow and intimate world. The forest today was full of plant and animal life. The imaginary fire behind me lulled me into a sweet dream, different from a recent experience on this spot.

I had been on this path only days before, riding my borrowed bike to get to and fro between Carsac and Sarlat. I had lingered longer into the early evening, thinking that, with the late setting summer sun, I would have plenty of light to illuminate my path. I was wrong. This valley was so steep and narrow, the sun set at least an hour earlier here than out in the open.

Thankfully, I had my headlamp (bless the modern little fire) in my pack and got it out and fastened it to my forehead. The path was so narrow, and the incline so steep, that to miscalculate with the bike was a tumble to an almost sure demise, or a very bad situation if I survived. I pedaled on carefully. I knew when I was passing Pech de l'Azé for the path narrowed, the hairs on my arm rose, and the familiar goose bumps flushed across my skin. I took a deep breath to calm myself when something moved on the lower slope opposite the caves. I turned abruptly and my headlamp picked up two bluish orbs looking back at me. I almost drove the bike over the edge.

I got off the bike. I really didn't want to stop there, but it seemed the safest move until I knew what was out there. I waited. The two orbs became two more and like disembodied spirits, slowly began to float like sine waves through the trees, moving down the slope into the valley, then suddenly, they snuffed themselves out.

I realized only then, as I saw the flash of white tails recede, that my headlamp had reflected the eyes of a pair of deer, their brown bodies remaining invisible in the dark. Pumped now with adrenaline, I got back on the bike and pedaled hard, refusing to look anywhere but at the black asphalt just in front of my tires until I arrived home.

While Pech is a puissant place, my imprinting happened at La Ferrassie, the place where I first touched humanity that was 70,000 years old. Like god's and Adam's index fingers in Michelangelo's Sistine Chapel, my finger touched the cosmic finger of another being and I was forever imprinted, a gosling attached to the mother goose.

I think the world around me became more vivid after that. I saw more. I could hear, not only see, the dime-sized forest frogs crossing the leafy floor. I could feel, not only hear, the heavy breath of the cicadas. I could see the feathered texture of the pair of turquoise and rust orange European bee-eaters as they streaked past. The dappled light penetrating the surrounding oak and hazel forest revealed the leaves' vein patterns as well as the undergrowth giving off the scent of five varieties of wild mushrooms. The small creek that flowed nearby had burbled for thousands of years. Even if altering its course by small increments, it was now audible like a fountain when before I heard nothing.

Yes, I understood imprinting. I now can close my eyes wherever I am and conjure La Ferrassie like a vivid and real place before me. It's in my cell tissue; its rust red *le fer ici* makes my blood more vibrantly red.

And Pech was Paul's, even more intimately and deeply now after four decades of returning here. So to have him as my guide to this famous cave, one of the caves from François Bordes's classic *A Tale of Two Caves* (the other was Combe-Grenal), was like being taken home to meet the parents.

I followed Paul around Pech IV, a gosling again, and learned many things, including that using food imagery was acceptable in describing geological formations. A favorite of his was the sausage, especially when telling me that Pech IV was originally thought to be an *abri*, a rock shelf, even when nearby, at Pech II and I, there was a surviving cave tunnel. He discovered upon closer inspection that it was, in fact, a cave and the cave's sausage-like passage emerged, going deeper into the wall. Both Peyrony then Bordes thought it was an *abri*, a logical conclusion at the time. But with Harold and Shannon's 2000–2003 excavation, Paul saw the signs of a cave and realized that all any of them had ever managed to excavate of this place was "the end of the sausage and the knot," he said.

"Or, as in the parable of the elephant," he continued, mixing metaphors as he liked to do, all the more charming given his Brooklyn accent speaking in Old World story mode, "we have here the tail and the hind legs. The rest of the elephant, the rest of the salami, the meat, is in there." He pointed at the back wall of the cave with an unlit cigar between his fingers and raised a questioning brow.

"So the whole enchilada is in there?" I asked, practicing my own food metaphors.

"That's right. You want to know, where's the beef? It's in there. Here, we're only looking at the entrance." Here was where everyone had excavated so far, from 1970 to 2004.

"If you want to look for activities or burials inside the cave," Paul added, "we haven't even begun. It might be tens of meters more, inside the cave." Holy smoke. I felt the weight of all those boulders that had crashed down and collapsed the cave. What a business.

"The nice thing about the geoarchaeology stuff," Paul had told me earlier in the week, "is you try to apply geological principles, which are fairly well-known, to archaeological settings, which are totally unknown, from the sedimentological standpoint. Geological principles are sort of standard. But when you start combining them with archaeology, then it gets kind of dicey. At each site, you've got to go back to square one. You hope to get enough experience so that you can see some patterns. But you can't predict it. There are no two sites that look the same."

That could be a good caveat for all generalizations made across a wide region, such as Europe, Asia, and Africa. Fire also seemed a good candidate for this sort of caution. Don't try to overgeneralize. Look at each site as unique.

"Do you think you'd ever like to come back here and reopen Pech IV and go in deeper?" I asked. Seeing now that a whole elephant, in terms of the parable and perhaps dinner's remains lay in there, it seemed to me like a dream to go deeper.

"No," he said without pause, "That's for the next generation or the one after that, the grandchildren."

He and Zenobia resumed working on refining the dating of the strata in the cave while all the food metaphors made me hungry and I pulled a bag of almonds from my pack to share. They reminded me of something else Paul had recently taught me, something that was going on back at La Ferrassie in terms of rethinking past interpretations of ritual burial at the site. Monticules. These almonds looked just like them, monticules in miniature, Paul might have agreed.

These were geometric smooth stones stacked near each other that for decades prior archaeologists had read as placed by humans near some of the skeletons at La Ferrassie. Paul took a closer look and found signs that these geometric stones were actually natural rock formations that can occur with prolonged frost action working on the stone.

Freezing and thawing will polish stones under the earth, often in perfect geometric forms, and they can even result in these curious pyramids. The originally interpreted ritual funerary pyramid was recently revised thanks to the geological eye: It was really Mother Earth rubbing her rocks.

Harold and Shannon were among the leading archaeologists in this field who specifically dedicated their efforts to sort out the natural causes of forms—taphonomy—from the human-directed causes of forms found in archaeological sites. The monticules and the two vastly different interpretations of their meaning is a great example of why this is important and why they like to work with the likes of Paul and Vera. Their whole effort in re-excavating these known sites in southwestern France was in large part toward sorting through these matters so that when we try to understand the actual human past here, we're not making up a fantasy.

"Monticules are like clouds," Paul said. His forte wasn't only food metaphors. I heard chagrin and humor, that life was fascinating and that people kind of know nothing. But by clouds, I wasn't sure if he meant they were forms made by the Mother as she worked her natural forces, or if it was like what we did as kids, watching clouds and seeing meaningful forms in something random.

Knowing him, it meant both.

# As if Written in Stone

NE RAINY SATURDAY afternoon, I sat in my barn *à la Bordes* and watched four flintknapping videos to hone my beginner's skills. On days when I worked under Virginie's sure direction in the lab at Carsac, I sometimes used part of our lunch breaks to sit at the flintknapping pit to try my hand at the craft. I recalled something both Dennis and Harold had said at different times, that craftspeople were rare, the really good ones, then as now. I was learning firsthand how complex and hard stone craft really was.

I also learned more deeply the reasons the knapping pit was there. Yes, Harold wanted people to learn firsthand how hard this work was to master, but he had a second motive: for us to see the debris we created and what a flint pit looked like after beginners-to-masters sat at it and worked away. The *chaîne opératoire*, chain of operation, is what it's called in the biz, the step-by-step process and decisions made while making a tool. It prepared the eye to see patterns and process, not just types, when we got to the dig site or analyzed a tool collection. Sometimes archaeologists could even refit the pieces together if they were all there, and determine the original *chaîne opératoire*, like reversing a film in slo-mo. After sessions in the experimental pit, we then had the privilege to see the real patterns preserved in sediment at the site and were better prepared to actually see them, not to make a whole bunch of assumptions.

In earlier excavation eras, excavator bias was a serious problem and sometimes the lead excavator, including Peyrony, would cast aside flakes and debris he considered meaningless while keeping the pretty bifaces and blades. He didn't realize he was throwing away half the tool kit and also the pieces that could, like a puzzle, be refitted to see how that person 70,000 years ago had made the biface, point, or scraper. Today, this meant modern excavators had also to dig in a prior excavators' back dirt—the dirt they had moved and tossed aside—to find the missing pieces to what was now in the museums' collections. The pit prepared the modern mind to see details and stop making assumptions about what was important and what was not.

If the debris at a site looked anything like our pit at Camp Carsac, then it was likely a place where novices like me got a taste for making tools. And if they were anything like me, they would remain novices and contribute some other way, perhaps in making birch bark pitch to fasten spear points to wood staffs, or gathering wild mushrooms and berries, or cooperating in the hunt to drive the big animal we pursued into our spear-thrusting trap, or working deer hide. I'd be really good at that.

So far, I'd been doing okay with the knapping. When I'd managed a pretty flake and proudly took it, as a kindergarten child would her finger-paintings, to show to Dennis, he would kindly say it was a good start and remind me that it took over two hundred hours of practice before a knapper learned to make a decent tool. Just a decent one, not a masterpiece. Thus encouraged, I'd show it next to Harold, who'd smile and say, "Wow, that's pretty crappy, Beebe, even though I can see that you think it's pretty. Pretty just doesn't cut it." He'd then giggle himself silly with his double-edged pun.

Jan, an undergraduate student from Canada, who was dedicating her life to lithics and was already one of the better knappers in our band, overheard this exchange and took a closer look at my tool. "Yeah, it's crappy, but the point is you're banging rocks and that's what counts. Keep banging."

I did. I still do. I'm still a novice, but I love nothing more than trying and when I hit the angle just right, I love the percussive sound and slick tactile feel that vibrates through the stone. It's like English toffee in consistency and brittleness, but smooth as silk and buttercream in character.

From watching those videos, I inadvertently learned that the term *flintknapper* was not first a Paleo term, but was built on from Middle English (*knap*) and popularized in the sixteenth century. It referred to the craftsmen who would shape flint pieces to fit into rifles to set off the spark that ignited the gunpowder.

But around 2.6 million years ago, hominids began choosing stones and shaping them to use. The ones that responded well to being struck to remove sharp flakes, also leaving a core that could be used as a chopping and smashing instrument, were the ones most sought and used. These earliest tools were a hammer, the stone that struck the rock being shaped, and the resulting core and flakes from the effort. All useful and all pretty much the shape of things until around one million years ago. These first stone tools are often called Oldowan tools, named after the Olduvai Gorge in Tanzania, where Louis Leakey identified them. They are very useful tools that can be independently invented on the spot, in a pinch. These were so useful and basic that they are found for a long time, not only in parts of Africa but also in Eurasia, with many variations of hominids.

One of the deceptions of identifying early stone tools and then trying to correlate them to only one variety of hominid that used them is that often more than one variation of hominid did so. Oldowan might have been made and used by some of the Australopithecines but was certainly the tool style the earliest member of our genus, *Homo habilis*, made, as well as overlapping in use with later hominids, such as *Homo erectus,* and even later early modern humans. It's important to not make hard and simple one-to-one correspondences between tools and the various human groups.

Ofer Bar-Yosef opened my eyes to this complexity, and the long-lived legacy of Oldowan-style tools—cobbles, choppers, and flakes—given his pivotal land-bridge perch in Asia, looking east, west, and south for signs of human migrations through tools. It appears that these industries were all that was necessary in parts of East and Southeast Asia in order to use stone to then fashion other tools in bamboo and wood, materials more plentiful in those areas in Asia where the early stone tool style persisted. Bamboo and wood are materials that decompose fast, especially in warm humid climates, and we have little record of them, while the stones remained. In those Asian geographies, early modern humans pretty much kept using basic chopper and flake tools right up until the beginnings of agriculture, when they swapped them out for stone axes.

*Homo erectus* was the most likely group of humans to take the Oldowan out of Africa on the first hominid migrations into Eurasia, around 1.8 million years ago. It was also around that time that *Homo erectus* began tapping out another widespread tool industry, the Acheulean, named after the site of Saint-Acheul in northeastern France, where it was first given an official name. Its most distinguished differences are its bifaces, symmetrical hand axes.

Acheulean is different from Oldowan in conception: where Oldowan removes simple cutting flakes and fashions the core into a good smashing and cutting tool, Acheulean is the first tradition that began shaping the core into a more complex shape while simultaneously deriving various shapes of flakes that could also be retouched and shaped into other tools.

As mentioned, the classic shape of the Acheulean tradition is the archetypal hand ax, or biface, those pretty teardrop-shaped stone tools that we most often think of when we think *stone tool*. These bifaces really are the defining signature of the Acheulean. They most commonly are large, from dessert plate–sized to the size of one's hand. They probably used the flakes too, as nice little cutting edges.

The Acheulean has been found in Africa, Europe, and large areas of Asia. A pliable and useful tool tradition, it lasted a good long time, from around 1.8 million years ago to around 200,000 years ago and maybe more recently. Mostly associated with *Homo erectus,* it was the likely foundation for a tradition that overlapped with it, the Mousterian, which began to appear around 250,000 years ago and lasted until around 40,000 years ago. It was made and used by Neandertals in Europe, by both Neandertals and *Homo sapiens* in Asia, and by *Homo sapiens* in Africa, all around the same general time period.

The Mousterian, too, is named after a place in France: Le Moustier, a lovely little sleepy village on the Vézère that gives its name to the tool industry discovered there. But the village also lives shoulder to shoulder with the cave that harbored two Neandertal skeletons—an adult and an infant—until they were unearthed in the early twentieth century.

The Acheulean and Mousterian both make bifaces that look very similar, so it seems that the Mousterian evolved in some fundamental ways from the Acheulean. However, Mousterian hand axes, in general, are more intricate, smaller, thinner, and sharper. But the signature difference between the two traditions, the thing that puts Mousterian in its own class, is the complex execution strategy called the Levallois technique. (Named after the site of Levallois-Perret, just a stone's throw outside of Paris to the northwest, where it was first labeled.)

Levallois is strategic and planned. Its goal is to arrive at a special flake or point, and to get this end result, all one's prior strikes on the core have to be planned and hit in exactly the right places with the right-shaped result to proceed and eventually end with a Levallois piece.

Levallois also has many variations on a theme, but all share this strategy. It's akin to the difference between home cooking (non-Levallois) and the must-follow-step-by-step molecular cooking that comes out of Ferran Adrià's Catalan restaurant, El Bulli (Levallois). The former is spontaneous and open to unplanned maneuvers and will usually work no matter what, and the latter is the exacting recipe of an intense scientist where if you get something wrong or miss a step, you ruin the outcome and have to start again.

The Mousterian and its techie Levallois had a pretty good long run, too, appearing around 250,000 years ago and lasting until the extinction of the Neandertals. By then, the early modern humans who had lived in the Levant around 100,000 years ago and also used the Levallois may also have gone the way of extinction; or came and went into and out of Africa, met up with new early modern humans who were doing their thing in Africa, and perhaps just picked up a new tool tradition and dropped the complicated Levallois in favor of the easier-to-make blades of the Upper Paleolithic traditions.

Upper Paleolithic blade industries are really geared only toward knocking longer, thinner blades off a core piece of stone. They can be mass-produced and really take less skill than a biface or a Levallois point. They also may or may not make any other use of the core than to produce blades, like peeling an onion, until the core is spent.

Ofer again set me straight about the patterns of emergence of the different tool traditions. "Making [Upper Paleolithic] blades is much simpler than making Levallois," he said. "Neandertals were able to do Levallois technique. These people were skilled workers, artisans, with stone tools. And there is more than one kind of Levallois. There is one that produces these beautiful big flakes like the tortoise cores and so on. There is one that is going both ways so that it produces both flakes and some kinds of blades. There is one that produces points. Each of these requires a high level of skill." He paused and smiled before delivering his punch line. "Neandertals had higher skills than the stupid modern humans."

I smiled. This was another major aha moment for me, akin to when Alain told me about Neandertal versus *Homo sapiens* adaptations as flexible versus rigid. I had tried to understand the Levallois, including watching more of those flintknapping videos, but found it so much more complex than any of the other tool-making techniques.

Monsieur La Ferrassie was nodding his head vigorously in complete and total agreement. *We give too much credit to the explicit production of symbolic objects we call art,* he seemed to say. *This, too, my friend, was art, just art of a different sort.* I decided that the so-called Neandertal pendulum had gone far enough and was built on a faulty premise. I climbed on Monsieur La Ferrassie's shoulders, taking my best Mousterian hand ax, and as soon as the pendulum swept past, grabbed its rope and cut. We were free now to move about the territory with fewer preconceived ideas.

The Mousterian was the main tradition of the Middle Paleolithic. In Europe, the Mousterian is found only among Neandertals, who seem to be the sole occupants of Europe at the time. In different but related variations, the Mousterian also appears in the Levant, also called the Middle Paleolithic there and where it was made and used by both Neandertals and early modern humans. And finally, the Mousterian also appears during the same time period in Africa—called the Middle Stone Age to distinguish it from the Middle Paleolithic in Eurasia—again in different variations, but only in the hands of early modern humans, since Neandertals never appear to have lived in Africa. It took me a while to sort all this out.

So in Western Europe, the Mousterian was entirely associated with Neandertals. It appears that Europe was the place where Neandertals as a distinct meta-population evolved, given the evidence from Atapuerca in Spain as the oldest site (so far) to turn up early Neandertals. Some 700,000 or 800,000 years ago, Neandertals-in-the-making and *Homo sapiens*-in-the-making seem to have separated from our common ancestor in Africa. Some went into Europe and Asia and some stayed in Africa. Just as early modern humans most likely emerged from *Homo erectus* in Africa, so Neandertals most likely emerged from *Homo erectus* populations that made Europe and Asia their digs, with some mingling back and forth (which needs to be factored in, since both genetics and human nature show that people meeting people tend to mate, no matter what else they do).

I HAD VISITED Le Moustier many times before, but in different ways. My first glimpse of the cave was from the other side of the river, having climbed up and into the massive rock shelf called La Roque St-Christophe, a place occupied intermittently in later prehistory but most certainly in the Middle Ages, when it was a fortified cliff dwelling. I knew Le Moustier on first glance across the river valley because it had its signature rectangular gaping-mouth upper cave hovering over the village beneath it. But it was a second cave mouth, below the visible one, where the two Neandertal skeletons had been found (dating to between 41,000 and 45,000 years old), the adult by Swiss prehistorian Otto Hauser, and the infant by Denis Peyrony.

I soon revisited Le Moustier, crossing the river with two friends, a painter from Bretagne and a baker and costume designer from Japan. We were on our way to visit the Tibetan Buddhist retreat center and monastery of Dhagpo Kagyu Ling, founded in 1977 on the plateau right above the upper cave. True to the outlook of the Four Noble Truths of Buddhism, that suffering comes from attachment, the village seemed to be endeavoring to practice nonattachment; no one was making a big deal of the two ancient celebrities who had lived there, other than to say they were smart chaps. This was unusual. Attachment was the game elsewhere, at other sites with similar ancient residents.

Take the village of Marillac. Their site is Les Pradelles, a 40,000-to-80,000-year-old Neandertal butchering camp filled with animal bones, flint, and a few human fossils, which also appeared to show the telltale cut marks of defleshing (and possibly cannibalism). In its honor, the village showcases a towering sculpture of a Neandertal carrying the burden of many layers of sediment, much as Atlas carries the weight of the world. Likewise, driving to the village of La Chapelle-aux-Saints and its famous purported Neandertal burial site, the visitor is greeted with a banner almost wider and longer than the site (which may not be so hard; it's a small cave) marking the larger museum next door. At Les Eyzies, a romantic limestone statue of Neandertal Man overlooks the valley from his perch at the rock shelf above the village, where the national prehistory museum is located. Atapuerca has my buddy *Homo antecessor bardem*, aka Javi. Le Moustier was decidedly Buddhist on the matter.

We visited the monks, turned the numerous prayer wheels, prayed at the stupa that marks a potent mystical apex on the Mousterian plateau, and returned back to village origins at the lower cave. "It's not a mystery why the monastery or the Neandertals are here," a local said and shrugged casually as I bought a postcard from him. "It's a place with good energy." He handed me my change and went back to reading his newspaper.

Le Moustier is a beautiful place, as is the plateau above it. You feel good here. The village itself is serene and harmonious—forgotten by time but with a restaurant serving up excellent local cuisine on red-checkered tablecloths. To visit their cave is a quiet exercise in respect for the ancestors, another interesting extension of what goes on uphill at the monastery.

The lower cave is slightly up the slope along which the village huddles, and is tucked between two houses. As you climb, the medieval church is right behind you across the small road, and in front of the cave, there is a little nook where you can have a picnic in the shade. At the very front of the fenced-off excavation site is a replica of all the layers of strata, striated and several meters high, to show to the visitor the wealth of artifacts—Les Moustiers—found therein. After the Neandertals, early modern humans also occupied this site.

VERY COMMON IN southwestern France are four variations of Mousterian, one of the most common being called the Mousterian of Acheulean Tradition (MTA), one of three other variations on a Mousterian theme that François Bordes identified and also considered distinct cultures. Harold changed all that. He was the third wrench in the system, as Dennis told me one evening at Camp Carsac, aptly offering a tool analogy for how Harold disrupted a nice smooth typology elegantly in place, which had been making everyone's life more certain in France. In America, Lewis Binford was rocking the Bordean boat. Bordes and Binford were the first two wrenches.

In the 1960s, the Binford–Bordes debate erupted, knocking across the Atlantic over how to read stone tool variability and what stone tools are telling us about who made them, how they were made, and why they were made the way they were. Bordes argued that the different styles of tools found were distinct from each other, as separate traditions made by different people: they defined cultures. American archaeologist Lewis Binford counter-argued that the same groups of people made the stone assemblages but that the variation reflected different functions of the tools.

Harold, almost two decades after the debate had begun, found that neither of the two typologies nailed it, and further that the Bordean typologies just weren't holding in the excavations and collections he was studying in France. It forced him to reexamine all the stone assemblages in question and he arrived at a different conclusion than Bordes or Binford: that they weren't necessarily from different traditions or made for different functions, but more likely they were different stages of a tool being worked, retouched, and resharpened.

One way Harold argued his perspective was by using the life of a pencil as an analogy: A new pencil looks very different from a used one and a used one has different reuse and retouching patterns, being sharpened, its eraser wearing down, until the pencil is discarded into a trash heap and the pencil user goes for a new pencil. Moreover, in flush times, a person may be likely to discard a perfectly good pencil for a new one with a fresh eraser. In more economically pinched times, they'll reuse that pencil until it is a stub.

Not everyone agrees with this perspective—in this business, if they did, you better check for a pulse. The biggest critics of Harold's process-oriented view still prefer to view static tool types and kits in the record, similar to the specialized tools they might have hanging on the wall in their garage—either culturally or functionally—as the dominant paradigm. Some say these tool collections were conservative cultural traditions that were passed on from one generation to the next and unchanging in that way. Still, across a range, as usual, many have incorporated aspects of Harold's ideas about retouched and resharpened tools.

Most importantly, the dominant contribution he made was that tools are now seen as having a dynamic, not a static, life. A tool's shape can change over its lifetime of use; a tool type, just like a fossil, was a proxy for something in the process of becoming something.

That was huge. It was also cheeky. He was young and challenging his own mentor's typology, one that had become the dominant way to organize stone tools across France and Europe and elsewhere. He arrived at and presented his ideas a few years after Bordes had died, but when he did, Madame Bordes came to his talk. He was nervous. He was about to stand in public and shoot down her husband's ideas. It was at a symposium in Liege, Belgium, in the mid-1980s, and the audience was pretty hostile. After he presented and was being harshly criticized as an American interloper, Madame Bordes couldn't take it anymore and stood up and said very loudly, "Michel Lenoir! Defend your colleague!" Michel Lenoir and Harold had worked together at the site of Combe-Capelle Bas (a part of Abri Peyrony), which was where his idea of scraper reduction—the life of a tool in process—came to him. Madame Bordes was dedicated to science, not factions, and this was science and needed to move forward. She had given her blessing, and in a sense, so had her husband from the beyond.

Thanks to Harold's work, life in the past looked more like what we know life to be: dynamic, changing, full of options and choices that never quite represent a whole culture in one slice of time, certainly not in one set of tools. Process was now in the picture and people who liked nice neat stories had to get used to the fact that their photograph of the past was really a single frame in a movie.

An innovative way that Harold is still getting at this issue is through a flintknapping machine he developed at Penn, which he endearingly calls Igor.

"It's a device I made to knap glass cores," he explained to me when I visited him in Philadelphia and stood before what looked like a giant's microscope. But instead of lens and viewfinder, at its center was a clamp grip holding a glass core. He could adjust knapping angles and record them, capturing the whole process from the beginning to the end result and shape. He was both getting at the processual stuff and also quantifying the choices a flintknapper makes. "I'm trying to test several things that the flintknappers say, since most of what they know is based on impressions or lore."

I had encountered this a lot, and it is still very widespread in France with prehistory buffs who are also flintknapping masters. They speak very intuitively about getting the feel of the stone and through it, actually saying this, *communing* with the mind of past flintknappers. It is believed by many of them that if you master this skill, you will almost be like a shaman, journeying into an altered state of consciousness and folding yourself into a past consciousness, understanding through skill, and feeling the mind of the prehistoric Neandertals or Cro-Magnons.

"This machine helps me control a lot of variables and get results that look exactly like what a flintknapper would do," Harold said. Where a flintknapper uses experience and intuition, the flintknapping machine maps mathematically what angles, velocities, and distances create a stone tool. This helps establish patterns, patterns of what a flintknapper can do, patterns of what creates the shapes archaeologists find on site, and also patterns toward what is a human-made tool versus something shaped by natural forces. It's essentially getting into the mind of the knapper but doing it less intuitively, as is the main trend, and more mathematically. Patterns.

"That's why we have science," he added, "to remove the bias," and offer something others can test and replicate, confirm or refute.

THE TOOL TRADITION that sits between the Mousterian and all the Upper Paleolithic blade industries is one called the Châtelperronian, after the site of Châtelperron northwest of Lyon, where it was first identified and labeled. This is considered a blade industry, too, but one that is very different from any that came after it and a definite break from the Mousterian. Some consider it the first of the Upper Paleolithic tool traditions of early modern humans. Others consider it the last of the Neandertal tools, but not Mousterian, so a sudden change in cultural habits among the last Neandertals. Ofer sees it as a modern human tradition simply because it is a blade tradition. João sees it as a Neandertal tradition because he sees Neandertals as exactly like us and considers them to be the first innovators of the blade tradition during "the transition." Everyone else seems to be on a sliding scale somewhere in between.

The Châtelperronian sits at that narrow band of time, around 47,000 to 41,000 years ago, and occurs in France and Spain during the overlap between the Neandertals and the newly arriving early modern humans from farther east. It is a sensitive time because it keeps getting recalibrated, which changes the amount of time for the overlap, altering a lot of possibilities over who influenced whom—if at all. A lot of blade-throwing takes place among specialists in the field over these issues.

Add to this the fact that among some 143 Châtelperronian sites found so far, most prehistorians consider that only about twenty-five of them have been dug well enough to offer valid evidence. And only two are associated with Neandertal fossils, but these two, Grotte du Renne at Arcy-sur-Cure in Burgundy and St-Césaire in the Poitou-Charente, have serious integrity issues, with mixed sediment levels that have made it impossible to really know who made the associated Châtelperronian tools (and ornaments, for there are animal teeth with holes drilled into them). It comes down to needing to find a new, untouched site that will be well excavated to begin to resolve this issue.

"There is still much to be learned about the Neandertal adaptation," Shannon told me when I asked him about this and related issues. "There are very basic concepts that after forty to fifty years of intense debate and analysis, we still haven't solved. You may remember the Bordes–Binford debate? This debate remains unsolved. We don't know what stone tools were used for and we don't know why they favored some technologies for making flakes over others."

"What do we know?" I asked.

"We do know that starting around forty thousand years ago modern humans replaced Neandertals in Europe. But we still don't know exactly what advantage moderns had over Neandertals. To address this we need to better understand Neandertals before moderns arrived and we need to better understand the adaptation moderns arrived with."

Shannon grew up in St. Louis, Missouri, and first tasted archaeology at age eleven when he dug at a site in Kampsville, Illinois. From then on, he knew that somehow archaeology was in his future. He took a course with Art Jelinek, Harold's advisor years earlier. That course oriented Shannon to a strong interest in the Paleolithic. His first dig with Harold was at Art's site of La Quina in the Charente in France. They've now collaborated for well over twenty years and have created a clearinghouse website for their collective Paleolithic research called Old Stone Age (OSA).

Dennis joined this duo when he first arrived in France to work with them at Pech IV in 2000. Setting high standards for strong scientific research, they also got along with ease and complemented each other creatively and intellectually. It grew from there, with Alain, Paul, and Vera and then the many others who weave in with equal clarity, competence, and cheer. It was almost akin to the sediment layers they studied, layering their histories over each other, beginning with the bedrock of Bordes, then Harold, Paul, Shannon, Dennis, Vera, and on to current and future students.


THERE IS ALSO a hospitality element to running a dig, such as making sure there is enough food for lunch, not only for crew but also for the many visiting colleagues and collaborators who may stop by any day during the season. Another hospitality element is that when many tourists drive by and see the dig in progress, some stop and it is important that someone show them around. This is in part to keep everyone safe—there are a lot of open trenches in the earth, ladders, bars, rocks, and buckets moving around and sensitive materials being gathered. And it is in part because digging at such an important site means also sharing the patrimony with the public.

I loved this part of the job. If I was free, I enjoyed introducing the new humans to the old. I loved watching the visitors' eyes light up and their faces grow stunned when they learned this was a Neandertal place and that at its oldest level was 90,000 years old. I loved watching the metaphoric sweater unravel—all their preconceptions of being human, of time, and of what "old" meant.

I loved watching the know-it-all husband from Paris be struck speechless. I loved the "*so*" that slipped out of the exhaling puckered Hummel-like lips of the little girl from Munich, not knowing what to do with someone who might be 89,994 years older than she. I loved seeing the magic wash across the face of the little boy from Holland to whom I showed a 50,000-year-old bison molar the size of his palm. He saw galaxies in that molar and stood there for long moments, staring at it, perhaps rebuilding the animal in his mind. I loved the look of contentment on the face of the mother from Düsseldorf who had said she wanted to be here with her three children where they could learn prehistory at its thickest in Europe. They had grown up near Mettmann, where the famous Neandertal, the fossil who put Neandertals on the map for us in

1856, was uncovered in the Neander Valley. It had been the Neander Thal then, but the German language modernized its spelling for "valley" and removed the "h," making it Tal. Neander Tal.

I'd noticed that some researchers who wanted to show a new era was dawning, since we were no longer so arrogant as to assign brutishness to these very sophisticated cousins, were changing the spelling of Neandertal, too. Dropping the "h" seemed a way of quietly saying, let's start again: a new, more enlightened era in studies of human evolution and relatedness is dawning. No more Neanderthals, but instead Neandertals. We're all growing and changing. It's a subtle, quiet movement and those who still use an "h" aren't in the wrong; it's just a wish to depart from the past.

Presenting La Ferrassie also gave me the chance to review it. I had to go over the nine distinct levels that had been identified: Levels 1–5 were Mousterian, dating from 90,000 to 45,000 years ago. Check. Levels 7–9 were Upper Paleolithic, beginning with Aurignacian and moving into Gravettian and perhaps Solutrean. Check. And then that tricky Level 6 that was sandwiched in between, the very brief Châtelperronian. Check. Sort of.

"There's a debate about who made the Châtelperronian," I'd repeat word for word what I'd heard Dennis say when he did tour duty. "Most think it was the Neandertals," he'd explain, "but others think they learned from modern humans or that it was just something made by modern humans. It would be great if we could find some teeth or something in that layer so that we could tell for sure, but we haven't."

When I wasn't trying to piece all this together by talking to the specialists or working in the lab or at the site, I sought different perspectives, and a clearing of my mind, two ways. One was to take off on my own and spend a long day at the Musée National du Préhistoire in Les Eyzies. My favorite museum of all time, it has a dizzying series of displays that lay out all these stone tool traditions so that you can wander and lose yourself in stone-craft geekdom to your heart's content. The village Café de la Mairie, right at the base of the museum's rock shelf perch, was a good place to punctuate the effort with coffee in the morning and beer at closing time. The liquids helped immensely in absorbing all the stone.

The second way was even more pleasurable and complementary: I'd hang out with the local amateur prehistory experts, who were close to the material but free from all the politics and contentions that defined the fields of paleoanthropology and archaeology. In fact, a common quality among all these prehistory locals was that they had little patience for the vitriol of the profession and stayed out of it, instead spending infinite time with the material, with the land, and with the publications and collections, without needing to take a stand. The pendulum, as well, was useless to them: They loved the Neandertals and didn't need them to be like us or not like us to do so. The whole point was to get *away* from us and into another way of being human.

A group arrived one afternoon at La Ferrassie, led by a regional guide, a transplant from England who was showing other British visitors the sites. Dennis showed them the site, from all the layers of occupations at the corner of the cave where we worked to the wider area of the larger cave, near where the French team with Isabelle, Antoine, and Asier were re-excavating the original site of the infant, La Ferrassie 8. He explained that it was a complementary but separate effort from the 1970s Delporte dig. La Ferrassie 8's skeleton was incomplete and the hope was that in reopening the area where it had been found, they might find more pieces. (They didn't but in the end it did bring to light that enigmatic adult molar.) He added that the child skeleton's angle and fragmented nature could potentially negate evidence that it had been buried intentionally.

Up until now, the guide had listened and smiled with her clients. Perhaps because of Dennis's warm nature, she decided to get a little controversial, and pointed out that he, as a North American, was suspect for denying Neandertals things such as burial or language. She really leaned in hard, not to mention committing an inaccurate statement but one with a lot of gossip that swirled around like a patchy game of telephone. Or the parable of the elephant.

Dennis, like Harold, and pretty much the whole team, left things more open and didn't make proclamations if the evidence wasn't strong enough to do so. It was better to say it was still unknown or uncertain. They wanted to keep the distorting lens of speculation out of the science.

Dennis said as much, in a very diplomatic way, and then added, on the theme of language, "I would have no problem with Neandertals having language. They physically seem to have the same physiology as we do. They have the same number of genes that we do that are associated with speech. They're cousins of ours and there's no reason to say they didn't, but it's impossible to say for certain." He then offered an example of experiments with a view toward trying to answer this question.

"There are some people who've done experiments with that. I knew a graduate student who was doing this." He referred to Shelby Putt, who with three other colleagues at the University of Iowa presented their findings at the Society for American Archaeology conference in 2012. They had set up three different groups of subjects who were asked to flintknap an Acheulean hand ax. One group was asked to just watch the flintknapper do it. Another group watched and was allowed to ask questions. And the third group never witnessed the knapper do anything, they only saw the finished product. All three groups were then asked to knap a hand ax. "With the first two groups," Dennis continued, "there was really no distinction in the quality of their work. The third group was terrible of course, they'd never seen anyone do it. This isn't proof that Neandertals didn't have language, but it's a compelling argument that language, as we know it, was not necessary to execute complex stone tools."

When I looked up Shelby Putt and her colleagues' subsequent publication on their experiments, I discovered that they found the nonverbal group that watched the flintknapper make a tool set up their striking platforms differently and actually made more efficient flakes, indicating that verbal communication might reduce focused learning, not enhance it.

This reminded me of the glassblower from Toulon I'd met in Sarlat on a recent Saturday in town. He was an itinerant soul, much like foragers of the Paleolithic, stonemasons of the Middle Ages, and archaeological excavation crews of the twenty-first century, all carrying their tool kits with them and all less bound to a place and people, wandering to the next site, camp, or town to ply their trade. We'd met with friends in the Café la Lune Poivre, where a lot of interesting conversations happen in Sarlat. I told him, when he asked what I did, that I was a writer.

He heard *words* and *language* in that, and said, "I find language gets in the way. The conventional view is that it is the cornerstone to being human, but I find it blocks me in my craft and in my experience in the world and with others."

Without knowing it—and no offense taken on my part at cutting down my chosen profession—he had tapped right into the heart of the issues in play when we try to guess at language's value and uniqueness to us and to Neandertals. Have we overestimated it?

"Language blocks our ability to fully absorb our human experiences," he said conclusively, more to his beer than to me.

Yes, I am a writer, and I find myself quite often trying to get the right words and narrative to get past potential blocks to eliciting direct and vivid experiences. My human mind is wired to allow me to guess at the mind of the reader—something the psychologists call Theory of Mind— and determine what experience the reader might seek. Then, using language, I do my best to conjure it up—which, at a distance, allows me to communicate it directly without us ever meeting in person to share the tale. *That* is the power of language, far more than teaching how to make a stone tool. The part of that equation that is very human and common to both Neandertals and us is the penchant for teaching, for learning, and for sharing with or without this thing we call *modern* human language. Besides, modern human language potentially is a phenomenon far more recent than we think.

# 9

## PIPER AT THE GATES OF DAWN

NE EARLY MORNING, when the fog that settled in the valley every night was still low and covering the ground and trees, Didier picked me up in Sarlat. He'd brought mud boots for both of us; I had chocolate and nuts. Soon we were standing in a farmer's field on a high plateau just outside of Sarlat.

"This field was recently plowed and will be left to rest for the winter," he said, "so it's the best time to see if anything new has come to the surface." I noticed tunneling marks across the field, with cloven hoof prints all around. "*Sangliers*," Didier said quietly. "The wild boar love it after a field has been plowed and they root out the earthworms and grubs." We too were opportunists, coming right after the boars.

I looked more closely at a stone that had been angling out of one of the boar-carved trenches. "Is that a stone tool?" I asked, incredulous. "Yes," Didier answered easily, with no drama, and shrugged.

"Once you tune your gaze, you'll notice the field is full of them. That's why I brought you here. Some are Middle Paleolithic and Mousterian, but many are younger and they're all mixed up, given all the plowing.

You will soon learn to distinguish the Neolithic from the Mesolithic from the Upper Paleolithic—both from their style as well as their color."

Flint is very much a living stone and over time it takes on a chalky or brownish patina. Upper Paleolithic tools still have some of the flint's sheen and are often a glossy light brown. Neolithic are a beautiful clear to foggy cherry red tone. One Mesolithic core—a period that sits between the Upper Paleolithic and the Neolithic—which I also discovered near a boar track, was glossy, clear, and dark gray.

I soon learned, as I showed each find to Didier, that if it were anything other than Mousterian, he'd frown as if in mild disgust and say, "Too young. *Homo sapiens.*" He'd say *sapiens* disparagingly. Like us. Dirt bags. Litterers. We had just found a cast-off cigarette lighter in the farmer's field and he'd said it exactly the same way, "*Trop jeune. Homo sapiens.*" Peh. "*Sapiens dégueulasse*, disgusting *sapiens*," he finished.

Lighter aside, this was bliss; and there was no better company than Didier, the knowledgeable, calm, and contemplative sort of person you'd want on a hunt, be it for boar, mushrooms, berries, or tools. I mimicked him as he paced and looked, jogging over when he called to show me something. Such as when he picked up a scraper that had the color and thickness of steamed milk in café au lait, just a touch of the light coffee color seeping in.

"Neandertal," he said with a smile. There was no accusation in his tone, only joy and rapture. These were his people. He then taught me how to read not only the tools but the soil.

"Each year the farmers plow their fields, and each year, also, through the action of the earth's warming and freezing through the seasons, stones that lie deeper under the surface work their way up to the top." Almost in a similar fashion, a deep splinter might make its way to the top layer of skin after some time and begin to jut out so that you could at last find a tip surfacing by which to remove it. "But all that over there," he pointed to stretches of dark, loamy earth, "it's just topsoil, fertile but recent." We walked a few more meters and he pointed to our left. "Over there. What do you see?"

I walked over to the area and studied it. I began to notice that the earth had little stripes of sandy silt coming through, and said so. "*Exactement*," he whispered. "Those are like little trails from deeper down, that there has been some earth movement to bring the sandier sediment from older earth up to the surface. That is where you may get lucky and find stone tools."

As if on cue, I looked a foot to my left and saw a slice of café au lait patina jutting vertically. When I picked it up, it was an intricately and delicately wrought hand ax whose tip had broken off. From the shine of clearer brown flint at the broken edge, I knew it had probably recently been snapped in two by a farmer's plow. But it was still beautiful and showed a master stone crafter in the fine details of the lower rounded end of the tool. I set it back in the earth.

I looked up at Didier's dreamy gaze and realized I was mirroring the same magic back to him. "This is addicting, to touch the deep past like this," I said.

"*Oui*," he concurred. "*C'est une drogue.*"

"*Oui*," I echoed, the perfect apprentice caught in timelessness, "especially when it's not *Homo sapiens* but Neandertal."

"*Exactement*," he punctuated, and we walked to a neighboring field to do the same. He then said, "I've saved the best for last, now that you know how to see."

We walked back to his vehicle and took off to another plateau a little farther north. As we did I learned that he had been born in a village south of Carsac famous for a-yet-to-be-excavated Neandertal site called La Gane. He lived a stone's throw from it all his life. Although from an Italian family that resettled in the Dordogne, Didier was considered a man from the Périgord, very much like the long lineage of people from this land. Alain said of Didier that they didn't come any more Périgordian than he.

The knowledge Didier had of the land was so precious that often Alain liked to have him work with him on sites. He respected the land and spoke its language, a subtle and quiet tongue requiring infinite patience and attention to detail. Moreover, he was even-handed with the Neandertals. He loved them but was far less willing to speculate about who they were than the scholars.

"All we really have of them are their stone tools and some fossils. That's not enough to build a whole story on, but it is enough to show they were successful, highly intelligent, and best of all, lived with the incredible knowledge about the world around them and did not alter it." That's actually saying a lot. How many of us can say these things about ourselves?

This plateau was higher up and had several small valleys and sweeping hills nearby. I could just make out the layers of the Massif Central to the east. "*Voilà.*" He swept his arm, "I call this the sanctuary of Neandertal stone toolmakers." It was his brotherhood. Didier could make all the stone tools, from Acheulean to Upper Paleolithic. He loved the Levallois, for it was the most challenging and had so many applications.

He called it a stone maker's sanctuary because this field, belonging to a local who had given him permission to come here as he wished, keeps bringing up exclusively Neandertal tools—nothing later and nothing earlier. No *Homo sapiens* tools, not even a lighter. Bliss. And it does so each season like clockwork, after each plowing.

I looked with a growing concentration, working toward the center of the scattered cloudy white stones. I saw cast-off tools, debris, and flint cores still plump enough for making future tools, left as a deposit for people who came here again and again until never again, after they disappeared from the earth. It was a mound in the field, another telltale sign of something going on underneath, and it was near a rich source of natural flint in the nearby valley just beneath us.

We fell into silence and paced and tracked in our own directions. After ten minutes, I found myself bending and picking up a beautifully formed scraper. Didier saw me and walked over to see what I had found.

"*C'est très jolie,* Beebe. I've scoured this field really well already and I assure you, finding something as pretty as that is a very rare occurrence. You must have the touch." I felt as if I had been knighted. He is a very kind and generous soul. He added that he would not have shared these sites with me if I were not so enamored with the Neandertals. He is a part of the local effort to protect the integrity of the land and its prehistory. I promised not to show a soul this spot, secretly happy that my love affair with Neandertals had given me this rare privilege. As the sun rose high enough to lift off the fog that had hovered head-high throughout the morning, we left things as we'd found them and ate the chocolates and nuts, which tasted so vibrant after the morning's hunt, and then Didier took me back to Sarlat. But I was not the same person who had left that morning. I had stood in the heart of an open-air site where over many visits, maybe generations, Neandertals had worked stone and made their tools to carry off into surrounding valley and forest and plateau and live their lives as they had for 400,000 years or more.

As rare as these *known* open-air sites are, it turns out they are more common than cave sites. But the obvious issues of preservation—caves being more stable and open-air sites having been plowed since the first farmers came here—has really jumbled the remains. It has created a distorted image, where most people imagine Neandertals, as well as early modern humans, living in caves. It is more likely they did only some of the time—probably during winter and cold seasons—and the rest of the time, in better weather and warmer seasons, moved, likely with the animals, out into moveable open-air camps.

When I spoke with Randall White from his terrace overlooking the Beune and Vézère valleys near Les Eyzies, he confirmed this and blew me away with what was already known about this reality.

"The crazy thing is that to this day, there's never been a survey project in the Vézère, in the Dordogne, or anywhere else, that systematically looked below ground as well as on the surface. We're really left with a complete lack of information about what's in the open air," Randy said. "The situation has improved a little bit recently because of salvage archaeology. When they built the auto route that now goes to Bordeaux and ultimately takes you on to Clermont-Ferrand, they discovered, just in the Isle Valley alone, one hundred ten Mousterian sites in the open air and all that material has been sampled. That's one hundred ten sites," he emphasized so that I could digest it, "that were considered worthy of additional excavation, and that's in the bottom of the valley." He had already told me that people occupied different levels at different times and that in a place such as the Dordogne, the valley to the plateau gave life to up to seven different vertical large-scale ecological zones on each face of the four different cliff-facing directions. So people weren't just hanging out in the valley but going up and down too, eating well, some twenty-eight options at least for varied meals.

"The bottom line is, if you run under fifteen-meter swaths, from Périgueux to Bordeaux along the Isle Valley, you're going to find one hundred ten Mousterian sites. Right?" he asked, incredulous, more as a statement than a question, and then laughed almost for comic relief. "That's like the width of this courtyard," he swept his arms to both sides on the terrace, "for seventy kilometers." That's a lot of occupations, all open air, on a narrow corridor, for a mere forty-four miles.

I was speechless. I also wondered if it meant that there were many more Neandertals living here at any one time than has been estimated. The most accepted idea, based on density and frequency of sites, was that Neandertal populations never got very big—maybe 10,000 to 20,000 at any time and living in groups that averaged between ten and twelve people, far smaller than the later invading early modern humans.

"People ask me," Randy added, "if I think there are sites to be discovered, and I say, 'We haven't even started.' The obvious ones have been found."

* * *

WHEN NEXT I saw Harold, I asked about the population thing. I added that population size here seemed as outlandish as in South and East Africa, recalling how much I'd heard about Acheulean hand axes just littering the landscape, hundreds of thousands just lying on the surface in some places, for seemingly small populations of *Homo erectus*. In his usual forthcoming way, he grabbed his calculator and cheerfully said, "Let's do some arithmetic."

"And replace preconceptions with numbers," I said.

"Exactly," he said as if firing up the engines of the *U.S.S. Enterprise* from *Star Trek*. I recalled he had been both a humanities and a math major before he'd switched to anthropology and archaeology.

"Let's just keep to East Africa." Start from the beginning, he said.

"Okay."

"Let's say we've got, um, do you want to go with five thousand toolmakers at any one time? Excluding the kids. I'm talking about whoever is making the tools."

"In how large a group?" I asked to get a feel for non-toolmakers.

"Let's say ten thousand people." He said.

"So every other person is a toolmaker?" I asked. "Isn't that a bit generous?"

He shrugged. "It's an assumption, but I'm going to calculate it based on how many tools. So we've got five thousand toolmakers. Now. Let's say that each of them makes one biface a year."

"Okay," I said.

"So that's five thousand bifaces a year being put on the landscape."

"Okay."

"Or is that really too stupid? Should we make it two bifaces per year?"

We both laughed. "How many bifaces does an individual need to make in a week?" I asked.

"I have no idea."

"Then, let's say, one a month," I ventured.

"Okay, so twelve a year," Harold said.

"But really, I don't know. What do I know about how many bifaces a person needs a year? I have no idea when one wears out or needs to be retouched."

"You want to go with one a year or twelve a year?"

I thought about it. "How about eight a year?"

"Okay, eight a year for five thousand toolmakers." He began punching in the numbers, a demonic grin growing on his face. "That's forty thousand bifaces per year. Now, that lasts for one and a half million years." He crunched more numbers and his face transformed from the Grinch to the face of a child opening Christmas gifts. "That's six to the tenth. That's sixty *billion*," his voice echoed like Carl Sagan, "hand axes . . ."

". . . dropped by a mere five thousand people every year for one and a half million years," I said.

"Yeah." Harold was totally satisfied, his mission on track to replace speculative reality with hard data anywhere he could. Had we gone with even more conservative numbers, we'd still have a landscape piled with hand axes by a small group of people. The situation was no different when applying the numbers to Neandertals in the Dordogne. A small population at any one time over the course of 400,000 years was still a huge number of dropped stone tools. Maybe they even dropped them on purpose, so as not to carry them around, knowing that there were caches of tools all over the landscape.

Warmed up from this exercise, I wanted Harold to give clarity to this whole stone tool issue, the one hard fact of his work that he found at sites, long after softer organic material had disappeared from the record. "How do you see behavior in the archaeological record? What do you see? Especially since stone tools are your main source of information?"

"I see it as incredible stagnation," he said. "Let's go way back, to early stone tools. Let's put it at three million years, it's a controversy right, but three million. Okay, three million to a million, you've got the same goddamned stuff over and over again." He said this last half of the sentence as if a cowboy with a big wad of chew between his lip and gum.

"Acheulean, i.e. bifaces, come in one and a half million years ago, something like that. There's a lot of overlap with the Oldowan. Distinguishing the early Acheulean from the older Oldowan is not always easy, right?" Didier had told me the same thing. "And it's really based on one thing, so the rest of the industry looks pretty much the same. The Acheulean goes on from one and a half million to let's say two hundred fifty thousand. Then you've got the Mousterian, starting at about two hundred fifty thousand. Distinguishing between the Mousterian and the Acheulean is extremely difficult. You cannot do it strictly on the basis of an assemblage. You have some really Acheulean-like pieces, bifaces, okay, that would tend to make it more Acheulean, but there's no strong line.

"So when you add all that up, you can't [easily] tell the difference between the Acheulean and the Oldowan, you can't really tell the difference between the Acheulean and the Mousterian, and you've got a continuity of three million years of very little change. And then," he says in a dramatic voice, "from forty thousand years to now—change, change, change—that's the nature of the game. Human recent history is unbelievably short. Then take the Neolithic," which marked the beginning of farming around 10,000 years ago. "*That's* when we had a transformation like nobody's business. The population was growing, the whole subsistence base was changing, the effect on nutrition. What has happened in those last ten thousand years? Everything that we think of, really, what most people think of." Agriculture changed everything.

He paused and then slowed down his response to make his point. With all the rapid change captured in the past 10,000 years, he sees nothing anywhere close to it in the Middle Paleolithic or earlier.

Everyone agrees on the rate of change but not on why. Some think it was a key mutation that changed our brains and brought on this rampant need to alter everything. Others think that's way too simplistic and neat and that it was a complex mixture of both mutations and cultural changes that went hand in hand and appeared a long time ago but didn't reach their expression or culmination point until recently. Others think culture, adaptable and pliant, like our brains, could have just adjusted and innovated as the demands came about, with no significant genetic changes: the potential was in there all along, just dormant. Others look to population growth and its pressures as the mother of all change and innovation, a position that is not a contrast to the other theories. What can safely be said is that no one is entirely happy with what anyone else is saying. But the fact holds that around 40,000 years ago we began doing things differently from all our ancestors of the past 3 million years, and that only accelerated into a mind-boggling alteration of the world as never seen before and in which we now live.

ALL THIS HAS been the story so far as written in stone. We know already that Neandertals used wooden spears and perhaps other wooden implements. Occasionally, archaeologists have found Neandertal bone tools, pieces of animal bone that have been knapped as if they were made of stone, turned into scrapers and flakes in a similar way. Also not uncommon is to come across a deer antler or femur that has been refashioned into a retouching tool, to fine-tune a stone tool with softer taps delivered by this softer material.

But the Paleo world stood still for a spell, when archaeologist William Rendu, a member of Marie Soressi's team at Pech I, discovered a rib bone in their collection that looked as if it had been used to smooth something. It had a polished rounded tip like a Popsicle stick, only even more rounded and polished, with micro-abrasions on it that showed an applied and repeating vertical direction.

Soon after this find, the team led by Shannon digging at Abri Peyrony, downriver from Pech I in the Dordogne in the Couze Valley, found three more of these rounded-tip bone tools in their site. They all collaboratively began realizing they were looking at a special bone tool made by

Neandertals that had nothing to do with knapping a sharp edge. Instead, it was a lissoir, a smoother, a tool still in use to this day by leatherworkers; it never fell from use since the first, which appeared to have been made 50,000 years ago at Pech I. The lissoirs at Abri Peyrony were not too much younger, dating to between 41,000 and 48,000 years ago.

Shannon explored the modern lissoir's use, visiting a saddle maker in the Dordogne. She showed him three types of lissoirs: bone, wood, and metal. She said the bone was the best; it was soft enough not to scratch the leather but hard enough to smooth it. Wood broke too easily; bone was supple. She used it not only to soften the leather but also to close the pores to make it waterproof. The wear marks on the prehistoric lissoirs looked to hold the same pattern that appeared on the modern tools. The bone lissoirs have all come from rib bones, often from deer and bison.

The earth had stood still because this was a departure from the pattern of tool-making and use found in the Middle Paleolithic. And a date of 50,000 years set it on the precipice of possibly being in place before early modern humans arrived in the area. They, by contrast, were already known to make and use lissoirs. It appeared that here was a case of independent invention and also one that gave the first strong evidence for hide working and perhaps clothing-making and -wearing among Neandertals. That took the chill off winter, especially without fire.

I gained better perspective on the importance of lissoirs by talking with Randy White. From his work on the Aurignacian in the region, possibly the first early modern humans in the Dordogne, he had found tons of these bone tools.

"So, I'm excavating at Abri Castanet," he said, "which is a classic Aurignacian site here in the region, and within a single layer we have three hundred fifty lissoirs." He laughed. "And somebody finds a fragment of a lissoir at Pech de l'Azé [and Abri Peyrony] and it makes the pages of *Science*." He says it with a good deal of humor in his voice, as in, *really?*

"Because it's Neandertal and not early modern human?" I asked.

"Yes." He replied. There is nothing remarkable about lissoirs in early modern human contexts but they are remarkable when found with Neandertals, "because they are so extraordinary and we have to look so hard for them."

But he also seemed amazed by the massive conclusion that so many people have made with those four lissoirs, which is that Neandertals were just like us, as João would probably argue. João was making this argument already with a few pigmented seashells he had found in southern Spain, dating to 50,000 years ago, and also with the new and earlier dates he had arrived at for cave paintings in El Castillo Cave in northern Spain, not far from the site of Altamira, making it possible that they were made by Neandertals. Like the lissoirs, these were all rare expressions among Neandertals, but were very common among early modern humans.

"It seems like a very curious conclusion," Randy said, "to say, 'Well, look, Neandertals are just like us.' They're not just like us because all that stuff," such as lissoirs and beads, "is completely banal in a modern human context; it's just background."

Not so in a Neandertal context; it becomes, to us, extraordinary, which to me was beginning to appear a banal attitude. Instead of saying, 'It's whether they were or were not like us,' it seemed more enlightened to ask without preconceptions or other attachments, *Who were they on their own terms, without resorting to comparing them with us all the time?*

I had to ask Randy, who was so forthcoming to discuss this with me, what these few lissoirs could tell us about Neandertals.

"I don't think that a very small number of these objects from a handful of sites suggests anything more than that Neandertals are in our lineage and they're curious about things besides flint and animal bone. But it also doesn't mean that they're behaving like we do."

BACK AT CAMP Carsac, Teresa Steele, the head of the zooarchaeology work with the team, and her student Naomi Martisius, set to broadening the search for lissoirs. It was Naomi who had identified one of the lissoirs in situ at the dig at Abri Peyrony when a fellow crew member had un-earthed it and called her over to have a closer look, as well as another that she found in the stored collection from a prior season. Shannon mused, "Now that we've identified lissoirs, we may begin to see more of them because we know what to look for."

If ever there was a good case for having a great lab director, such as Virginie, who made sure the materials coming out of the ground were well organized and identified, this was it. Many discoveries have this retro-view, seeing something emerge later, after the dig is done, then going back to the catalogued and stored collection to sort out the emerg-ing patterns.

In addition to looking at other collections—not only those of Pech de l'Azé and Abri Peyrony, but also Roc de Marsal and Jonzac, a site Shan-non and Teresa dug together in the Charente—was to understand through experiments how these lissoirs were made. All they needed were a few fresh rib bones from an ungulate, a hoofed herbivore—maybe a cow or a deer would do the trick—and they could start working their own hides with bone and see if the wear and breakage patterns were similar to those on the ancient pieces.

FRANÇOISE WAS A local volunteer who had recently joined our team. She was a little older than I was and dressed like a jazz quintet, riffing on variations in red, orange, and yellow. There was color with shade nuances and saturation, there was color with texture, and there was color with couture, from her bright orange and speckled-with-yellow eyeglasses to her heathery tricolor sweater, red T-shirt, orange-and-yellow-striped scarf, and white jeans, and, if I recall well, tangerine leather runners.

She was a rare person, comfortable with change, and had reinvented herself many times, each time stepping closer and closer to her destiny with prehistory. I gradually pieced together her story, usually as we sorted bone and flint from each bucket into analytical categories for others to then study once Virginie made sure they were in their correct places in the catalogue and storage.

Françoise had once been the owner of a very successful French-fry joint in La Rochelle. She then traded in fries for inspecting cargo at the port, then moved on to making jewelry, then her favorite job, to working as a night clerk at a hotel, where she'd read Jean Auel's *Clan of the Cave Bear*. That was a major pivotal moment for her, as it was for many, including Dennis, who gobbled up the novels and then decided to get into the dirt.

She next drove south to excavate at Le Piage, a Mousterian to Aurignacian site in the Lot, the region just south of the Dordogne. There, she'd met Alain, a man who had volunteered for over forty years, digging wherever François Bordes was working. It was Alain who introduced her to prehistory buffs and professionals, including Alain Turq.

After the dig at Le Piage, she sold everything she did not need and drove south again, this time permanently. Alain (the volunteer) let her park her camper on his land. She had come exclusively to be in the heart and soul of all things prehistoric.

Alain, the fellow prehistory buff who had also worked with Shannon and Harold at prior digs, could no longer spend long days at the dig or lab sites, but Françoise was able to join us. Harold and Dennis were especially appreciative of her contribution upon learning she loved lab work as much as digging. We needed more help in the lab, processing all the incoming buckets of sediment and artifacts. She was invaluable in the lab, and moreover, she listened to all the conversations, so when she heard that the zooarchaeologists, Teresa, Naomi, Susan—another of Teresa's students—and Anna, were looking for a way to procure fresh bovine ribs, she filed that intelligence and let it be there as a part of her radar system.

*     *     *

IT WAS ENTIRELY an accident, but a common occurrence for drivers along the narrow and dark roads of the Dordogne and the Lot, that a deer ran in front of her car. Traumatized, Françoise jumped out and checked on the animal only to find it dead. It had been a long day, working at the lab and then staying for dinner with the crew before returning to her camper. She decided not to let the creature's death be entirely in vain and loaded the body into her trunk, turned around, and, late in the night, as the crew was still up but enjoying the campfire and after-dinner wine, walked over to them and reportedly said, "I have a deer for you. Just save me some venison steaks."

It was a feeding frenzy. Everyone went and took the deer from Françoise's trunk and she drove home. The lithics people in the crew set to making stone tools at the pit and then were joined with the zooarchaeology folks to use them to open, gut, hide, and cut up the meat. Steaks set aside in the freezer for Françoise, ribs and hide procured, flint tools proven worthy, they took the skeleton and buried it in the yard, far from any runoff or the creek and far from the tents. They eventually realized they needed to bury the organs as well, or there would be a butchering camp stench too close to the reality it had been in prehistory. Not every aspect of the Paleo past needed to be a part of the experience.

When I arrived early the next morning I learned of the late-night experiments. Even the buried bones were marked, for they were a part of yet another experiment, to be dug up at periodic intervals to see how they decomposed, turned color, took to the particular soil of the Enéa Valley. Apparently, said one very groggy crew member who may have had only four hours of sleep, there were more dead bodies in the backyard. There was a boar Harold's son Flint had buried. There was also a badger, roadkill I believe, from people going too fast on the passing village road, and many, many small rodents. Only the boar and deer were in marked graves. The zooarchaeologists couldn't wait to dig them up and see their life after death.

Archaeologists love this sort of experimental effort to get at the material in a different way. How can you properly understand why deer were so often hunted until you've hunted one yourself and learned how easy it is to process them? I had the opportunity to have this conversation with Jean-Jacques Cleyet-Merle, the director of the national prehistory museum in Les Eyzies, who confessed he loved spending time in nature, especially watching animals, that it cleared his head. But he confessed that with deer, it was hard not to think like a hunter. A prehistory specialist, especially of the Upper Paleolithic, he could not but help see them through ancient human eyes and how "easy they are to cut, clean, and dissect. *C'est zip et zip.*" He concluded, making a vertical and then double horizontal gesture with both hands in the air, as if holding a flint tool and casually dressing down a deer as if it wore a zippered coat that easily slipped off.

This might be a very good reason why deer and reindeer were among the most hunted animals in both Middle and Upper Paleolithic sites. Good meat, easy processing, great leather for all sorts of uses went a long way when you were hungry and all too often, cold. We humans owed a huge debt to deer and other ungulates.

Françoise arrived that morning, also worn for wear but happy. Her sad accident had led to several scientific experiments and one freezer full of meat. I learned all this before I'd had any coffee, so I went to retrieve a cup and overheard Teresa talking to Naomi, Susan, and Anna, all excited about their fresh ribs.

It's a living.

ZOOARCHAEOLOGY IS A specialized area in paleoanthropology that largely looks at patterns in how humans ate—their diet, their migrations, and their use of a local ecology in the drive to eat and live—and used the animal beyond just food. Its main focus is on animals, mostly vertebrates and mollusks, which preserve far better in the record than any other edibles. Plants are simply harder to find but most Paleolithic sites are chock-full of animal bones.

If there were a lot of reindeer, that was more likely a seasonal thing, with these migrating animals moving through in early spring. Other animals were in the region year-round, especially horses and bison. Roe deer were also ubiquitous. Faunal patterns at Middle Paleolithic sites in southwestern France showed Neandertals were flexible in adapting to their environment. When the coveted reindeer weren't around, they didn't go off running after them but made do with more perennial game. Animal bones at a site could tell a lot about hunting and the diet choices made, but they also could speak, when found, to how the animal remains beyond food might have been used.

Most of the time the faunal team was sorting through and processing thousands and thousands of bone fragments, identifying the animals they came from and also looking for any marks or impressions on them that pointed to human alterations. Cut marks were the most common, from using stone tools to deflesh a bone. But all in all, it is a lot of focusing and training the eye to see both patterns and anything that stuck out.

I saw Teresa one morning at the dig house table sorting a huge bag of bones. "I'm like a kid in a candy box. I love this stuff," she told me with glee. "Even just going through these little bits," she indicated the tray of animal bone fragments she was sorting. "You have to remind yourself, this is showing marks of a Neandertal butchering it fifty, sixty, seventy thousand years ago, and not lose sight of how incredibly cool it is to be handling stuff that was alive so long ago. For me the power is in the sample sizes. It's not the one-offs. In fact, I get kind of annoyed with the one-off cool finds."

"It's like the Indiana Jones mentality," I offered. Also I realized the lissoir had been a one-off too until three more were found, and possibly a fifth from Pech IV that was being closely studied.

"Yes. That's not what it's about. It's the sample size and it's the data coming into a pattern. That's why it's exciting for me to work with these guys and compile large data sets that we can compare together. All of these bits are exciting because you never know what's going to be in the next bag. Every little bag is a potential Christmas present." Like Naomi going through all those bags trying to find those lissoirs. Something a one-off can never offer is insight into a whole context, a whole way of life. Patterns, on the other hand, can do this.

Three years before the lissoirs came to light, João Zilhão unearthed four seashells in two separate sites in southeastern Spain near Murcia—Cueva de los Aviones and Cueva Antón—with naturally perforated holes but with clear applications by human hands of pigments of different minerals that created yellow, red, orange, and black colors. Both were located at Mousterian layers and dated to around 50,000 years ago. It was evidence that Neandertals selected pretty shells and colored them or used them to hold pigment for other decorative purposes; they engaged in symbolic actions similar to early modern humans.

It was almost a parallel situation with the lissoirs, where a small handful was found at two sites in a Neandertal context. If they had been found in an early modern context, as Randy said, they'd be seen as totally banal. The four pigmented shells, like the four lissoirs, remain extraordinary in their rarity.

Ochre and manganese oxides are more than one-offs or even four-offs. Many Neandertal sites show a high concentration of these two minerals being gathered and manipulated—smoothed like crayons or shaved with scratch marks to make a powder, perhaps. They speak of something beyond basic survival. Manganese dioxide can color things and also help wood ignite at lower temperatures. Ochre also has many uses. In addition to wide applications as paint or pigment, it can also cure and preserve hides, be used to repel insects, decorate both living and dead bodies, and possibly be used as medicine. Ochre has been found at several Neandertal sites in the record since at least 250,000 years ago and was as much in use by Neandertals as by later early modern humans. But with Neandertals, we have little evidence in how they used it. It wasn't rubbed onto dead bodies, for we see this in the Upper Paleolithic and it leaves physical evidence. There is little evidence for its use as a pigment or decoration or other more esoteric symbolic applications. The hard evidence is there, the presence of these minerals, but how to interpret them?

Physical evidence for symbolism is tough, period. But what if your way of expressing your symbolic life is not material and you never felt a compulsion to make it so, beyond producing Levallois—which was more complex than any tool technique before or after it? *Why do they have to be like us to be smart?*

Maybe we're misled to think that innovations led the way, even in spite of the rampant levels of change witnessed in the most recent 10,000 years. Maybe it's really about opportunity and timing. Maybe as a general trend, humans, Neandertal and early moderns both, were not so open to innovation—suspicious even, total Luddites—the first time a rare inventor developed or discovered and presented something new. These innovators are rare today; most of us are mimickers, followers, and copiers, even more than the chimpanzees prove to be.

Experiments with human children and baby chimps proved that the human children were more prone to follow instructions exactly, even when the instructions were full of useless actions toward getting to the goal, a tasty treat. The baby chimps saw the flaw, skipped the useless stuff, and went right to the goal: the food at the end of the task. In so doing, they seemed to skip the need to be taught: they watched and innovated as they went. We, on the other hand, anticipate being taught and also are inclined to follow instructions. In truth, chimps ape less and we modern humans ape almost all the time.

It seems to be a factor of how much more oriented we are toward teaching and learning from each other through instruction. Baby chimps learn, too, but their elders do not teach; they just go about their day and the baby chimp watches and replicates when he or she has a chance to try something out. But she or he does not always replicate exactly. Sometimes there is no replication whatsoever and the chimp invents a way to get at nuts or termites or fruits that makes sense—smashing with a rock, using a stick, maneuvering on a branch.

"How many of us, honestly, could invent the iPhone?" asked Dana Walrath when I asked her to tell me what she thought about this whole debate revolving around the sudden changes we began to see around 40,000 years ago, after a very long and more conservative material record. She is an anthropologist at the University of Vermont who worked on Neandertal material with Alan Mann at Penn and also excavated with Randall White at Abri Castanet in the Dordogne. She knew well the nature of Café Neandertal.

It was an efficient and rhetorical question and she didn't need to say any more: There are few such innovators in any generation, past or present. Many copied Apple and Apple was a whole tree with only a few brilliant fruits that could innovate at that level of Appledom. Even a hundred years ago, people would have scoffed at the iPhone. Graham Bell's telephone was varyingly accepted as it entered towns and homes, but people made sure it suited their social norms, that anyone who called at dinnertime had better be in an emergency state, or better yet, dead. Now, we more readily embrace the next social-fabric-altering innovation since the simple phone because we have already chipped away at the earlier idea of the sanctity of dinnertime. Our social conservatism has shifted from the sanctity of family to the sanctity of connectedness. Dinner can be interrupted for the network. All that has changed is what we deem most valuable for our own survival.

I wondered, how many of those one-offs in the archaeological record concerning Neandertals (and later ourselves) were such a thing, a rare shift from the day-to-day norm that was rejected by the group because it was something new that could destroy things as they were.

Maybe the rare ochre-colored shells João found in Spain were before their time, handled by a foresighted Neandertal who felt social media—communicating beyond one's immediate group—was the way of the near future. Maybe he or she had presented the pretty colored shells and pig-ment use, suggested they could help mark them for others to know, and instead of excitement, received criticism. "No way," said the others, "we have enough to do with butchering and curing hides to waste our time making personal adornments and to what end? We know who we are and who we're with. Who else is there?"

The pigment adorner dropped the shells onto the cave floor and never raised the issue again. But maybe later, with more humans arriving in places where before there had been smaller nomadic bands in wider landscapes, people were meeting up with more people as they roamed, people they'd never seen. Maybe body adornment became a convenient shorthand and new innovation to cut to the quick and know who had friended whom in the social network out there. Suddenly, who you are and who you are with means something in a wider and wilder social terrain. Before then, those rare super-creative members of a society may have been inventing all sorts of things that fell onto the cave floor, aban-doned because they didn't meet the social conventions of the times.

"We think with the *Homo sapiens* mind," Didier said, as we walked along the stone crafter's field. "We can't possibly know the Neandertal reality." Look how much we've changed just in the past 10,000 years. "We're too modern," he concluded the thought and paused to pick up a side scraper with a lovely creamy patina. He carefully studied it, smiled, then set it back down and looked at me, having taken all the galaxies into his face.

"*Les Homo sapiens, ils sont jamais contents.*" *Homo sapiens* are never satisfied. "Maybe that's why we keep fiddling and altering. Enough for us is never enough. And," he bent and studied another tool, this one a Le-vallois point, "we know very little about Neandertals and probably will never know. We have their stones," he set the one in his hand back on the earth, "and every now and then we find a skeleton. And that's it." He shrugged, looked at me, and smiled gently again, and together we walked in contented silence deeper into the morning fog.

# 10

## LOVE IN THE TIME OF
## NEANDERTALS

WHEN OLD MAN La Chapelle either lay down to die or was interred in the small cave, he bore already the marks of someone who had been cared for in life. Maybe even loved. Common to many Neandertal skeletons, his bones—discovered in 1908 at La Chapelle-aux-Saints in the Corrèze just east of the Dordogne—showed all manner of stresses that came with being a nomadic, big game hunter who worked with others to get close to wild animals with nothing but jabbing spears. It was a hard life, and many Neandertal bones, not only his, show a story of healing after severe injury.

The others didn't abandon the severely injured to die, but instead cared for them and extended their lives. Some think it was sentimental human love at work and some think the injured individuals carried knowledge and valued skill, such as tool craft, that was important for the group. As usual, the answer is more complex. They were human and like us, emotional. We all have been for a long time. Chimpanzees and bonobos prove it, for they too are a sentimental bunch. Outside of genetics, scars and healed bones are the single best evidence for the nature of relationships in the Paleolithic. Unlike genetics, they carry a more certain emotional valence. We can't imagine so well how the genes got exchanged, but to aid a handicapped person speaks of empathy, compassion, and group identity.

Old Man La Chapelle lived around 50,000 years ago and is called that because he died older than many of the same era, somewhere in his late thirties or early forties. He suffered from terrible arthritis, had a healed broken rib, had a lot of degeneration in his hip, and had lost most of his teeth. All of these features would have cut his life short if he had no help from others.

As María Martinón-Torres, one of the key fossil specialists with the team excavating at Atapuerca, said, "It's good! If you had scars, you survived!" This she exclaimed enthusiastically during her recent talk at the Collège de France in Paris. Presenting the findings from Sima de los Huesos, and going over the seventeen of the twenty-eight individuals who had skulls associated with their bodies, she was giving a pretty macabre profile of how they all lived and died. The audience especially appreciated her enthusiasm as they learned about arthritis, tooth infections, and crushed bones. Almost all of the Atapuercans had scars of one form or another, scars that they could not have earned had they been abandoned when their wounds were fresh. You have scars, you survived, this is good, because you were strong and had a strong social network that didn't toss you into that pit of bones before your time. As far as we can tell.

The skeletons at Shanidar tell a similar story. They are a collective of skeletons, eight adults and two infants, of individuals who lived there at different times (so not a related community). Some of the skeletons came to rest in the cave due to collapse from the cave ceiling, hardly an intended burial. But even these show the signs of healed old injuries before the final crush.

The best-studied skeleton is Shanidar 1, none other than the inspiration for Jean Auel's endearing father-uncle-shaman character, Creb. In the novel as in real life, he was handicapped from several severe traumas. He, too, was considered old upon his death sometime in his forties; he had healed from numerous dramatic injuries before then. His face's left side had been crushed in and that most likely took out his left eye. He had a huge gash that had healed on the right side of his skull. His right foot had a broken bone in the arch that had healed but would have severely handicapped his gait while doing so. He was missing his right forearm—it appears to have been lost or amputated—and his right upper body shows atrophy compared to his left side. He also had advanced arthritis in his right foot and up to his right knee. All these things occurred long before he died and spoke of someone who was helped many times along the way. He may have lived 35,000 to 45,000 years ago.

By contrast, another, Shanidar 3, who may have lived around 50,000 years ago, had a gash sliced into his ninth rib, a cut very much like those caused by a flint edge. While he too had healed wounds from prior traumas, it appears that it was either the deep jab that killed him, or rock fall in the cave soon after his injury. One of the troubling aspects of his wound is that he may have been attacked by early modern humans, who would have been in the Levant by then and in possession of spear-throwers—atlatls—that had the velocity and projectiles to make the deep gash that Shanidar 3 suffered. Were these early modern humans intentionally attacking from a distance, or had Shanidar 3 been hurt in a hunting accident as they tried to take down the same large game animal?

Likewise, at Atapuerca's Sima de los Huesos in Spain, where several of the skeletons show the signs of care and healing, one shows signs of possible violence, two sharp puncturing blows into the skull.

Then there are the cases of cannibalism, such as at El Sidrón in Spain, Krapina in Croatia, and Les Pradelles in southwestern France, which we can hardly decipher and sort between ritual versus survival cannibalism (or simply funerary defleshing of the bones without eating, though the smashed bones that look as if the marrow has been sucked out make this harder to argue).

These issues about relationship that show up in the archaeological record, from cooperation to competition, have been with us a long time.

Chimpanzees also exhibit this polar set of traits. So do wolves, and many other mammals, but the difference among humans, both Neandertals and us, is not only the degree and style, but that cooperation became stronger among us. Evolutionary biologist Edward O. Wilson calls this "group selection," when natural selection goes for group-level traits that help everyone survive better, rather than selecting at the individual level. Such traits are both cooperation and competition: the two sides of tribalism.

Our coordinated hunting and foraging, living together against the elements and others, is a part of what made this form of selection strong. It is deeply apparent in Neandertals. First, it can be seen in the types of hunting that they did, which required incredible planning, coordination, communication, and cooperation. And second, it can be gleaned from the acts of empathy that led to healed bones, to greater longevity, and to selecting for the group socially and emotionally, rather than leaving individuals to fend for themselves.

These two odd bedfellows—cooperation and competition—are within us and have been for a long time. In a sense, they are the root of all modern human mythic stories of the battle between dark and light and the incessant need to balance these forces all the time. The side of light is strong within us and so is the dark side. Experiments with chimps and bonobos have shown that while they have cooperation, it is a feature stronger and more complexly expressed in humans. Given, again, that Neandertals are our closest kin, from whom we split off around 700,000 years ago, if we've got it, and chimps have it, surely they did too. But beyond cooperation in the hunt and caring for the ailing, we have little idea how else it was expressed.

Once, I naïvely asked Jean-Jacques, "What would be the best discovery that would help bring more definitive insights to our understanding about the Neandertals?" I was sure he would say, "a skeleton, in situ, never disturbed by us moderns." It seemed obvious to me. A skeleton that hadn't been dug in a manner that removed precious evidence and context or that declared something conceptually huge, such as a ritual burial, before all the data was considered: that could offer such a fresh start. It could help lay to rest these unresolved debates in the field.

So his answer surprised me. "I don't want a new Neandertal skeleton," he said. "I want to know what his or her relationship was with his or her family-in-law! This is a bit hopeless I know, but maybe we'll learn more in the future about developmental aspects that have strong social implications, like, for example, the age of weaning. I'm more optimistic on this side."


WHEN I SAT in the reclining dental chair, I began right away to talk about Neandertal dentition with my dentist, Dr. H. He had told me that in dental school they study the evolution of human dentition as par for the course, so he was familiar with Neandertals and their oral health. It aided modern dentists in understanding the human lineage and dental issues. It also horrified them to see the levels of decay we moderns have with our high-carb, high-sugar, and processed diets. Neandertals may have had wear issues, and broken teeth that caused infections, but decay was rare compared to today. The Paleo diet is good for your teeth, provided you don't use a flint blade near them to cut the meat, or use them as a third hand to process hides.

Wanting to hear Dr. H's take on things, I planted a seed before having to open my mouth for investigation. "From looking at the Old Man of La Chapelle's lack of chewing teeth," I said, "they say he was cared for, that others helped him eat." I leaned back and opened wide.

Dr. H began to probe, much like a paleoanthropologist, using his own excavation tools, going into caves and analyzing fossils. Teeth are the most mineralized bone in our bodies and in a sense are already fossils while we live, a reason why they survive longer than other bones in the paleontological record.

"That he was cared for," he said of La Chapelle while checking my molars, "doesn't mean he was necessarily liked. It just means he was important to keep alive. Maybe people feared him. Maybe he carried important knowledge. Maybe he told people bad things would happen to them if he died, if they didn't chew or mash his food for him. Maybe he was a terror of a patriarch and held magical powers." My romantic bubble burst. Dr. H moved his probing to other areas of my dental cavern. "Maybe we just don't know if it was compassion or fear or even a mix," he continued. "Look at how we handle growing old today; it's a mix of compassion and fear."

I swallowed this as he worked in silence for the rest of the time before asking me to rinse. Maybe Mr. Chapelle was a conjurer of dark, inexplicable forces and people were frightened that if he was not content, he'd bring these forces down on them. Maybe that was also why he was set in a small cave. Equally, he could have been beloved, set there for respect and reverence. Or convenience. Obviously, we can spin this a lot of ways.

I prepared also for what I knew was the next line of conversation (it always was), that I grind my teeth. It was an unfortunate habit probably acquired during the high-anxiety years in graduate school, working and going to school full-time, and I never shook it off. No matter how much yoga and meditation I practiced—both recommendations from Dr. H—my grinding habit didn't diminish. It was my existential crisis as a creature with a grammar that allowed me to speak about, not only think about, the past and the future, share it and hear it from others, amplifying our anxieties over past regrets and future fears. The glassblower from Toulon was right: language was a block to living more fully—to being in the present tense. It was rigid intellect, one that defined and minced things that were not present and didn't even exist. Yet. Grind.

This time, I thought I'd preempt the discussion. I rinsed and said, "Neandertal teeth show bruxism more radical than my own." I rinsed again and spit. "I bet their teeth looked worse."

He didn't skip a beat—he cares about his patients, even when they apply heavy coats of denial. "But, Beebe, they didn't have the processed foods we have now. And they didn't go through the agricultural revolution that tamed and domesticated tough-to-chew foods as well as dramatically reduced the size of our teeth. They processed wild seeds, nuts, and meats with their teeth alone and that would cause the wear and tear. That's different from unexamined nighttime anxieties and unconscious grinding, which don't do anything to feed you. And they also used their teeth as tools, like a third hand, which I certainly hope you do not."

Slam dunk. My mouth hung open of its own accord.

"Do you think Neandertals needed to meditate?" I uttered the thought aloud as I met my friend Bruno for coffee at the Café de la Mairie in Les Eyzies. He'd been immersed in all things Neandertal and early modern human as a neighbor to Les Eyzies all his life. These woods and cliffs had been his playground as a boy. Later, as a teenager, this café had been his scoping grounds with other teenage boys, riding their bikes here in high anticipation of the pretty foreign girls who came to their prehistoric shores to visit the caves. Prehistory had sex appeal, and he was a native son.

"No, I don't think so," he said after a long quaff of his coffee, and serious thought. "We're the uptight humans, not they." *Homo materialensis uptighticus.*

Everyone in Les Eyzies knew Neandertals had the more flexible and Zen intellect. This was common knowledge here in prehistory central. Neandertals didn't show the compulsion to control the world around them as we do. Anxiety and OCD levels of control may be in some big way the origins of religion and the birth of conscious meditation. (When you hunt, gather, fish; work stone, wood, and bone, you naturally meditate. It seems its when we stop doing these sorts of things that the modern mind shows its discontent.)

With the new era dawning thanks to the genetics revolution and also cleaning up our nineteenth-century bigoted ideas about our hominid kin, let alone our own kind, Japanese fine artist Kentaro Yamada recently came out with a new fragrance called Neandertal. A master stone knapper made him a flint Mousterian hand ax of the Acheulean tradition, and he used it as the prototype for a ceramic perfume bottle, one in white for women, and one in black for men, and then worked with a Scottish perfume designer to create the fragrances with which to fill them. They strove to hit the perfect fragrant notes that would capture who Neandertals would have become had they survived into the last 35,000 years.

"If Neandertal[s] had survived," Yamada wrote whimsically on his website, "they could have created [an] extremely sophisticated civilization differently shaped from ours. The fragrance is designed for the Neandertals, and it will reflect their life in the past as well as their sophisticated future, which they could not see themselves. As we possess 1–4 percent [now revised to 1.5–2.1 percent] Neandertal DNA within us, this perfume can also be applied to humans. Smell triggers memory above sight and hearing, and it can unlock doors to their shadows hidden within our DNA."

Channeling Harold as I read about the new perfume (of course, I wanted a bottle), I knew he would add that both of us—Neandertals and early modern humans—had been pretty smelly, what with all the rotting meat we processed in our cave and open-air sites, and the lack of regular showers and deodorants. *Smelly, cold,* and *hungry* were some of the frequent adjectives that arose around the campfire as we tried to re-create life in the past.

We modern moderns, living now with our baths and toiletry products, have lost a lot of the signals our sense of smell tells us about the world and beyond. Smell not only triggers memory but can pleasantly or unpleasantly, depending on the situation and subjective sniffer of the person, trigger personal contact before anyone touches. A few long hot days on the dig, and we had direct experience of this and how a cave and trench can funnel smell into more concentrated bombs. Those days, we romanticized the past less and couldn't wait to hit the showers. On other days, with pleasing temperatures and a soft forest breeze, the romance returned. *Neandertal.* I liked that Yamada also had dropped the "h," which went further to unlock doors to their shadows and light hidden within our DNA.

DURING THE FLOW of five dig seasons over five years at La Ferrassie, from 2010 to 2015, news from genetics delivered several bombshells, first about interbreeding with Neandertals, then about the discovery of the new archaic humans called Denisovans, whom we had never known about. Moreover, we learned that in our many episodes of interbreeding, there was potentially one other (and maybe more) unidentified archaic human population(s) whose doors we had yet to unlock within our DNA.

The very day in May 2010 that I had spied Harold and Dennis fleeting through the market square as I purchased shallots, Richard Green, Svante Pääbo, and a consortium of some forty-eight more coauthors and collaborators on the Neandertal genome project published their influential paper in *Science* on the first successful sequencing of nuclear Neandertal DNA. Its impact was huge. It was hard evidence that gene flow was frequently going on between Neandertals and early modern humans. It was hard evidence for what paleoanthropologists saw in fossils they'd identified as hybrids. It was hard evidence for what we all know, that humans of all ilk have a healthy sexual appetite, going at it with adventurous gusto, seeking the exotic as much as the familiar. It was hard evidence that we had not only enjoyed liaisons with Neandertals but that those liaisons contributed to adaptive genetic traits that helped us overcome new diseases and afflictions unfamiliar in the new environments of Eurasia. It also opened a new door, and genetics became a third major player with paleoanthropology and archaeology in the study of human evolution. From that moment onward, each week it seemed, breaking news kept, and continues to keep, hitting the journals and news on new findings from the burgeoning field of paleogenetics.

This path in the field in many ways began to change in 1987 when Allan Wilson, Rebecca Cann, and Mark Stoneking at Berkeley published their work on human mitochondrial DNA. Mitochondrial DNA is a single circular structure composed of 16,569 nucleic acid base pairs found within every cell's mitochondria, the energy producer for the cell that exists outside the nucleus. It is one of two varieties of DNA humans have, this one almost exclusively inherited from our mothers. Nuclear DNA is far larger (3.3 billion base pairs) and more complex and is made up of forty-six bundles of DNA in the form of chromosomes. We get twenty-three chromosomes from our mothers and twenty-three from our fathers, each set carrying genes for the same functions but in different variations from each parent. It's the way we each turn out looking both similar to and different from our parents and their parents and also keep evolving (plus adding our own mutations to the pool) and having diverse options for adapting to present and future situations.

Wilson, Cann, and Stoneking sequenced and analyzed the mitochondrial DNA (mtDNA) because it was the best place to start in the burgeoning field of genetics of the time: mtDNA is smaller and more stable than nuclear DNA. They took mtDNA samples from 147 people around the world who represented the most diverse sampling of humans living today and discovered that we are all related and we all originated from a related maternal lineage from Africa. That undid a lot of prior theories about human evolution and also rebuilt some more complex and accurate ones.

It also mapped a possible chronology that our variation of human, *Homo sapiens*, began to emerge as a distinct meta-population around 200,000 years ago, though we we have changed a whole lot since then, especially in the last 50,000 years. It confirmed that we did all this in Africa and then migrated out into the rest of the world (and back again, for nomads are not unilinear). It also proved that all humans living today are incredibly closely related, in fact, so closely that it seems we are survivors of a bottlenecking event that reduced the wider number of ancestors we had (who therefore did not pass on their genes) down to what appeared as one specific population, one small group of women, all who carried the same related mtDNA, which we all carry.

This work became the foundation for the "Recent Out of Africa" theory, which has become a dominant idea about our recent evolutionary history. Another theory, the "Leaky Replacement Model," factors in the evidence for the low-frequency (but still frequent) interbreeding among different human groups—what the pros like to call admixture. It sees Africa as the origin of *Homo sapiens* but also that regional histories of interbreeding with other, more archaic groups are also a part of the formula, rather than all-out replacement by *Homo sapiens*. Both are theories and reflect how different scientists interpret the data from the fossil record and the new genetic evidence. The work from 1987 began this development toward more nuanced ideas about human evolution. But the work more recently, on sequencing the more complex nuclear DNA, both of huge samples of modern human populations and also of archaic humans—Neandertals and Denisovans—has deepened our ideas and loosened us up for more unexpected twists and turns in the future.

Dash any idea of those simple lineage charts we all grew up with. They are artifacts of an order-and-neatness-loving brain, not true maps of what happens in real life.

In 2008 Pääbo and his team first sequenced the mtDNA from a 38,000-year-old Neandertal bone from Vindija. This initial result showed that, based on only the mitochondrial genetic material—which is matrilineal—Neandertal genetic diversity fell outside of the range of our own widest range of mtDNA diversity among living humans around the world. It made it appear as if we had no interaction, an idea that was to be proven simplistic.

The nuclear DNA sequence from three Neandertals from Vindija made up the sample sequence, which was published in 2010, and this has become a part of a growing database for documenting Neandertal genetic diversity. It has also been a source for comparisons with us. In 2010, the scientists saw that we modern humans from Eurasia had received 1–4 percent of our DNA from Neandertals. With the growing and more accurate work since, that number is now adjusted to around 1.5–2.1 percent DNA that Eurasians have in their genes from Neandertals. Moreover, North Africans possess around 1 percent, filling in a gap that was glaring, that there had to have been migration back into Africa as well. Even though Neandertals never lived in or migrated into Africa—we have yet to find their fossils there—modern humans bearing their genes did come and go in Africa. For sub-Saharan Africa the percentage is smaller, perhaps around 0.7 percent. Africa is the second largest continent and has the world's most diverse populations living within it, the latter a legacy of our own origins there. We began there so we've had the longest track record there; genetic diversity will therefore also be the most expressed there.

All these noted percentages will likely continue to be adjusted as the database increases with more samples, but the bottom line is that we all have a little bit of Neandertal ancestry in us. Those who have more selected traits from Neandertals are likely here today because those traits helped them thrive in those early migrations into Eurasia. They in many ways can thank Neandertals for their survival. The 2010 paper and ongoing work since have shown that natural selection played its hand many times, positively selecting for certain advantageous traits from the Neandertals, such as in areas affecting our skin and hair, metabolism, cognitive development, and skeletal development.

Right around the same time, in 2010, Pääbo, David Reich, and their team also published on a sequence from a pinky bone of a young girl from Denisova Cave in the Altai of southern Siberia, thinking it belonged to a Neandertal—as they were known to have occupied the cave site. But the sequence had a different pattern, outside the range of variation in modern humans and in Neandertals, and this was the first time genetics discovered a new fossil ancestor rather than paleoanthropologists and archaeologists.

The genetics indicate that these ancestors, called Denisovans, were closely related to Neandertals and had branched off sometime after we and Neandertals had branched off from each other, from our common ancestor, around 700,000 to 800,000 years ago. We went on to become modern humans and Neandertals went on to become Neandertals and then somewhere in that process, Neandertals split off from a related population as well and that population went off in its own isolation to become Denisovans.

That little Denisovan girl and her powerful pinky had lived around 50,000 years ago in the Altai. Since the discovery of distinct genetic signature, a few more small fossil bones that also reveal Denisovan genes have been sequenced from the same cave. The work has been expanded to see if modern humans might also have Denisovan genes in the way that we have Neandertal genes within us.

As one would expect, given our track record for liaising with everyone we meet, we do carry Denisovan genes. Living people from Australia, Papua New Guinea, and some South Pacific islands carry as high as 4–6 percent Denisovan genes. People in mainland Asia carry less on average but more than Europeans. Denisovans seem to be an ancient form of humans who inhabited eastern Asia and then the southeast, and who encountered early modern humans who were moving into their territories around 50,000 years ago and perhaps earlier. They potentially mingled—admixed—in Asia, before the early modern humans then made their crossings into Australia and the Pacific islands.

But the Denisovan fingerprint also appears in the mtDNA of the Sima de los Huesos Neandertals, Europe's earliest Neandertals known to date—which doesn't say Denisovans lived in Iberia, but does confirm that they and Neandertals were a sister group that split off sometime after 800,000 years ago. Perhaps the Sima Neandertals were members of a more recent splitting. It's clear that they were firmly on the path of Neandertaldom, though, because their nuclear DNA—much more involved in the dance of genetic inheritance—is firmly within the genetic signature defined by the Neandertal meta-population.

One useful way to think about human evolution is a phrase straight out of all the genetic publications: "turnovers and migrations." These terms capture well the bushier and bushier lineages in our evolution, some that were successful and passed on their genes, and others that went extinct and their genes with them. Human evolution is a study of turnovers—gene flow, expansion, extinction, mixing, and mingling—and migrations, always on the move, wanting to see what's good to eat over the next horizon. (It's safe to say, then as now, as much as we love sex, we are even more motivated by what's for dinner.)

It seems dizzying but it is in keeping with human nature. More recent breaking news from genetics is that eastern Neandertals were different from western Neandertals and that ancient *Homo sapiens* from Africa some 100,000 years ago gave the eastern Neandertals a good time, leaving some genetic signals to prove the fact.

John Hawks, a very publicly engaging paleoanthropologist, wrote in his blog, The evidence now shows that introgression from Neandertals into modern human populations happened multiple times, and likely in multiple places." Paleoanthropologist Alice Roberts wrote more colorfully on Twitter, "Prudish paleoanthropologists are struggling to come to terms with the promiscuity of ancient humankind."

Genetics, coupled with fossil morphology and archaeology, is showing us that there were many migrations out of Africa, and back again, that define who we are today. And who we are seemed to show a trailhead toward modern humanness that showed up around 200,000 years ago in Africa, both genetically and morphologically, and that had several turnovers and migrations within Africa as well as without.

Beyond Africa, the first major turnover and migration concerning early modern humans appears to have happened around 120,000 years ago, aligning with the early modern human fossils found in Israel at Qafzeh and Skhul that date to that period. They occupied the Levant, which had already been occupied early by Neandertals, and also later by yet more incoming Neandertals on their own path of turnovers and migrations from Europe. Somewhere in all this the two meta-populations probably interbred here several times when they intersected and co-inhabited the region. Some of those Neandertals and their hybrid and fertile offspring may have migrated farther east, where the earlier early modern human genes have been found in the Altai Neandertal population. Curiously, no human living today has genes from that population of early modern humans, so we know they went extinct.

The same seems true for an early modern man who lived 37,000 to 42,000 years ago in today's Romania, found at Peştera cu Oase. He had Neandertal relatives four to six generations before his own and he too carried early modern genes that have gone extinct from the contemporary population. It's another reason why we probably have less Neandertal DNA in us than we could—because many groups within our own meta-population went extinct. It also reinforces the idea that some sort of a bottleneck event, or events, took place to define the relative lack of great genetic diversity found in living people today. We are more related to each other now than we probably have ever been in human history or prehistory.

Genetics was helping to break down cemented conceptual walls in paleoanthropology to get at real behavior, recorded in mating outcomes. One of those walls was a prudish attitude toward past sex lives. Another was the simplistic labels and overly bounded ideas regarding different categories of being human. People have now begun to speak about Western, Central European, or Eastern Neandertals instead of Neandertals as a single undiversified group. Any day now—from what I hear from the experts—China will recognize that it has had Neandertal—and Denisovan—fossils all along and soon the natural corridor of turnovers and migrations in the past, before limits imposed by national boundaries and border controls, will be open once again.

While genetics can tell us what sorts of gene-swapping we did, and even estimate when based on models for mutation rates, it can never tell us how or what these encounters were like. Were they romantic or violent encounters? Probably both and a variation in between and to different frequencies, all depending on the people and the circumstances involved. Taking into consideration modern humans and our other surviving closest relatives, chimpanzees, it is a safe bet that all ranges of cooperative to competitive dynamics were possible. But, still, we can't know.

Genes aren't the only thing being analyzed on DNA. So are the extra-genetic molecular signatures, the epigenetics, those molecules attached to DNA that regulate what genes are expressed, how, and what genes are turned off, on, or kept turned off. It is an area that helps explain how we can share so much common ancestral DNA and yet look so different. Epigenetics also can effect faster adaptive changes to an organism than full-on genetic sequence changes from mutations and natural selection. It's essentially a way that the same gene is shared between species but used—regulated—differently within each.

One way to get at this dynamic is through tracing the pattern of deterioration left by methylated groups, areas on the genome where a methyl group, CH3, is attached. This is a part of the mechanism involved in regulating—turning on and off and expressing—a gene. The patterns for areas that are methylated and not methylated are different between modern humans and Neandertals, even when associated with the exact same gene, and this may help explain why we look different in signature ways.

Not only this, but consider these wild and nutty facts from genetics, courtesy of Jean-Jacques: humans share 18 percent of their DNA in common with plants, 26 percent with yeast, 44 percent with fruit flies, 92 percent with mice, 98 percent with chimpanzees, and 99.7 percent with Neandertals. It's a different sort of family tree, one on the full tree of life. It tells us how interconnected we are with all life on earth and also that something more dynamic than just genetic flow and changes is at work to come up with the vastly different appearance of a human, a mouse, and a chimpanzee. It gets more subtle but as dramatic to contemplate with our closest kin, Neandertals, whereby a dance of switching genes on and off in a complex orchestrated methylation ballet, we still carry very similar genomes but can turn out looking different, best suited to adapting to where we are.

"Similarity between genotype," Jean-Jacques concluded, "does not mean that the phenotypes are similar. We are ninety-eight percent similar to chimpanzees but we are far from looking like a chimpanzee." It's not just the *pow* packed into the 2 percent that is different, but what epigenetics is uniquely doing to the whole package.

UNDERSTANDING THE DIFFERENT percentages can still be confusing, especially what might be going on in that .3 percent that is unique to Neandertals, portions of which we carry within us. To nail this down better, I turned to molecular anthropologist Theodore G. Schurr at the University of Pennsylvania, who works on dozens of human ancestry projects around the world and is as deeply trained in the four fields of anthropology as he is in genetics and molecular biology. His broad experience and open manner made it easy for me to ask seemingly basic questions. We met in his office in Philadelphia at an opportune lull between his field projects in the Old and New Worlds that take the study of turnovers and migrations to the widest possible scope.

"The science now estimates that modern humans share 99.7 percent of our DNA with Neandertals," I began, "and it also says we got about 1 to 4 percent of our DNA from them. Does that mean that it is this remaining 0.3 percent that is unique to Neandertals where we received our 1 to 4 percent?" (We talked before 1.5–2.1 percent became the more recent revised estimate.)

"In a basic sense, what this means is we are far more like Neandertals than we are any other hominids that we know of so far. We're closer to Neandertals than we are to Denisovans, in terms of sharing some large component of our genome. And we're certainly closer to any of the Denisovans and Neandertals than we are to the chimpanzees—which represents not our common ancestry with chimps, but an entirely different lineage, which extended from a common ancestor six, or seven, or eight million years ago. Each lineage is the result of a long process."

"So the 99.7 percent that we share with Neandertals is our common . . ."

"Our common genetic makeup or ancestral stock, if you will," he said.

"And that remaining 0.3 percent? Is that where they diverged separate from us, in their own unique genetic expression?"

"That's right."

"And that's where we're getting that 1 to 4 percent [1.5–2.1 percent], from interbreeding?"

"Yes, that's right," he said. "There are different models for this but essentially, in a basic sense, you have a common archaic form, whether it's *heidelbergensis* or whatever [*erectus/ergaster/antecessor*, for instance], out of which you have both Neandertals and modern humans arising. The Neandertal branch somehow makes its way into Europe and it begins to diverge from that which existed in Africa, from which modern humans came. So there's still hundreds of thousands of years of time that separate those lineages back to when they had a common stock. That six hundred thousand years or whatever amount of time that goes on is when you have a divergence of those two forms so that you can distinguish their makeup—Neandertal-specific markers and modern human–specific markers—so when they come together later to mix, you get hybridization." So we parted ways for a while but then came back, each different for that separation, and met up and were still able to get it on and have some viable offspring.

I had heard some paleoanthropologists say that early modern humans absorbed them, that we folded Neandertals into the whole flow of things. These scholars are largely associated with influential paleoanthropologist Milford Wolpoff's philosophical position, which proposes Neandertals were never a separate species because of gene flow and never went extinct. If that were the case, wouldn't we see more genetic material from Neandertals? I asked Theodore.

"If that were true," he replied, "then we would see much more extent of Neandertal markers than we do; if there was extensive admixture, then we would see much more extensive admixture."

"You mean, if we really absorbed them, then we would have far more DNA from them than the percentage we actually have?"

"I would say we would have a greater extent of admixture," he said. "We don't have a complete replacement of Neandertals. [Likewise] you don't have people who are 97 percent Neandertal and 3 percent modern, or even people who are 50–50. There's not a clear mixture or merger of the gene pools. That just didn't happen."

He reminded me of something Svante Pääbo had recently told the audience in Paris at the Collège de France, about the way these percentages add up. He was there just a week before María Martinón-Torres arrived to deliver her exuberant talk on the Atapuerca twenty-eight.

Of possessing 1.5 percent Neandertal genetic ancestry, "It's as if you have a Neandertal ancestor six generations back," he said, which meant a Neandertal great-great-great-great-grandparent. "But," he continued, "it's distributed differently in the genome, in small pieces everywhere. If it were a [direct] ancestor, it would be in big pieces." Because these small pieces aren't coming from direct ancestors but from distant ones whose genes have remained in us but get recombined in each generation. What this also means is that all of us carrying this 0.7 to 2.1 percent (to include Africans as well as Eurasians) have different pieces of the Neandertal genome within us. If we took all our little pieces and pooled them, then how much of the original Neandertal ancestors do we all collectively carry around within us today?

"It's still a bit unclear," Svante answered the Parisians regarding this very question, "but somewhere in the order of forty percent or so of the Neandertal genome still exists in people today."

So, to Theodore's point, had there been more admixture and total absorption of Neandertals into our modern populations, we would be seeing that 40 percent or so in one person, or at least more than the 1–2 percent on average that we do see in any one person.

"That's probably because we were diverged biologically, that it couldn't happen in part because of hybridization issues and fertility issues and other things." Theodore finished his explanation. "So. We're a bit Neandertal for the most part, and some of us also have a bit Denisovan admixture in there. But what is interesting is that there's a persistence of the admixture, which suggests that it's a part of the formation of the modern human populations in their dispersal over the world. And then, even though we share a lot with Neandertals, we also share a number of things that are different. The differences we have with the Neandertals, it's not just the number of markers we have, it's actually which genes and what form of those genes that we actually have."

"What about the FOXP2 gene?" I asked to this theme. We carry the same version of it as is found in the Neandertal genome. It's the so-called language gene, another recent hot topic, though more accurately, there are a few hundred areas on the human genome, unknown to date, that are involved in bringing about what we call human language. Or almost any other trait: If there are over 697 places on the human genome that work together to express a person's height alone, imagine what complexities of many genes are involved in something seemingly more complex, such as language.

"The FOXP2 gene has an important role," he said, "in the development of the areas of the brain related to language comprehension and production. There's a unique form of this that was identified in humans that's different than any other form found in apes, but it is present in Neandertals. It could be some kind of a hominin-type of thing, which would allow for some kind of communicative skills, abilities, language or proto-language, whatever you want to call that, in these earlier hominins." *Hominin* refers to the collective of modern humans and all forms of extinct humans, including all lineages of *Homo* and extending even into earlier ancestors, such as the Australopithecines.

"But the form of language that we have now," he elaborated, "our brain has also grown, we aren't just looking for language areas in the brain;

basically the whole brain is connected in some way, to symbolic work and so forth, but that's a very important one, the FOXP2, because it has developmental implications." If one copy of the gene is mutated, one copy of the two we each have, one from each of our parents, a person will have significant difficulties with language learning and communication.

ON ANOTHER LEVEL, we modern humans, those of us on the dig team at La Ferrassie, were merging, swapping, and admixing with Neandertals—not via our genes, or by making alchemical fire, though I suspect that went on too (I was blissfully oblivious, sleeping in *la belle grange* Chez Cécile)—but through our psyches. The psychic infiltration began deep into the second half of the dig season; everyone seemed to be reporting strange dreams, ones that showed the experience of camping and digging for a few weeks was altering us and had sunk into our subconscious minds.

Dennis was having those usual dig director dreams, but more vividly than the others: a lot of driving and logistics dreams, sorting out and troubleshooting all manner of issues, from finding Harold to getting everyone to the site. If he had any about Neandertals, he kept them to himself. But a crew member, Dafne, and I each had dreams that exposed our ideas about Neandertals and turned them into feature films.

One morning, she reported that she'd had a dream about visiting a medieval village, an archetypal one like the many villages that speckle the shores of the Vézère and Dordogne Rivers. She walked along cobbled streets, past stone homes, through winding village lanes where lots of tourists were visiting and eating at their outdoor cafés, consuming lots of truffle omelets, roasted duck, and perfectly poached foie gras, while sipping lots of local wine. In all this she walked until a crowd began to form around a man dressed in hides. Perhaps he had wandered in for the same reasons, to get a mouthful of the succulent fare offered up by his beloved Dordogne, but soon he was frightened by all the attention he received for looking different. The closer she drew, the more she realized he was Neandertal and no wonder all these modern types had frightened him. She woke up trying to catch up to him as he ran away. She wanted to help.

I had two dreams, both taking place at La Ferrassie. In one dream I was in the upper cave and looked down at myself and saw I was Neandertal, dressed in heavy furs but still cold. There were many others with me, a few adults and a few more children. We were cold and mildly hungry but had just managed to have something to eat before a huge storm blew in and snow swirled all about. Accurate to the record, my dream showed no fire. I heard a thundering outside and went to the edge of the upper cave's mouth and looked outside and saw a towering mammoth, all white with long shaggy hair and tusks thick as his swinging trunk. He was lumbering toward us and crashed into the cave and everything tumbled and I woke up before, I think, I blacked out.

In my second dream, some days later, I was again in the upper cave but this time I was watching a female shaman holding a stretched-hide frame hand drum and beginning to beat it in order to alter her consciousness. She was doing a journey for a man who sat before her. We were all dressed in hides. Soon, a fourth person, a male shaman who was Neandertal, appeared and sat near the woman. She explained to me that to journey to the modern man's past, she needed a Neandertal shaman to help because the modern man had been part Neandertal and the consciousness was organized differently.

I thought this was odd but soon found myself watching the two work together. The drumming began and I saw—saw as if someone were painting a graphic visual in the air above us—her "consciousness" take on the visual appearance of concentric circles like a round striated tunnel, a classic form reported by people who do drum journeys. Simultaneously, her male counterpart's "consciousness" also appeared in graphics in the air above us, next to hers, and showed a different pattern.

His was an organic maze, no tunnel but a lot of folded-in passageways that rounded to and fro like folds of the brain. I watched the two forms in the air and felt two different kinds of electric pulses pass through my brain. Suddenly I was pulled into the maze pattern and found myself going deeper and deeper into the earth, landing in a chamber with dense crystal-like structures all around me and rectangular mosaics on the cave walls, also like crystal structures. The whole world was rust reds, ochre, and deep browns, like the different sediment layers at La Ferrassie. I looked down and saw a river of human bones.

That's when I woke up.

I love dreams and strive to remember them and sometimes am rewarded with full Technicolor dreams. This one was of a different order. I sat up in Cécile's childhood bed in my loft in the barn and wondered what I might have eaten, or drunk, the night before. Nothing that I could recall. It must have been the growing intensity of the dig season and how much time I spent thinking about Neandertals.

Just as the second half of the dig season was bringing up intense dreams, conversations during the lunch break were also riffing on more esoteric themes, almost as if it were safe now, this deep, to go into harder-to-chart territory. The waking and more rational sort of dream.

Harold and Shannon were talking about Neandertal and modern human behavior, mulling over the possibilities. They were riffing on a familiar theme, the different ways, it seemed, Neandertals and early modern humans went about solving their problems, that Neandertals worked out a unique solution each time and modern humans followed already established rules that made them think less and effect more conventional and commonly held ways to deal with something. Harold was uttering one of his favorite lines when I settled in.

"The Neandertal way requires a lot of smarts," he said. "The modern human way of doing things, you don't need to have as much smarts. Anybody can learn the rules." And stop thinking too hard to solve something, limiting our creative solutions to those bound by the rules, not looking outside of them.

"Maybe rephrase that in a little different way," Shannon said, ready to bring his usual calm counterpoint to some of Harold's more brash statements. "Both folks are smart but the modern human 'smarts' is embedded in the culture. The culture is carrying that accumulative knowledge."

Or what if Neandertal smarts weren't so embedded in—or dependent on—cultural forms, I thought to myself, but more fluid, able to break cultural forms to conform to other norms such as the immediate environment and what was possible there? Modern humans were known to go well out of their way—waste a lot of energy in a sense—to get flint or hunt exactly the sort of animal they wanted to eat. It was a lot like people today who will drive out of their way to go to a grocery store that carries a special product rather than make do with what the local stores have in stock or alter the recipe to accommodate it.

"The Neandertals," Shannon added, "were not all that concerned; they just wanted to get their stuff, figure out how to get it." Without complicating it by adding new or further steps.

It was another way of getting at the same point Alain had made, that Neandertal adaptations seemed to have a more flexible—less rule-governed—intellectual approach that allowed them to solve each problem uniquely each time. Modern humans seemed, by contrast, to have a more rigid, culture-controlled, rule-governed intellectual approach that limited the solutions but assured that everyone agreed on what the options were and didn't have to invent them each time.

"The Neandertal way to me is the smart way," Harold said, popping a piece of cheese in his mouth and savoring it. "The trouble is, there's a cost. If you've got a family that's, you know, not playing with a full deck, well, you're not going to figure things out all the way, all the time, and that's going to put you at a disadvantage."

"Well, it's also not going to get you to the moon," Shannon added. "The system of storing knowledge and passing it on has tremendous benefits in the long run."

"That's why you see a stasis for so long in the Middle Paleolithic,"

Harold agreed. "There's not much variability because it's constantly rein-vention, reinvention, reinvention. They have a repertoire in terms of technology that they can call on, but they're not robots: It's intelligent behavior. They're actually figuring something out, appropriately. I would say that modern humans are more like robots: I get on a plane and I stay American the whole time. I get into France and I'm still American, whereas I picture more, well, this wouldn't happen, but imagine it does: a Neandertal gets on an airplane to France; he's going to see what the resources are and do it that way, the French way. Though," Harold chuck-led, "we'd probably both wind up wanting *chocolatines*."

Shannon busted out laughing, as did Dennis, Vera, and Paul, who had been listening in on all of this. Beyond them, so had the crew and every-one was hungry again. *Chocolatine* is the local name for *pain au chocolat*, those crazy delicious buttery croissant creations that have a brick of dark chocolate baked in the center.

"And you'd still want *vin de noix*," Shannon added with a straight face, mentioning the regional walnut wine.

"Exactly. Nothing wrong with that," Harold replied. "But I'd take mine with ice." Mad dogs and Englishmen! The French do not put ice in their *vin de noix*.

"Well," Dennis entered the discussion, "*you* would eat the *chocolatine* and *he* would eat you with the *chocolatine*."

The whole site erupted with even louder laughter.

"I'd make a nice dessert," Harold defended, pretending to be miffed. "But to even say something like that," he returned to the original part of the conversation, that Neandertals may have had a smarter adaptation than us, "nobody can get it. 'Oh, you're bashing the Neandertals now,'" he said sarcastically, "'you're calling them *smart*.'"

"What about the FOXP2 gene?" I asked. "Culture and language are very bound up together as symbolic products."

"It just means capacity," Dennis answered.

"Right," Harold said, "capacity versus performance."

"So, couldn't you say then, that there was also the capacity and the foundation for symbolic thought?" I prodded.

"Of course," Harold said. "But you've got to see the performance take place to conclude that they did it. I think that's one of the big hangups here, all the time, is that people look at Neandertals and say, 'Well, physically and brain-wise they're so similar to us, they must have had a capacity.' Everybody since the Magdalenian could have had the capacity to make spaceships. And in the Aurignacian, they had the *capacity* to play pianos," added Harold, "but they did not."

"Hey, hang on, hang on, hang on," Shannon said. "If the Châtelperronian was made by Neandertals, then the deal is done."

"Right," Harold replied. "Then it shows by *performance* that they had the capacity."

"Yeah. And you don't even need genetics."

"Exactly." Harold popped another piece of cheese in his mouth and chomped with glee.

It was time to return to our respective trenches, inspired again as we worked hard and carefully to gather the material meticulously so somewhere down the road the experts could discern actual behaviors with evidence to back it up. But I also looked forward to Scotch Time, a tradition—rule-governed maybe, but adaptively flexible, especially because Harold was such a forthcoming and cheerful person—at which to ask more about this whole capacity-versus-performance thing.

As a cultural anthropologist, I got both from modern human culture, so I could test my theories just by hanging out in the field long enough. Not so in archaeology. You needed material evidence to show that the more abstract stuff happened.

Once we were back in Carsac, I rushed to Cécile's for a quick shower and to report to her the dinner menu that evening: roasted pork, garlic-sautéed green beans and salsify, a special kind of white asparagus-like tuber found in the southwest, and buttered noodles.

"Tell Harold I'll be there for dinner," she said. This was our ritual.

Harold reminded her all the time that she was always included in dinner, but she liked to take a very French approach and hear the daily menu, mull it over, and then decide to come over anyhow. The French love to talk about food, a wonderful cultural development.

Clean, back at Camp Dibble, the scotch chilled as ice crackled in our glasses, soda on the rocks for us both, very refreshing after a hot day in the sun—I asked Harold to elaborate on the lunchtime conversation.

"There are all sorts of different adaptations out there," he said. "So when we talk about Neandertals as being a member of our species, it doesn't mean they're exactly like New Yorkers. It doesn't mean they're exactly like anything. They could have a kind of adaptation that doesn't exist anymore on the planet. It's still is a human adaptation. I think that we're looking at human adaptations going way back, even beyond the time of Neandertals. So it's a *kind of* human adaptation. But does it mean it's ours?" He took a sip of the very fine liquid adaptation in his hand and paused to enjoy it.

"So okay," he continued, "they're the same species. They can still have different adaptations. Do they do things, then, exactly like we do them? I think they're just as smart as we are—there's hardly any way that you could argue the contrary. They've got brains as big as ours; they're technologically savvy; they're long-lived . . ."

"And looking at the way neuroscience understands the way the brain functions, there's really no way to say that their brains were any different," I added, swirling my glass as he did, the sound of ice against glass pleasing backup music to pontification.

"No, there's no evidence." He agreed.

"The brain is flexible, it's plastic," I added. I had been reading more in neurobiology to get a better understanding of the brain and was learning that it's still largely a huge mystery but a very pliable one.

"Exactly," Harold agreed again. "It's hard to characterize brains. That's why I say, look, they've got brains just as big as ours. They're smart. They're technologically savvy. They use technology, a complex technology. So, in that regard, they're just like us. Then that leads to the question, okay, do they have other things that we have? Do they have language? Everybody wants to equate language with intelligence, right? But that's saying, we're intelligent, we have language, so that means, we're intelligent, we have bipedalism. Does bipedalism make you intelligent? That's dumb. They're two independent things."

"Those are just questions again to make them just like us," I said as I picked up the scent of roasting meat and frying garlic wafting in through the open window from the backyard below. I took a sip. I loved this hominid life.

"That's right," he said. "When I say Neandertals are doing something differently, it's not saying that they're further down the line, that they're stupid or anything like that. What I say is, 'Oh, you know what, it looks like they are behaviorally different, so in what ways are they different?' By looking at it that way, suddenly we've got a sample of two humans to compare. We've got us and we've got another that is very similar to us. Now what is the difference? Let's get at the behavior and see what they were *doing*."

Cécile arrived in the doorway, signaling it was almost time for dinner. She joined us for an aperitif and we shifted from brains to interior décor, she as ever trying to introduce more color into the dig house, not realizing that just by being there, she did.

# 11

## A Foot in the Grave

ÉA, Bruno, AND I made an early Sunday of it and drove to La Chapelle-aux-Saints in the Corrèze, east of Sarlat, toward the slowly rising, drier foothills of the Massif Central, birthplace of many rivers,
among them the Loire, Vézère, Dordogne, Lot, Cèvenne, and Tarn. A
less-known mountain range in south-central France compared to the
Alps and the Pyrenees, the Massif is a wealth of ancient volcanoes and
volcanic soil and a place considered the most ancient heart of France,
with old mythic associations among the locals. It is a part of a richly
variable biosphere as well, with such diverse plant and animal life that it
still holds mysteries yet to be discovered. Perhaps the Corrèze wasn't as
rich in fertile soil and forest as the Dordogne, but it was a part of the
continuum between the Dordogne and the Massif and the good life, in
Neandertal times as well as our own.

After driving through wild, largely unmarked places, as a contrast we
arrived at a huge banner across the road, "Musée de l'Homme Néandertal," our destination, identifying the building nearby. The building had
to have been shorter than the banner. The Neandertal museum was at
one end of a hooked path that connected us to the village of La Chapelle,

also no larger than four or five stone houses anchored by a pretty twelfth-century Romanesque church.

Between the museum and village lay the village cemetery, and right next to it, the Lilliputian cave where the arthritic, practically toothless, and beloved Neandertal Old Man of La Chapelle had been found over a hundred years earlier.

"Let it never be said," Bruno offered his most theatrical voice, "that there was no intentional burial here in La Chapelle-aux-Saints." He then broke into a chuckle as we stood practically with one foot in each gravesite, one with hundred-year-old tombstones, and the other with a plaque over the cave mouth announcing the historic discovery of a local who had died around 50,000 years ago. We decided to visit the museum first, and then return to the cave, cemetery, and chapel. We turned around and went to sign up for the guided tour of the history of the pre-history of the place.

In 1905, as the Western world struggled with the mental paradigm shift that science was placing on religious outlooks, grasping the truth that we are creatures in nature and evolved from other creatures, two Catholic priests, Jean and Amédée Bouyssonie, with their younger brother Paul, began to dig here. This seemingly small place was to have a huge effect on our collective psyches.

Being amateur prehistorians as well as professional priests, the two were a part of a modernizing trend in France to harmonize and attune religious doctrine to the emerging facts of biological evolution. Why not let god's universe be more complex? But making sense of the world was still the order of the day and so when in 1908 they unearthed a Neandertal skeleton, the two priests reported it from the beginning as clearly an intentional burial.

The skeleton was in a tucked, fetal-like position, in a shallow pit, and was surrounded and covered by hundreds of Mousterian stone tools and animal bones that covered most, if not all, of the small cave floor, all artifacts typical of living spaces of Neandertals. Most modern human burials similarly contain ordinary items of everyday life far more than blatant symbolic bling. But these artifacts really appeared to be a part of everyday life, ones that occurred before and continued during and after the body arrived there.

Their find and declaration was *"une veritable 'bombe' scientifique et religieuse,"* a true scientific and religious bomb, wrote Bordeaux paleoanthropologists Jacques Jaubert and Bruno Maureille in their recent book, *Néandertal.*

Both influential institutions—science and the church—each with their selected ways of knowing, took burial to mean Neandertals must also have had a rich emotional and spiritual life. As much as all mortuary rites are first rites for the living to deal with the loss and grief of the deceased (emotional), and second, to work out what to do with the body (practical)—when looking at how people handled their dead, we also tend to extend beyond the emotional and practical to a possible spiritual life, maybe even to ideas of the soul and a hereafter. This purported burial led the discoverers to see a rich emotional and spiritual life among Neandertals and with their vision the Bouyssonies widened the door for people in 1908 to embrace Neandertals as kin and to stop seeing them as deeply other.

Ironically, the find also had the opposite effect, to deepen the divide in the hands of Parisian-based paleontologist Pierre-Marcellin Boule, who was given the bones to analyze. He misread the severe arthritis as a natural stature, making Neandertals stooped across the board, not just in this one individual who suffered from a painful deformity thanks to the fact that he lived a longer life than usual and had been helped by his people to do so.

That Boulean image, now in hindsight, we understand, came from heavy biases in Boule's mind that kept him from seeing arthritis and instead he imposed his preconceived ideas of an ape man. The public gobbled this image up—equally gullible to run with bigoted preconceptions—and one would think they entirely forgot the possibility of burial and what that implied about relatedness to us. This, even, when the Bouyssonie brothers spoke and wrote about the origins of human spirituality based on what they thought they had found here.

The little cave in one of the smallest villages in the Corrèze was a huge platform for the whole raging spectrum of ideas about Neandertals, from coarse brutes to the spiritually illuminated. The stakes were high for humanity that burial should win out over brutishness.

Those are still the stakes.

One will never hear an anthropologist, no matter what his or her position on similarities or differences, crack the coarse jokes for an easy laugh that still come off so readily from the lips of the public—even the well-educated public—when calling someone a Neandertal. It is known as wrong and inaccurate—indeed, racist—but so hard to extract from the public mind that does not know the deeper dangers. It is so embedded into our culture that this is okay that we still don't stop to think just how terribly close it is to othering others and making them subhuman, too.

The stakes are high.

So science steps carefully forward.

On corrective physiology, paleoanthropologist Jean-Louis Heim reexamined the bones in 1983 and found Boule's errors and biases and realigned the Old Man of La Chapelle to his rightful upright posture. Heim further added that repositioning the skull to sit atop the vertebrae as it originally had been in life changed the shape of the throat and showed that spoken language as we express it was an anatomical possibility among Neandertals as well. While the skeletal record has been set straight, we the public inherited a bad dish from Boule and are still crooked, dropping our mean Neandertal jokes without thinking.

The topic of burial has been revisited as well and has even more sensitivities around it, also thanks to the bad press from Boule. When studying burial among humans, seeking the earliest evidence for such behavior is one of the hardest things to prove because of preservation issues and what will constitute solid evidence for human behavior versus natural actions. And because so much hinges on burial, because we've made it so symbolically potent as an issue for humanness, it is especially touchy. But ironically, burial is also only one of many ways humans past and present handled their dead and even burial has a wide range of variation, from simple and practical depositing of the body and mourning the dead (burial) to more elaborate and ritualized matters of giving body and soul a proper send-off (a funeral and rite of passage).

There are also primary burials, such as placing a body in the ground and covering it with earth; and secondary burials, such as laying it on a platform to be picked clean by birds and other creatures and then gathering the cleaned bones and burying them, or defleshing the bones *tout de suite* and handling the flesh and bones separately. Cremation is also a secondary burial because it involves first burning the body and then distributing or burying the ashes.

Of interest, the form of secondary burial involving defleshing usually leaves cut marks on the bones, offering new possibilities for all those sites where cut marks and cannibalism have been equated. They may also be funerary activities, not just culinary. Defleshing and even cannibalism aren't uncommon among humans historically or cross-culturally, and moreover, defleshing of bones is found frequently enough in Upper Paleolithic contexts among early modern humans to blur the lines even more regarding how Neandertals and modern humans have handled their dead.

A recently excavated 18,000-year-old early modern Magdalenian site in southern Germany revealed the fragmented bones of two individuals who had been so heavily defleshed that the cut marks on their bones were more frequent than the same style of cut marks found on the animal bones in the same site. Also, there were no clearly symbolic items mixed with the bones, only lots of stone tools and animal bones. Though no one yet seems to have analyzed the frequency of cut marks on Neandertal bones, there is already a growing precedent for cut marks and fragmented bones mixed with animal bones and stone tools in some Neandertal contexts, such as at Les Pradelles. Beyond this, it is anyone's guess what happened to the nonskeletal part of the bodies and why. The level of fragmentation, and smashing of bones for marrow, suggests eating, which in turn could be both nutritional and ritual.

To deal with the lack of better-documented data from La Chapelle to address the nature of the burial, or if there was in fact such an act, archaeologist William Rendu and colleagues from across France more recently reviewed the Bouyssonie documents and then spent twelve years re-excavating the cave in order to discern better evidence for or against intentional burial. They also excavated the other small caves in the same hillside to better understand the natural processes of the hillside caverns and to understand the wider use of the landscape by Neandertals. Mousterian tools and animal remains were found in the other caves as well as in the burial cave. In the Old Man's cave they even uncovered fragments of other Neandertal individuals, one adult and two children. Theirs was definitely not a burial but more a placing, a dumping, or a scattering.

It was hard to reconcile the original documents with the current dig's findings. Some evidence was simply gone, but they eliminated the likelihood of the cave as a bear den and other natural processes that could have resulted in a pit and a well-preserved skeleton, and concluded that the most likely case was still that this was an intentional burial, that others had used a natural depression in the cave floor to carve out a place to set the body and then did a quick backfill to cover it. There is no hard evidence for the backfill sediment, but the good preservation of the human bones, especially when compared to other animal bones in the cave and surrounding caves, implied to them that the body had to have been better protected. In essence, the evidence can't confirm or negate burial so the team seemed to go with what they thought was the most likely scenario, perhaps to be sure that the door from 1908 remained open.

"It's a big deal," Harold said. "This is no small thing, but a big deal that changes the direction of what Neandertals did or did not do. We need to be certain about it before we make it a fact." He, Dennis, Shannon, Paul, Vera, and Teresa wrote a response to the Rendu team's publication about their work and called for more stringent criteria. They listed what these criteria best could be—the issue of determining the fill in the grave as laid down by nature or by human action—to test for certain for intentional burial. Rendu's team considered the critique and responded, after serious consideration, that they felt the same conclusion was the most reasonable, even with the lack of good evidence for the original nature of the backfill or sedimentation in the cave.

Critics from outside these two collaborative teams threw in their two cents on the debate. Some felt that the stringent criteria suggested by Harold and team was setting a good standard for gaining better and testable evidence—real science where outside and independent researchers could test the findings using the same measures. Others said the opposite, that Harold and team hold standards that are too strict and that even most modern human burials would not pass the test, let alone earlier burials. This, to Harold's mind, is fine and also missing the point.

There is a great deal of similarity in the appearance of Neandertal remains in the Middle Paleolithic up to early modern human remains in the Upper Paleolithic, from simple shallow pit burials to the fragmented human bones with cut marks mixed with animal bones and tools. Then there are the burials found in the Levant that reverse the order of things. There, the earliest burials among humans are among an earlier migration of early modern humans into the area around 100,000 years ago. Qafzeh is the most famous, with a proven intentional burial because the pit is clear and the body was accompanied with ochre and beads—it goes the whole distance and is both a burial and a funeral: emotional, practical, and symbolic all in one. Kebara and its purported Neandertal burial nearby and farther south is some 30,000 to 40,000 years younger than Qafzeh and can only be considered a burial (and yes, some contest this, though most see it more than even La Chapelle as a hands-down burial).

The fossil record also complicates things because despite the Qafzeh remains and a few others, we still have more fossil remains for Neandertals than early modern humans anywhere, even early modern humans much later in time than the Neandertals. Why the Neandertal fossils preserved so well is an important question.

"That's the sixty-four-thousand-dollar question," Harold said when I posed this to him. "We don't know what preserved the bones." But the conundrum is that there is no hard evidence for covering the bodies with dirt, which is the reasoning most archaeologists give to explain the preservation mystery. And it still doesn't address the related conundrum, that Upper Paleolithic burials that showed a similar possible practice of backfilling still preserved fewer skeletons and from more recent time periods.

The famous skeleton of Kebara in Israel was a nearly complete skeleton of a man but for his upper skull (the jaw is still there) and a few limbs. Near him, another partial skeleton was uncovered. It was a child, and its relative wholeness may point to some form of burial. But the child could as likely have been "dumped" into a zone the excavators identified as a "dumping zone," where they found fragments of another twenty-one infants and children, none of them buried. At the very least, there were two different burial practices going on in Kebara, yet it has similarities to other possible burial sites.

But Kebara is also less debated in the burial question because in the Levant there was earlier mixing and contact between Neandertals and early modern humans and the story is different here. The Kebara Neandertal "burial" is younger than the ones of early modern humans at Skhul and Qafzeh by about 30,000 to 40,000 years. The same story extends to other Levantine Neandertal locations, such as Shanidar in Iraq and Dederiyeh in Syria, which are near contemporaries of Kebara.

La Ferrassie has two somewhat complete adult skeletons and five partial skeletons, some very partial, of children and infants. La Chapelle has the famous Old Man nearly whole but fragments of three others, an adult and two children. Maybe some people were buried and others placed and left. Maybe different people used the sites in different times or the same people in different times, as temporary hunting and camping occupations. There are so many maybes, again, including ideas about infant mortality and differential treatment of adults and children that are pure speculation, that one needed to advance with caution.

Another conundrum is that we just don't have as many skeletons for early modern peoples as we do for Neandertals. "The uncomfortable fact," Randy White said when I visited him near Les Eyzies, "that people don't know what to do with is that *my* people the Aurignacians," early moderns who appeared right after the Neandertals disappeared, "didn't bury their dead. The whole premise of the Middle Paleolithic transition was that the Upper Paleolithic people were burying their dead, but they weren't. It's the opposite. Neandertals appear to be, in some contexts, burying their dead.

"But what we know is that through the twelve thousand years of the Aurignacian," Randy continued, referring to the time from around 40,000 years ago to 28,000 years ago in Europe, "we don't have a single burial. I'm sure they were doing something with their dead, but it wasn't burying them or it wasn't burying them at living sites."

The first burials in Europe to appear in the Upper Paleolithic are associated with the Gravettian people, who lived around 29,000 to 22,000 years ago. These show full-out burials as we recognize them, people buried in dug holes with personal items, such as the beads they may have worn while living. Later Magdalenian people handled their dead in ways that appear very similar to the Neandertal mortuary remains: either mostly placed in natural shallow pits, or defleshed and scattered with animal bones and stone tools and nothing much else.

"What the Neandertal record says," he continued, "if you believe indeed that those were burials, is that people were burying dead people in places that they were living. When you get to the Aurignacian, you don't know whether they were burying their dead. They could have been burying them out in the valley bottom or other contexts. They could have been doing other things: hanging them in the trees, throwing them in the river, or whatever. It's very uncomfortable to have these moderns who have all this symbolic stuff, but guess what they don't have?"

"Burial," I say, happy to oblige.

"The thing that's allegedly made Neandertals human. Well, what do you do when you have the first humans who follow the Neandertals who don't do it?"

In my mind, it seemed like different cultures, where some do one thing and others another. I grew up aware of Zoroastrian funerary rites in Iran and India, which, similar to those practiced by Tibetans, were to place the dead bodies on high platforms—sky burials—in the mountains and let birds of prey, rain, wind, and sun deflesh the bodies. But the whole debate here wasn't just different cultures but different pathways of being human that both intersected but also walked in unique directions.

"I think there are all sorts of conundrums," Randy said. "You probably already know that all of this stuff about burial started with La Chapelle-aux-Saints and its excavation by two Catholic priests." I told him I had just been there with my friends. "And then Bouyssonie," he continued, "writes this book on the origins of human spirituality. I mean, they have a really big stake in it that has nothing to do with archaeological theory or the evidence itself. It's about something else. It's about being a priest. It's about the role of the Catholic Church in scientific research."

I recalled a central quote, attributed to both the Bouyssonie brothers, on a display at the museum that confirmed as much: "Insofar as philosophy and science show that burying the dead presumes religious beliefs and sentiments, one can assert that during the Mousterian period there existed religion among humans."

This can apply to all of us, Mousterian Neandertals in Europe and Mousterian early moderns and Neandertals in the Levant. But the key pivot, the one that trips people up, is the difference in how philosophy and science arrive at their evidence. Philosophy has its logic and theorems about humanity that can use just the mind to confirm its ideas—*feel* and *reason* what makes *sense*. (As if what makes sense is logical.) Science has to use more hard physical evidence, provable beyond the mind of the beholder—and other like-minded beholders who agreed with each other's poetic logic—to test criteria that anyone, no matter what they believed, can confirm. Hard physical evidence for the softest, most abstract of substances.

"It's curious," I emailed Harold, "that more Neandertal skeletons have been found in the Dordogne, or anywhere, in general, than early modern human skeletons." I told him about my recent visit with Randy and what he'd said about bodies and burial.

"That's true about the Aurignacian," he wrote back, "but by the time of the Gravettian, and again in the Magdalenian, there are lots of burials."

"So this really argues for widening what the handling of the dead looks like, right?" I asked.

"Sure. As I always say, moderns don't always bury their dead. It's only one of many ways to handle the deceased. People like to make the argument that 'well, if a modern group doesn't bury their dead, it doesn't make them less than fully modern.' That's true. But that's not the point. The point, and the bigger question, is this: Did Neandertals have modern culture, which we are more and more defining as the heavy use of symbols, which in turn means language, symbolically mediated social structure, etc.? If Neandertals practiced burial, it would heavily imply the use of symbols in ritual, and therefore all of the other stuff, and therefore the conclusion would be that they had some kind of equivalent to modern culture."

He was on a roll, which I appreciated, because I wanted to sort out how all this mattered.

"But it has to be kept in mind that modern culture began at some time, just like domestication of plants and animals. The question is when. We cannot simply assume that bipedality = modern culture. We cannot assume that tool use = modern culture. Or hunting = modern culture. What the consensus is now is that the use of symbols = modern culture. But like any evolutionary development, if something exists at one time, we cannot simply *assume* that it was present earlier as well, rather, we have to try to demonstrate that it existed earlier."

The problem in archaeology is that it will always be limited to what can be found physically in the record, and symbols in our minds have probably been around far longer than symbols outside of our minds, left engraved or carved. When did we decide to express symbols beyond fleeting, oral utterances and turn them into a record? It had to exist long before it showed up in the record.

Paleolithic archaeologists such as Alison Brooks and Sally McBrearty, working in Africa on the origins of early modern human behavior, are finding more and more that these features of a symbolic life don't just appear suddenly, but are present somehow in earlier forms, or unexpressed but evolving with a suite of traits that positively reinforce each other. The earliest example of this, going beyond the question of just early modern humans, but back into our common genus *Homo*, is the trend toward a larger brain compared to body size that emerged around the same time as increased lateralization in the brain, tool-making, right- and left-handedness, and, some would argue, language in some form, even if not language as we know it today. This suite of traits may have eventually led to fashioning things more into outward symbolic forms. Perhaps it lay within for a long time but the need to cooperate and communicate with growing groups of people and strangers pushed it to outward expressions, such as beads, paintings, and engravings.

La Chapelle is as much a part of our collective human legacy as it is a French legacy. Bruno Maureille, one of the coauthors on the study with

Rendu, told Noémie Fraiche, for his biographical portrait (which he dedicated to his grandfather) on *Chercheurs d'Aquitaine*, that he first visited La Chapelle-aux-Saints when he was eleven years old. He was on vacation and visiting his grandfather, who wanted to take him to the site. It made such a deep impression that he went on to dedicate his life to studying Neandertals. La Chapelle is also *une veritable bombe emotionelle et intellectuelle*. It is a place where people wear both science and emotion on their sleeves and to do otherwise may be impossible.

Most purported Neandertal burials were excavated years ago at a time before archaeologists documented geological strata as exactly as they do today, explained Leiden-based archaeologist Wil Roebroeks at his recent talk in Paris at the Collège de France. He was advising a steady approach to this emotional debate. "This debate will probably remain an open discussion," he said, "until we find new sites" that can be excavated with better techniques. "We can't answer this question with what we have today," he concluded.

Roebroeks also stressed the need to make a distinction between burial and funeral behavior, one addressing emotional and practical issues and the other ritual and symbolic. Even in cases for burial among early modern humans, very few offered evidence for strong symbolic behavior beyond the act of burying. He noted the recent survey made of the entire Upper Paleolithic across Eurasia by archaeologists Julien Riel-Salvatore and Claudine Gravel-Miguel. They found that the majority of burials, which are coming from a small known sample so far, were clustered around the years 28,000 to 20,000 years ago (in the Gravettian) and later, around 14,000 to 10,000 years ago (within the Magdalenian). Very few of them could be called typical burials and fewer still bore such ritual aspects (such as elaborate grave goods or art) to be considered anything other than "sober affairs." The two authors found that early modern human burials varied quite a lot, but for the most part were simple. In fact, these burials seemed to not be all that different from what were being called purported Neandertal burials. In other words, most lacked the strong symbolic evidence to make the difference between burial for emotional and practical reasons and burial of a highly ritual and symbolic nature.

As I FOLLOWED Béa and Bruno into La Chapelle's museum, I heard Béa telling the young woman behind the counter that we were interested in the guided visit to the museum. Bruno added that they were professional guides—hoping for the more detailed tour if possible—and that I was an anthropologist-turned-journalist. As those last two nouns left his mouth, the woman who led the tour stepped out from the back room. "An anthropologist and journalist and two guides! Good! Excellent!" We would get all the details.

I decided to come clean from the start. I was a *cultural* anthropologist but as a journalist I was writing about Neandertals, especially about the work in the southwest of France. And I was digging with Harold and Co. I held my breath.

"Harold Dibble!" She said. "I know him! He was here!"

"Yes," I said, waiting, wondering if we would be welcome.

"The one who wrote the strong critique of the recent work here and that this still was not a burial."

"Yes," I said again, waiting, wondering.

She turned to Béa and Bruno and filled them in. "I remember when he visited with his colleagues." She mentioned Paul and Dennis. "I told them, 'Come back, visit the cave, and you will change your minds.' They never did."

I later learned that they actually did, wanting to completely take in the recent report, the past reports from the Bouyssonies, and also the cave and how it had been excavated, but she just didn't know that. I didn't at the time either.

"I'm not a specialist," I reemphasized, "and I just want to learn about this place and see how you see it."

"Of course. Very good," she said as two French couples and a family from New Zealand arrived. No more was said about Harold, as if he had somehow been involved at Hastings and had tried to resist the Normans, but we all know how AD 1066 turned out.

The tour began in French. I later learned from the New Zealanders that though they spoke no French, they had found our guide's enthusiasm so infectious that they were pulled along and worked things out from museum displays, maps, and charts.

The guide was incredibly knowledgeable and on top of all the current debates and theories, not only on burial, but about human evolution from 2.5 million years ago to the present. Before she went full-tilt into the material, she wanted everyone to know that the Old Man of La Chapelle was not that old, somewhere in his thirties and forties, even if the name stuck because of its charm.

The central and most important display was a replica of the grave and skeleton. As a part of her explanation for how he ended up here, in Europe—the wide sweep, not the grave-digging—she delved deeply into human evolution, beginning with *Homo erectus*, who effected the first series of migrations out of the African continent, one bushy branch wandering off toward Europe and giving rise to Neandertals as other bushy branches inhabited Asia and another for the most part hung out in Africa. Over a long time, isolated from the others in East Asia and Africa, the folks in Europe and West Asia took on features we identify as classical Neandertals. Of course, it's all about flow and we already know flow continued to be possible much later, with the likes of us and our encounters with Neandertals and Denisovans and who knows who else on all those bushy branches including our own.

When she came to the later *Homo sapiens* migration, around 60,000 years ago, she let us know it was not a first migration but one of many before it and soon after it as well, as well as flow back again into Africa.

Everyone listened carefully and then one of the Frenchwomen asked, "Why did *Homo sapiens* migrate out of Africa around fifty to sixty thousand years ago?" By now we had been standing around the display of the burial for several minutes. It was set into the ground level of the floor, the Old Man in his cozy curled position, and for some reason we all stared at him simultaneously, as if the answer lay there with him.

"It's not known," the guide answered. "But there are theories that population growth led to movement and expansion, to find new means to eat and live. This trend continued into the Neolithic and hasn't really stopped."

It could be our population growth and bigger numbers that pushed Neandertals out of their traditional territories to more marginal ones. That may even be the reason we made that big pulsing series of migrations out of Africa around 60,000 years ago—too many of us there for a nomad's tastes. Perhaps Neandertals had smaller numbers than we did, which the evidence for density at their sites is telling us. But maybe, she added, we also brought new diseases with us from our long life and separation in Africa that they had never been exposed to. Maybe it was a combination of things, as life is prone to be.

She then worried that people would make the old mistake of thinking Neandertals weren't as smart and so couldn't adjust, and added, "We and they are simply two different types of intelligence and adaptations. One is not smarter or better than the other." It was a matter of chance and the randomness of life. "In the end," she said, "Neandertals were driven into Iberia."

This, in current thinking, is considered one of the marginal places Neandertals retreated to, given that the latest occupation sites seem to be there, though Mezmaiskaya in Russia (just north of Georgia in the Caucasus) is recently dated to around 39,000 years old, about the same age (and perhaps a little older) as many southern Iberian sites. And more recently, work from the Altai in southern Siberia is also showing a potential last marginal range of retreat as well, to the north. The prime areas to live apparently were in the band in between and we moderns, in our sheer numbers, seem to have been flooding into them. Maybe.

Add a *maybe* to everything in this field, and also, don't let the ink dry.

"*Homo sapiens* had an especially developed frontal lobe and the Neandertals' was also extremely developed," the guide concluded, "but with important differences. We were genetically programmed to do different things. We're just different, not better." Her Neandertals were also masters of fire, decorated their bodies with shell beads and ochre and manganese oxide pigments, spoke their own languages, and used symbols. They were different from us but a lot like us, too. Her collective of Neandertals was a certainty of all the issues that are still unresolved and continuously contested, while everyone agrees, at the same time, that they were very, very smart and as human as any other humans who have ever existed.

The tour over, we thanked the guide and made our way back to visit the cave site and then to the church, a walk of 50,000 years in two hundred meters. As we peered over the fence toward the cave, Béa said, "It was very clear that she is very proud of this place and deeply connected to it."

"Yes," I agreed. "She is definitely a deep part of all this and I can see why." I looked at the cave opening where the three brothers had stood in 1908 and revealed a small place with a big impact over one hundred years ago and counting.

All the caves in that hillside were small and low, like hobbit holes inserted into the slope. The middle one had a huge plaque on its arch, which marked it as the famous one where the Bouyssonie brothers found their man. A person even of modest stature could not stand straight inside it without hitting her head.

But as I stood as close to the cave as the fence allowed, I found myself being pulled into that emotional force-field that grabbed people when confronted by time and mortality. How much stronger would it have been had I been born French, or better, Corrèzienne and this too was the land of my own origins?

Speaking entirely emotionally now, just knowing this famous personage had been found there was enough to fill me with wonder and a suspension of time. It was perfectly logical that this was a place a nomadic person might come to die and be surrounded by loved ones, or after the fact be laid in and set away from scavenging carnivores, such as lions and hyenas. But this was purely my mind's imaging and wouldn't add anything to the debate except that we humans are emotional and impressionable when faced with things to which we would do better to say, "I don't know." But we really want to make meaningful stories instead. Stories are the most fundamental products of our symbol-making mind and rarely get written down because their nature is simply to make sense, offer calming effects, be communicated, and then morph into the next *meaningful* situation. Invisible.

It seemed to me that Rendu and his team went for drawing the line on burial in a moderate place between emotion, politics, history, and science by saying that, though they felt they have documented enough hard evidence to say burial was more likely at La Chapelle than not, they do not claim that this means it was absolutely certain, nor that burial was practiced all the time, everywhere.

"Some of the Neandertals in some regions," Rendu told *Archaeology* magazine editor Zach Zorich in 2014, "in very particular moments, made these kinds of burials." Rendu had read the report from Roc de Marsal and agreed, as noted in *Archaeology*, that it was a burial from natural processes, not by human hands.

We walked from there, past the cemetery, and to the Romanesque church with its octagonal steeple and Gothic archway on the edge of the old village with its small cluster of houses. Locals had dedicated their church to Saint Namphaise, an officer in Charlemagne's army who, tired of war and violence, retreated and became a hermit in a remote forest in Quercy, the region including the Lot just south of us.

I smiled to myself. Saint Namphaise wasn't the first to think of retreating to quiet solitude and a little cave and he now was the namesake of a church near a small, remote, and quiet cave with another in reclined retreat. Béa went off to gather the huge cast-iron skeleton key from a neighbor that would unlock the chapel and let us inside.

It was a simple chapel and mostly unadorned, but with harmonious Romanesque arches and columns that allowed for perfect acoustics and, dare I say, a primordial cozy cave feel. As my friends turned to leave, I walked a little farther along the aisle before turning to join them. I found they had stopped at the entrance, reading a sign posted on the back wall, and were beginning to chuckle.

"Fees," it noted at the top, with a list beneath it for different services the parish would perform regarding important rites of passage:

Mass—17 Euros

Marriages—160 Euros

Interments—160 Euros

Baptisms—free

When I caught up to them and read over their shoulders, Béa was saying, "I can't believe marriage costs the same as burial. I always thought it cost more." I thought I could almost hear a personal statement in her tone: marriage *should* cost more. "Burial must be really important here," she finished and walked out.

"Or it is as important as marriage here even if elsewhere it is less," Bruno said to me. I wondered what the cultural norms for costs of rites of passage were across France. Did marriage normally cost more than death? Death to my mind had a naturally higher price, but then, it was a one-time deal and marriage could last a lifetime and might need a bit more mass and ritual to get it onto the right groove.

"But," I reflected back to Bruno, "you still have to pay for both. There's no way around that."

He laughed. "At least admission is free." He then stepped quickly through the door—not wanting to be irreverent in church—before bursting into a good belly laugh outside.

•　　•　　•

THE FINAL DIG season folded in 2014 and soon the team was dispersing but for the core members and graduate students who were working the material into their own research. As everyone analyzed more material, consolidated the geological observations, worked out strong dates with several dating methods, all the team leaders met in the summer of 2015 for a powwow session in Carsac, including dating specialist Guillaume Guerin and fossil expert Bruno Maureille from Bordeaux, to consolidate what they all were seeing and offer sound assessments. I think they astounded themselves when they came to swift and aligned agreements about what the evidence was saying.

They agreed on the defined strata and the different occupations and the dates laid out for La Ferrassie. "The other thing everyone agreed on," Harold told me afterwards with chagrin, "is the La Ferrassie 8 child is at an entirely different level than the other two, La Ferrassie 1 and La Ferrassie 2. So it can't be a whole family. It can't even be a cemetery. You've just got a coincidence that you've got other humans there."

"How different are the dates for the two levels?" I asked.

"Well, we've got a level difference. Guillaume's dates put it at a good 10,000 years earlier. It's also probably true for La Ferrassie 5 [another of the children], which is looking as at the same time as La Ferrassie 8."

La Ferrassie 1 and La Ferrassie 2—the two adults—were separated by 10,000 years and younger than the two children for whom there was good data. It seemed information for the other three children was too incomplete to say much.

"Those are some major things as far as the evidence," Harold said. "We weren't talking about the symbolic aspect, but those data are hard to make it work with the traditional interpretation of burial."

"So it's true to your mantra 'Show me the evidence.'"

"Yeah. And when you look at the evidence, it turns out it's nothing." I could detect a bit of disappointment, that he had hoped more would come out of all this. But the evidence is like that when you stick to it impeccably: it won't let you tell stories. Perhaps Wil Roebroeks was right, the time to dig new sites and take a chance on them was upon us.

It was a typical Saturday morning at Sarlat's weekly market and by midmorning I ran into Aurelie and our friend Christian. They made a ritual every Saturday of stopping for coffee at the market café and asking about any new findings regarding Neandertals.

The Saturday prior to this one I had summarized the paper Dennis and the team had published on the lack of evidence for burial at Roc de Marsal. I had seen the knitted brow of mixed curiosity and concern in Christian. He was French so had inherited the strong emotional and historically paved affinity for burial. Aurelie too was French, and a hundred percent from the Périgord, and the Roc de Marsal child was also one hundred percent from the Périgord, but she too knew Harold, Carsac, and archaeology well from the inside out, so little could surprise her and she just smiled. *Never let the ink dry on any of this.* Christian listened, asked hard questions, and filed it all away.

This week we resumed where we'd left off and found the last available seats at the café at a table occupied by another friend of Christian's. "My friend is interested in prehistory and Neandertals, too," Christian told me by way of introduction and added that he was a retired teacher. We shook hands and the waiter came, took our orders for three espressos, and Christian dove in.

"I considered the report on Roc de Marsal," he said, "and I looked into it and I have to say, I totally agree with their science and their conclusion. The taphonomy bears it out."

Christian's friend, the teacher, leaned forward, intrigued. They batted this about, Christian offering further details from the study, and I saw Christian begin to win the taphonomic cause.

"How do you come to Neandertals?" I asked the teacher once the Roc de Marsal discussion waned.

"*Bien sûr,* ever since I read Marylène Patou-Mathis's books. Especially *Neanderthals—Une autre humanité,*" he noted the most influential. "Her title says it all: another humanity, equal but different. She is an advocate for Neandertals, correcting our false and bigoted views of them inherited from the past."

In a sense, Patou-Mathis is to France what João Zilhão is to the rest of Europe. Here in France they had their own special spokesperson who really spoke to the people, not just the scholars. It reinforced the idea that the French public really did have a more intense relationship with their prehistory than any other people.

I had heard about Patou-Mathis before, many times before. Nearly all of the French volunteers who came to work with us for a week or two at a time at La Ferrassie had told me, just as a casual part of conversation, that Patou-Mathis was *la grande dame* of all things Neandertal.

A leading prehistorian and zooarchaeologist at the Institut de Paléontologie Humaine in Paris, she worked especially on the faunal remains of Neandertal sites in Eastern Europe but also had quite a public outreach toward representing Neandertals everywhere. I think her Parisian Joni Mitchell style, part hippie chic, part Parisian panache, further extended her public persona as Madame Neandertal.

Second only in popularity to her nonfiction *Neanderthal—Une autre humanité* was her novel *Madame de Néandertal—journal intime,* in which she imagines being inside the mind of a Neandertal matriarch as she records the day-to-day observations of her Middle Paleolithic life.

"How did her books pull you in?" I asked Christian's friend.

"They're thorough and engaging and put human flesh onto the bones," he said. "They made me really think about Neandertals as human and a part of our shared humanity."

A man at a neighboring table, an acquaintance of both Christian and the teacher, overheard our conversation. "Oh *mon dieu, encore?* There you go again, about Neandertals. Are you in love? *Madame de Néandertal?* Can you think of nothing else?"

The teacher blushed. I leapt to his defense. "It's my fault. I asked him about them."

"No, *Madame,* you cannot take the blame. I know him. He's always talking about his beloved Neandertals."

"That's an exaggeration," the teacher said, "but what would be wrong with that if I did?"

"How about you?" I asked the eavesdropper. "Why don't you think more about them?"

"*Baf.* I'm too busy checking the rugby scores," he said, puffing out his chest and acting the very manly man.

"Humph," Christian's friend replied, "compared to how Neandertals hunted, rugby is a game of sissies."

The man's chest deflated.

*Voilà. Touché.*

Marylène was doing something extra for the Neandertals, something João never could; she was acting as a *woman* advocate. Not only was she a successful woman scientist in a field infamous for its testosterone and male dominating behavior, but she was also putting a female face on Neandertals—who also have a rather testosterone-defined public persona. I bet when you think of them, you think of the males first, right? It's a common bias.

Svante Pääbo, in his autobiography *Neandertal Man* (notice the title), wrote that when his team published their groundbreaking work on the first sequenced Neandertal genome in 2010, he received a lot of positive emails from the public saying they knew they were part Neandertal and his work confirmed it. Curious, he went back and counted how many of the writers were men and how many women and found that out of forty-seven such emails, forty-six had been men. Another twelve that came from women were claiming that their husbands were Neandertal, not themselves. He worried, correctly, that the negative image of Neandertals was persisting into the new era, this one celebrating burly men but not burly women.

I found it both disturbing and fascinating that the public was still fixated on the physical appearance of not only our kin but ourselves, rather than the deeper implications of our wider shared genetic wealth that allowed us to adapt better to new circumstances. While all of this fell outside the realm of science and was fully a part of the public and human hunger for storytelling, having a woman in science speak for Neandertals in a positive light has helped close this gap.

I realized too that I had been egregiously excluding Madame La Ferrassie, and needed to bring her into the fold. From there on, not only would Monsieur La Ferrassie be looking over my shoulder, aiding and abetting, but so would she, adding more interesting perspective and dialog to the effort.

I MET DIDIER for another trek into the wild prehistoric past of the region and Christian joined us. We went this time into the Corrèze, not too far from La Chapelle-aux-Saints. As we climbed into a cave near a farmstead that Didier knew about, one that might have been occupied in prehistory, I asked him what he thought about the idea of a cemetery at La Ferrassie. I liked his insights: he had the expansive skill of listening to everyone and reading all the literature and staying on top of the most current evidence. He also tended to keep his ideas to himself unless asked.

"I don't think La Ferrassie was a cemetery," he said softly. "That many bodies, especially spread out by so much time, do not make a cemetery. It speaks more about a highly frequented place where people died and were set aside or just simply died right there."

Further afield, Kebara in Israel has evidence for around twenty-three individuals having been left or having died there. Only one of the skeletons was nearly complete and well preserved. Another is partially complete and in more fragments, and the remaining twenty-one individuals are only small fragments and most of their skeletons are long gone. It comes across as if there were a lot of visits, activities, and deposits over different times and by different people. It, as at La Ferrassie, seemed to be more telling about the life of nomadic foragers than any significant statement about Neandertals or us. I thought also about La Chapelle and its one whole skeleton and thirteen fragments of three others found in the Lilliputian cave. This all made me think of what Dennis had told me recently when we talked about the issues of Paleolithic burial.

"While the vast majority of modern cultures, including simple hunter-gatherers, do have some ritual behavior associated with the treatment of their dead, there are a rare few who did not. There are examples of recent/historic hunter-gatherers who did (at least on occasion) simply abandon the bodies of their dead when they moved on to a new site. We would obviously not accuse these people of being cognitively inferior to other modern humans or incapable of 'modern behavior.'"

"What about the idea of a cemetery, such as it is attached to La Ferrassie or Shanidar?" I asked.

"The cemetery concept—a special place where an ethnic group/culture would regularly transport the remains of their dead to—is not in keeping with the behavior of simple forager societies," he said, "who do not view the landscape in the way that more complex hunter-gatherers and food producers do. True cemeteries really only appear with the development of sedentism when people begin to live (and die) in one location.

"There certainly are examples of cemeteries among hunter-gatherers, but almost all undoubted examples of these appear relatively late and their development is likely associated with higher demographic densities that limit free movement by any one group across the landscape."

I also caught up with Alain to ask him about the whole burial thing.

"I prefer calling it 'treatment of the dead,'" he said, "'not burial.' It's a Judeo-Christian idea to call things 'burial' as well as 'cannibalism.' Not all cut marks mean eating, and not all eating means survival or symbolic cannibalism, either." He revealed the absurdity to our easy way of force-fitting the past into more recent cognitive categories. He next elaborated on the vast diversity across different cultures regarding human mortuary practices.

"The possibilities are infinite. All the more reason not to interpret how people handled their dead without solid data. I prefer the deductive approach, where I observe and observe and build a foundation to put things together when I see patterns. The patterns also need to repeat, to show themselves as real patterns. But this takes time and a lot of work. But," he added, "the terrible thing today is that to get money and positions, people have to publish very quickly and too soon." This was especially the case for junior scholars who were just starting their careers and navigating such a contentious field. There's a lot to balance, all of it precarious.

WHILE PALEOANTHROPOLOGISTS SPEND a lot of time with the dead, their bones and dropped stones, Elisabeth Daynès, a celebrated reconstruction artist, does the reverse and brings them back to life.

Applying knowledge from anatomy and physiology, she closely studies every mark left on the bones, for muscle attachments and how strong they were, and then works with a complex calculation of facial and body proportions for muscle, fat, and skin, and layers these onto casts of the skeletons. She folds in findings from genetics to come upon the most likely phenotypic expression of skin, hair, and even eye color. She has refleshed several of our lineage Homo as well as a few Australopithecines, and these people wander about from exhibit to exhibit across museums around the world. In the Les Eyzies museum and the nearby prehistory didactic and conference center, the Pôle International de la Préhistoire, reside several of Daynès's creations, including two favorites, La Ferrassie 1 and the child from Roc de Marsal.

One day, after making a run with Susan to store collections in Campagne, a château and grounds donated to the government, which in turn donated it to archaeology for ample and lush storage facilities, I suggested we stop briefly in Les Eyzies to pay homage to the ancestors. A zooarchaeology graduate student with Teresa Steele, Susan was excited to see something whole after working with thousands and thousands of fragments of bones. Exuberant and comfortable with expressing herself, she is also an adamant scientist, dedicated to keeping all speculation and sentimentality out of the research effort, an apple not far from Harold's tree.

So it hit her hard when she turned the corner and saw one of Daynès's creations staring back at her through his soulful dark brown eyes. She was struck still and silent as he reached toward her, holding a rabbit he had just hunted, his other hand holding his spear like a walking staff. His long brown hair and warmly wrapped hides added to a sense of comfortable familiarity. It took a few long moments before Susan pried her moistened eyes away and could speak. "I didn't expect that," she said. "This is why we do what we do. I just wanted to stay there and ask him about his life and who he was."

When a grown man in furs holding a dead rabbit can elicit this level of emotion from a staunch scientist, imagine what a three-year-old infant with his soft tender skin, wrapped in a deer hide, can do to the heart. He is the refleshed Roc de Marsal child and in the museum, when he is not on tour, he sits on the ground watching and listening to La Ferrassie 1 (my Monsieur) in avid conversation, teaching him something key about the life around them. Once the visitor gets caught up in the space unfolding between them, the glance, the movement of lips, the gesture of the hand, the glass case in which they sit dissolves.

Emotions connect us. They have from the beginning in a very primate way through our common ancestor with our closest living relations, chimpanzees and bonobos. Emotions underpin things before symbols and language ever do. Emotions are not symbolic, even though people mix them up with symbolic ideas in such highly charged contexts as death and burial. Emotions do not represent anything other than exactly what they are. I recalled my visit to Atapuerca and the young child and her mother standing next to the re-creation of the Neandertal burial.

*"¿Qué pasa aquí, mamá?"*

"A friend is sad," her mother had answered, "because his friend is dead and is honoring him and showing his *tristeza* with the flowers."

That was it. The mother didn't say anything more, nothing about assuring a peaceful journey to the other world, nothing about meeting god, nothing about preparing for an afterlife. It was about showing strong emotions of grief and loss, the one solid thing we can say, from chimps to us, about death and burial.

WE HAD FOUND no new skeletons at La Ferrassie but the pattern of some places as a deposit for the dead as a part of living camps made it seem possible there were more. Maybe. I listened in as Alain, Harold, Paul, Dennis, Shannon, and Vera pondered the site and its strata and their data so far and worked out the original orientation of the seven skeletons—an effort that led to realizing these were at least two deposits made at least 10,000 years apart.

As they spoke, that back wall taunted me. I wondered if it taunted them too, knowing future generations of archaeologists would have a go, but that for them, they had gone as far as was feasible for the current research proposal. Like Pech IV, the tail and the hind legs were before us but the rest of the salami, the whole enchilada, the beef, the bulk of the elephant could still very well be in there. Holy coprolite.

I pondered too, again, about the molar that Isabelle, Asier, and Antoine had found, pointing to a possible third adult left at La Ferrassie. I pondered again all the roof fall beyond the child's final resting place. I considered beyond it that the whole hill still remained a mystery and that the three excavations from 1905 to 2014 were still only a beginning of sorts. I wondered again what the story had been here, even though we're not really supposed to tell stories. I wanted a sign, a hint at least, about the direction of things.

As I looked around, I saw *tout les deux*, Madame and Monsieur La

Ferrassie, watching with me. It was time to see them in person, to pay a proper visit to their fossils. It was time to head to Paris. Maybe there, a piece of the mystery, a hint, a message, was waiting to direct the story to its most likely direction.

*Allons-y,* I said, and we made our journey north.

## Morphing Neandertals

⚜

WALKED DOWN THE center of the wide dirt park lane of the Champs du Mars through throngs of visitors from all over the world waiting to ascend the Eiffel Tower. There were many large groups and all of them displayed the outward signs of their national belonging. Such as the big sunglasses-and-floppy-hat-clad Tokyo teenagers with canvas walking shoes and current photo apparel, including selfie sticks. Or the group from Mumbai in kurtas or jewel-toned saris and elegantly draped scarves and tailored leather sandals, also with selfie sticks. Or the Russians with form-fitting earth tones, chicly wrapped neck scarves, and leather loafers, feeling oh so very self-consciously Parisian, also with selfie sticks. There were the icons that distinguished and the icons that pulled everyone into the same feeding frenzy, tribes and the Tribe, the most recent being an obsession with photographing oneself everywhere one migrated and to widening one's network, invisible and present—an obsessive signature only of modern humans.

I was on my way to meet Antoine Balzeau at his office in the Musée de l'Homme, just on the other side of the Seine and in the Place du Trocadéro. The visitor's Paris out here was so different from the one I was about to encounter in there. Or was it? It was still all about us humans and what we're doing here on this beautiful blue planet.

Ever since meeting Antoine, I liked him. He had been hunched over a microscope in the Carsac dig house, working with Harold the evening before he, Isabelle, and Asier were about to join us to dig at La Ferrassie for two weeks and where they would unearth the adult tooth in the infant's square. He was a solid scientist, always cheerful, and had a penchant for wanting to share his knowledge with the public. So much so that he had been the scientific consultant for a televised program in France, *Les Pouvoirs extraordinaires du corps humain: Dans la peau des premiers Hommes.* (The Extraordinary Powers of the Human Body: In the Skin of the First People.) It had aired on France 2 and resulted also in a book. In both, there is Antoine walking and discussing matters with celebrity hosts Adriana Karembeu and Michel Cymes and others, all dressed in beautifully tailored fur and hide trousers, leather shirts, and fur overcoats in the forests of France, exploring bipedalism, stone tool-making, fire, spear hunting, living in rock shelters, and foraging for a living. The same cheerful, happy-go-lucky smile was there as the one that greeted us every day at the dig and that now walked toward me at the museum just before opening hours.

"Thank you for making the time," I said after we greeted each other.

"*Pas du tout, pas du tout,*" he waved one hand lightly. "It's a pleasure to share what we do here."

The museum had recently renovated and revamped its halls and exhibits on the entire journey of being human, from the deep past of our evolution and its many branches and stops and starts, to the present, to the waves of the potential future. Descartes's skull even was here, just meters away from earlier thinking-therefore-being celebrities, such as the original Cro-Magnon skull of the early modern human found in Mr. Magnon's hole in Les Eyzies, as well as the skull of the Neandertal child from Pech I, and my two favorites of all, Mr. La Ferrassie's skull and Madame La Ferrassie's right foot, the latter still encased in the original sediment in which it had been found. I was excited to visit them in person, a special pilgrimage to me, which I kept to myself. But there they were, smiling, too, and walking in step along with Antoine and me, almost as if we were in an additional segment for *Dans la peau*.

No one knew how often these two stood next to me as I journeyed in their world, my special guides. It was my own secret interior life, à la Descartes, of thinking things into being. One day, when I'd gone to revisit a favorite prehistoric cave in the Dordogne, I'd spoken with the guide about our affection for prehistory. She said softly, sharing a secret away from the earshot of others, "I love prehistory because it lets me travel back in time *et toucher un mammouth*, and to touch a mammoth." She said this as she simultaneously stroked her thigh and then laughed timidly because she had revealed that it wasn't just an imagined touching but a real one, and very seductive, even if only real to herself.

"My father is Jewish and my mother is Catholic," she elaborated, "so I grew up aware of different ideas in one home. But I also wanted to leave the political world of modern humans. Prehistory let me do this, where I could just *touche un mammouth*, touch something untouched by all *this*." *This* being the messy, political world in which we stood. *Madame et Monsieur* were my equivalent of touching a mammoth. They were my steady guides to a world that was untouched by all *this*.

Antoine gave me a private tour of the whole museum, a walk through the prehistory, history, and beautiful diversity but unity of humankind, saving the best for last, a visit to our celebrities from the southwest: the Old Man of La Chapelle, the child from Pech I, the original Cro-Magnon from Mr. Magnon's hole, and best of all, Madame et Monsieur La Ferrassie. He left me to linger a moment longer over the latter two. He seemed to understand without my needing to explain. He got it; this magic was his life's work. From head to foot I pondered my friends. They were set in a black case with lights set on the fossils so all else was obliterated and one's eyes went right to them. There was still so much mystery locked inside of them into which we still had not tapped.

Before Antoine showed me the private section of the museum with the researchers' offices, he had one more treat in the exhibit space to share. The museum had installed a new interactive contraption, the Morphing Neandertal, that on approach looked unremarkable, like a box-shaped car without doors. It had two seats like the driver and passenger seat of a vehicle. He didn't explain to me; he just invited me to take a seat. Together we went and as soon as we sat down the screen came to life before us.

Oh my god.

Our faces appeared as two ovals floating in a sea of black, side-by-side, eggheads. Suddenly the computer laid down proportions onto our oval visages. At first they looked like the lines and dimensions one learned to make in a portraiture drawing class. The computer was measuring our brows, foreheads, cheekbones, and chins; the width, length, and shape. It next took these dimensions and recalculated them to the measurements that paleoanthropologists have documented for Neandertal facial proportions and their range of variation. Once the measurement was done, a note appeared on the screen below my face, "Morphing Neandertal."

I watched, mouth hanging partially open, which was now being factored in, as my face and Antoine's next to me morphed into proportions and the look I might have been born with had I been born Neandertal. Staring into the would-be car's windshield, my face was recognizable but I had bigger teeth, a receded chin, more pronounced brow ridges, a larger nose, and the biggest, bluest eyes I've ever had. I closed my mouth and saw my expression turn serious and philosophical, mesmerized by the transformation. I stole a glance at Antoine's face and he had taken on similar changes, only he was grinning at me, a full set of large teeth in joyous play. I smiled back and was stunned by my own teeth and then saw the two of us at once, both a bit shocking but more and more quite human and quite attractive. I was amazed how in seconds I had gone from feeling I was watching someone else's face to quite physically embodying the image before me and feeling as if the changes had actually happened on my own face. I smiled again and Antoine smiled back; a smile is all it takes to see fully our interconnected humanity and our beauty.

We were beautiful as Neandertals, as beautiful as we were as modern humans. The morphing stopped and the screen went black, waiting for the next pair.

We continued to the back of the museum, and slipped behind a rope barrier and through a hidden door into a sweep of hallways to Antoine's office. He opened the door and let me step in first, waiting for my reaction. A picture window looked directly out across the park below, across the Seine, and framed perfectly the Tour Eiffel. All the many groups I'd passed earlier in the morning were specks of color, ants—the other amped-up social animal.

"*Pas mal*," I said and began to wonder if all paleoanthropologists in Paris had offices with a view, thinking back to Jean-Jacques's office with the Seine and Notre Dame as constant companions.

Antoine went to a special cabinet, unlocked it, and gingerly pulled out a box and picked up an item wrapped in plastic within. Leaving it in the plastic, he gently handed it to me. I held it in my palm; I didn't dare breathe or move.

"This is . . . ?"

"A fragment of the child's skull, La Ferrassie 8, that we found when we recovered Delporte's boxes of materials." A jolt of electricity ran through both my arms.

He set it back and took out another piece of precious cargo, this one in a clear plastic box within the larger box. Again, I held it gingerly.

"The tooth," I said, "the mysterious third adult's tooth."

"Yes," he answered. "But this is the *other* one. There are two. The one we found at the site last summer, and this one, which we found in Delporte's collection. We identified it when we looked at the whole collection more closely." That collection was supposedly only the infant's bones.

"So with the one you found last summer and this, it really confirms there's another adult there?"

He smiled like a kid.

My heart stopped. With a second adult tooth near the child, the third adult was now even more real. If one pinky bone and a few teeth can identify a whole species over in Denisova, two whole teeth from a new individual (or two) could potentially change the story at La Ferrassie. I was transported back to the site, standing before that wall, the one we'd contemplated so much, the one the dig directors had faced, like a sacred wall of contemplation. It *was* sacred, it held more beyond it, under all its collapsed stone and earth. "Will anyone consent to testing these bones for viable DNA, to analyze them genetically?" I finally asked when words returned to me.

"Yes, it would be very informative," he paused, "but it's complicated."

Many others from the dig had said the same; this business was not only of discovering but also of protecting bones. No one had said more but I'd pieced together that those who gave the final okay on such procedures weren't yet ready to take the risk. Maybe it was because the genetic science was too young and it inevitably had to destroy a part of the fossil, grind a small piece of it to powder, for DNA extraction. They seemed to want to wait until things looked more certain. Once that day arrived, some of the mysteries of La Ferrassie could feasibly be answered, including if any of the Neandertals found there had been related.

"No one knows where the origins of the Aurignacian comes from," Harold said one lunchtime *à la Ferrassie*. A lot hinged on the Aurignacian as a clue holder to the mysteries of "the transition," that period when the last Neandertals overlapped with the newcomer early moderns into Europe, bearing in mind also that tricky bit about the Châtelperronian.

"It could be that Aurignacians came to Europe from the Zagros," Shannon replied.

"Came from the Zagros," Harold echoed.

"Came from the Zagros," echoed Shannon, as if they two were each making the trek in real time in their heads, deciding where to cross: farther south near Shiraz, or up north near Kermanshah or Tabriz.

*Came from the Zagros*, I echoed too, but quietly in my head. I went into my dream world too, recalling flying over the Zagros as a child on summer visits to see relatives in Iran. I couldn't wait for the last leg of the connections from Denver to Tehran to look out the airplane window to see the ancient folds and wrinkles of the gray-green-brown mountain range sweeping all along Iran's western flank. Some of my people came from the north Zagros and the rest come from areas just south of the Elborz or deeper north and in the Caucasus into Armenia, Georgia, Azerbaijan, and Russia. Some relocated to the Colorado Rockies in the USA, my parents, and hence there my brother and I were born. We were mountain people through it all. After the Iranian Revolution, when those trips ceased, I never forgot that view or those gray creases.

I had been talking about the Zagros a year earlier with Amir and now with Aylar, both Iranian doctoral students, one in Paris and the other in Philadelphia, both of whom had joined the crew. They were exciting windows into a world from which the rest of us had been cut off, me emotionally and the scholars intellectually, including some of the most important archaeology in Asia. The Zagros remain an untapped wealth of human evolution even though archaeologists within Iran are currently excavating some of the known sites.

The Zagros mountain range was a place where everyone it seemed had passed through. First was *Homo erectus*. Next Neandertals, then, most likely, the earliest of the early modern humans, the ones who also went to places such as Qafzeh and Skhul around 120,000 years ago. Neandertals kept passing through before, during, and after them. And last, those even more widely roaming moderns from Africa passed through, possibly around 60,000 years ago. They would keep exploring the next horizon and one day dream of inhabiting other planets, so insatiable their obsession for the next horizon. Maybe they already did when they looked up at the stars that they used to navigate. Who knows?

But in those early days of 60,000 years ago or so, the places Neandertals had inhabited often became places the later-arriving early modern humans inhabited. The Zagros was one, along with the Caucasus and the Levant, because they were a part of the huge geographical bottleneck where three continents come together.

Our crew was such a bottleneck. There were days when my brain felt particularly spent, more than my body, when I realized that in this crew I got to use the four languages I knew well and sometimes smashed all into one paragraph as if it were normal. We were the bottleneck writ small, a microcosm for the macro. And we proved that cooperation was a heavier skillset among humans than competition, considering the many times we efficiently solved problems and moved largely in concert without conflict, submerging other drives to be stronger as a group than as individuals.

Biologist Edward O. Wilson was right: besides ants, humans were the only other social organism on the planet that really uber-selected for the group. And that selection for the group went back early, extending to other hominids, especially Neandertals, from whom we now have a lot of group fossils. In fact, we have more for them than for early modern humans.

"I love this whole experience," Virginie said as we set the sieved sacks of fauna and flint we'd cleaned, sorted, and labeled into trays with their catalogued numbers for careful documentation and storage and later analysis. "I love working together with all the nationalities and people. You feel like you are somewhere else. You don't feel as if you are in France. You are in *Carsac*." A universe unto itself. "It's really peaceful and you always meet new people. I really like that."

And all these people are unified by one thing: The desire to understand our most closely related relatives, the Neandertals. They are as much seated around the campfire or washing dishes, sorting in the lab, drinking Harold's booze, and swapping dinnertime recipes, as are we.

Virginie, who grew up in southeastern France, in the Côte d'Azur, came to all this as a youngster. During summer vacations, her mother opted to go on archaeological digs instead of swank poolside vacations. Virginie grew up with prehistoric dirt encoded in her bones. She was sixteen and serious when she joined the team at Roc de Marsal, and when she enrolled for her master's at the University of Bordeaux, Harold and Dennis saw a lot of skill and promise and assigned her to be the lab director. She loves science, order, logic, and clarity along with Neandertals and us.

"I'm really fascinated that they survived for some three hundred thousand years before the time modern humans arrived here. There are so many questions we can't answer for this period, or we do and we realize that we're wrong. Neandertals seem to be so close to us but at the same time they're different. Little by little, a hundred fifty years later," she referred to how long we've been studying Neandertals and how long it's taken us to cut through culturally inherited biases to see facts, "we realize that they were quite sophisticated."

"How do you imagine them?" I asked.

"I'm not sure that they would have been that different from us. Little by little, we'll find more. Like the lissoirs. That gives us something more to think about. And there are still a lot of questions."

Such as, after such a successful existence, longer than we've managed so far, what happened to them? I later turned to someone who has been pondering the question for over six decades (he began his archaeological career when he was eleven). Ofer Bar-Yosef, of course.

"So what you have," Ofer told me on that spring morning from Brooklyn as he sat in one of the world's most diverse human geographies of our era, "is you had Neandertals in Europe. Modern humans came in. The Neandertals disappeared. The earliest modern humans are of the Châtelperronian." Not everyone would agree with this, but his reasoning is compelling, that it is a blade industry and conceptually more like later blade industries and also far less complex than the Levallois of the Neandertals. "And you find them in different spots," he continued. "And then, and I think, that other modern humans came, not as one group, one wave, but different groups. Then another group is coming, then another. Then you have the local emergence of the Aurignacian culture." He sees the Aurignacians as a native European culture, not one that came in from the east.

Most people, including Randall White and Harold, say it really isn't clear where the Aurignacians came from, that no one knows. Others suggest that this is because they didn't come from anywhere but Europe, as Ofer suggested; they were an indigenous phenomenon emerging from prior people who had been there and stayed, so, no trail from elsewhere would appear. But even local emergences can have trails, right? It's another conundrum. How does a group of people just appear and with a different tool tradition and a whole engraving-rich craft industry in bone and stone without leaving some bread crumbs of their emergence? Let alone bodies. Another mystery.

"What happened," he brought me back to the transition, "is that the Neandertals became extinct because their meta-population was splintered. Modern humans took the best areas." Places like the Dordogne, across the swath of central zones between northern and southern Europe, though southern Europe was an appealing place with rich flora and fauna, so, this too strikes me as a curiosity. Perhaps it was more the isolating effect and, as Ofer said, that the different small groups that had probably managed to stay in touch with each other and keep the meta-population looking as unified as it was were splintered and could no longer come together.

"So, in bad years, Neandertals—hunters-gatherers-foragers—couldn't go back to other places, and this is a death sentence." Ofer emphasized the phrase *death sentence* and referred to how among small groups of hunters and gatherers in areas with limited resources, one bad choice during hard times was all it took to finish the group. It was as true then as it is now.

"They were extremely successful, intelligent people," he emphasized also, but early modern humans pretty much delivered a death sentence by cutting them off from their traditional seasonal hunting and foraging grounds. "There is a continuity biologically," he added, "a continuity of general humans remained with us, but there were lots of extinctions along the way. There were a lot, at the same time, of mutations." We're always changing and we carry it all, or a good lot of it, within.

"You must be asked a lot, 'Who were the Neandertals?' What do you say?" I asked Alan Mann and Janet Monge that day in autumn when I visited them at Princeton and we sat in a swank modern classroom surrounded by casts of famous fossils from human evolution, including the requisite standing skeleton so famous in medical circles.

As physical anthropologists they have collaborated in many ways, one of the most involved being the analysis and inventory of nearly nine hundred bone fragments from some seventy-five Neandertals who lived 130,000 years ago at Krapina in Croatia. It is a project that has reconstructed Neandertals closely, finding many individuals with healed bones, many who suffered from osteoarthritis, and overall, a group that was pretty hale and hearty until whatever it was came along and killed each of them.

"I would say," Alan answered, "look inside yourself. Because they're in there along with the rest of us."

The truth was, I'd already done this; I was looking for someone like me but different who might have a secret to share about being human in the world in a better state of balance than we moderns have managed. I thought of Alain Turq, Harold, and Didier's insights about Neandertal adaptations revealing a people in greater alignment with the world around them—without needing to change it. *Neandertals adapted to each environment, but we adapted each environment to ourselves.*

"What would I look for inside of myself?" I asked Alan, searching for his take on this.

"Well, okay, so you're a human," he offered. "What does that mean? Neandertals are human, too. So when you describe your humanness, you're describing theirs."

Cool. But then. "What happened to them? Why did they go extinct?" I asked because we knew that they no longer walked the earth today, at least not in the form that he and Janet found morphologically in that huge collection of bones at Krapina.

"You have met the enemy," he said softly, "and they are us. They are us."

"You mean we killed them off?" I ventured, naïvely, simplistically, knowing this was not the likely scenario. Harold also had said one day at La Ferrassie, "There's no evidence that we killed them off, absolutely no evidence." If we did, we killed them softly, with splintering, as Ofer suggested; and perhaps with diseases that we carried with us from Africa for which we had evolved a level of immunity but that did not exist in Eurasia, and these hit Neandertals hard.

"Considering the amount of Neandertal DNA in modern humans," he said, "rather, we have to postulate a series of Paleolithic singles bars." He said this deadpan and held his straight face but smiled with his eyes as Janet launched into a belly laugh.

I prodded him for more details. "So, you walk into a Paleolithic singles bar. What happens next? What does it look like?"

"Well," he looked up at the ceiling of the Princeton classroom, "first you look at the roof to be sure it's stable because so many cave roofs have fallen in on you and that's how we get Neandertals."

Janet couldn't stop laughing now as Alan animated the full crush. I moved my Bar Neandertal out into the open air in my mind's eye, under the moonlight. *Madame et Monsieur* enjoyed that, too. It was a starry night. They ordered pastis.

I think Alan may also have answered another question, not only mine, but Harold's $64,000 one, as to why we have so many well-preserved Neandertal skeletons. They had lived during many periods with a lot of temperature fluctuations, with extreme freezing and thawing that could cause such roof collapses. So add to some possible cases of intentional burial, some other cases of unintentional burial.

"They were just like us because they were human," Alan added more seriously, something that needed to be said, joking aside, "only they were not just like us because their way of life is extinct."

And what do we know about that way of life that is now lost?


NO DEAD BODIES were found this time, or any human remains at all, or even any stone tools, but deep in a chamber, 330 meters from the entrance—just less than a quarter of a mile—Neandertals seem to have visited a dark cavern in Bruniquel Cave along the Aveyron River, forty-three miles north of Toulouse and sixty-five south of Sarlat. They built two stone circles, one large and oval around four meters by seven meters, enough for a few people to gather around, and another smaller, two meters across and seemingly big enough for one or two people. They were built from broken-off stalagmites, the conical mineral towers that form in a cave from the ground up. The stalagmites were fairly uniformly broken, using the middle portion and leaving the stems and tips, though the stems and tips aren't on hand nearby, so they could have been carried from other parts of the cave.

In dating the stone circles using several techniques and repeating the tests, the large research team led by paleoanthropologist Jacques Jaubert, geologist Sophie Verheyden, and paleoclimatologist Dominique Genty learned a surprising fact: these stone circles had been built around 176,000 years ago. This is the sole reason that they think the stone circles were made by Neandertals, because they were the only known humans living in Europe then. And human action seems pretty certain. Cave bears don't stack relatively uniform stones, break off tips from elsewhere, and make fire.

Some four hundred pieces of broken stone, stacked in low walls, made up two circles and also four smaller piles of stones in and around them. Several areas on the stone circle had discoloration from fire. The team also discovered some burnt animal bones, possibly from a bear and some herbivores. These cannot offer too much evidence for anything more than burnt animal bones. Were they dinner, had they been used to make a torch for fire in this dark space? No idea. Was the small circle for small people or someone undergoing initiation while the rest of the group sat in the larger space? Total speculation (in this case, on my part).

The cave was first discovered in 1990, but with stops and starts the full investigation began in 2013 at Verheyden's instigation, as she was curious about dating the stones. The results went public three years later and created exciting ripples in the public and the profession, but when the waters calmed again, it seems we still knew about as much about Neandertals as before, only with better vision to look for built structures, not only deep in the earth but also aboveground.

It's exciting nonetheless because it adds one more thing to look for and consider in the evidence: the performance, as Harold or Dennis would say, of what that extinct way of life might have been. It also served to regalvanize and deepen the mystery while adding to it a new layer. It's likely that something different was going on there in Bruniquel, different from what we can even speculate. We may not even have the capacity to figure out what that difference could be, for our way of seeing things might frame things differently, even with the lens of science.

The stone circles certainly confirm that building was a part of the repertoire but not always necessary or useful. So why here? Mystery. It may help researchers tune their ability to see, to look for more structure, both above- and belowground, in different ways than usual. If they discover more, they will help turn a one-off incident into a body of data that may reveal a pattern. And with patterns, we can start to say something about something.

So what are the patterned somethings we already know about our closest kin, the Neandertals?

They lived social lives in small groups. They moved about and kept contact with other groups but also seemed to like to stay near home territories. They knew the earth very well, so well that they used what was there rather than moving far distances or altering the world around them to suit preconceived ideas of what's good to eat. They made really complex tools that were more masterful than the blade industries of later *Homo sapiens*.

They most likely had language, but what would they have called language and how did it work? It could very well have been different from ours, or applied differently given different priorities. The more I read about experiments chronicling how *we* use language, the more it appears to be a skill with a weirdly heavy marketing aim. From gossip to teaching, we are arranging ourselves in social structures and dynamics; keeping up with the news, passing on the news; seeing how we can prepare, get ahead, and benefit—as well as keep tabs on what we owe others and what others owe us; advancing our cause; preparing for the future; making myths from the past to advance our cause and prepare for the future, and so on. Even our outward symbols and texts show a lot of this marketing behavior. Our first written texts were either to keep tabs on commercial inventories and exchanges or to make offerings to the gods, a spiritual marketing effort. The fact that we don't see frequent symbols among Neandertals, in the form of beads or painted shells or written texts, is not so much evidence that they did not have a symbolic life but more that if they did, they did not apply it as we do. We are *Homo marketer* and perhaps they were *Homo let's-be-here-now* without needing to get ahead or keep up with the *Homo Joneses*. Adapting to the world each day, rather than adapting the world to them—which, indeed, takes more manipulation and keeping tabs on the project.

Back to what we know. Neandertals had fires, sometimes and sometimes not, just like us. They worked hides and most likely wore them, given the wear patterns on their teeth as a third hand to hold the hides and also the occasional lissoirs that appear, but a good stone side scraper with a blunt edge also does the trick more crudely, and they had many of these on many sites.

Neandertals probably built or augmented temporary shelters. The one deep in Bruniquel Cave survives because it is protected. As Randall White illuminated, open-air sites are everywhere in the southwest. Potentially, they may have contained evidence long gone that could confirm shelter building, if we could find intact sites. But the lack of frequency of finding these things, compared to finding them for early modern humans, may be more than just a preservation issue and more about a behavior in general that did not need to build as much for permanence or posterity. Permanent shelter building among us also didn't happen for a long time.

Neandertals certainly ate a lot of meat, preferring large game but also adapting to the environment in which they lived. They also ate many more plants than we ever realized before.

We also can say that they had complex cooperation, social organization, and intricate multifaceted intellects. Their hunting techniques and their tools show this. They planned, they projected, they organized, and they made Levallois *à la Michelangelo*, seeing in the raw flint the form they wanted before they began to systematically and abstractly knock it out.

They cared for each other and had rich emotional lives. Courtesy of their genetic gifts to us, we also know they liked to make love a lot.

Their way of life is extinct but their humanity is not.

Had we never come along as the aberrant world-dominating cousin, they'd probably still be around, as would many other life forms that have gone extinct courtesy of our peculiar adaptation to adapt less and alter more.

When in 2014 the final dig season folded at La Ferrassie, I said good-bye to the dogs and the cats and the crew and the dig directors and Cécile drove me to Sarlat, where I said good-bye, for now, to her as well. I had a little over a week in Sarlat before needing to return stateside.

I was there in time for the Saturday market and as usual at the café with Aurelie and Christian by midmorning, Christian waiting to take a first sip of espresso before launching into this week's question.

"What may have caused the extinction of the Neandertals? Was it us?" He looked up expectantly, almost steadying himself in his seat to prepare for the verdict. A retired wood shop teacher at the local school, he still did his own woodcraft and created wonderful pieces, and usually his body language—wiry and always in motion—connected somehow to craft, as did his questions. I knew he imagined Neandertals working their stones and probably wood much as he did, making choices, executing a plan he visualized into the wood just as Michelangelo had seen and then released form from marble.

I thought of everything I had learned and heard and tried to sum it up: "There are lots of theories and as usual, probably not one is an answer; that might be too simple. Some say we outcompeted Neandertals just by our sheer numbers and different hunting techniques. Along those lines, some think it was largely peaceful, just a fait accompli and others think it was violent, like tribal warfare for better real estate."

"I recently read about the idea of weak sperm," he added, sounding doubtful.

More recent news, from the geneticist who managed to talk about sex without titillation: "It seems more like fertility issues that arose because as much as we were related and alike, we had spent so many thousands of years evolving separately, they in Eurasia and we in Africa, that some fertility issues were bound to occur. But we were still close enough to create many viable offspring, even if not all of the matings resulted in children who then in turn went on to reproduce. One theory was that something selected out male children offspring, maybe that they had less viable Y-chromosomes or couldn't father children as easily." But it sounded silly to utter aloud so new a science. I went back to the extinction list.

"Disease is another possibility. When we arrived with our own set of germs, to which we had adapted a long time before, but that were new to them."

"Like smallpox and influenza when Europeans arrived in the New World?"

"Yes."

"And then there's climate change and natural disasters," I finished.

"Which is less likely according to new thinking," Aurelie chimed in.

"Right. Because they had managed to survive pretty well in pretty harsh conditions. If anything, it seemed they had the advantage."

"And it appears that they gave us an advantage, in the disease department," added Aurelie. Because our offspring who survived and went on to reproduce incorporated immune gene variations that had helped Neandertals adapt to the more common diseases found in Eurasia, or metabolic issues too, different for the climate there. We took these and incorporated them and adapted better, most likely thanks to them.

"Then, of course, there is the final piece: that they are still within us," I said. "Some will go as far to say that they are not extinct at all but right here in you and me."

They are very much among us: 40 percent at least, according to Pääbo, of their genome survives if we were to take everyone's 0.7 percent to 2.1 percent and knit it together, eliminating overlap and filling in fragments. But around 35,000 years ago, their unique meta-population look and adaptations stopped appearing both in the fossil record and in us. Some paleoanthropologists say it is because they evolved due to all the interbreeding and morphed into humans, as we appear today, a harmony and blending of all our traits. But others, especially the geneticists, point out that the percentages of shared DNA would have to be higher for a total absorption. It's a part-absorption, part-extinction situation.

THAT LAST WEEK in Sarlat, post-dig, I desperately needed to undo the kinks of the physically demanding season. In that spirit, I made a space on the floor and switched on the television and settled into a good long session of yoga. It was a Sunday afternoon, which always promised a family after-lunch movie specially aired for this festive time of the week. I stretched and waited for it to come on, and when it did, I almost doubled over in a fit of laughter.

Café Neandertal extended into the television and there before me began a Paleo feature, *L'Odyssée de l'Espèce*, Odyssey of the Species, a reenactment of human evolution with heartstrings attached, from the Lower Paleolithic and Australopithecus through to all of our ancestors into the Upper Paleolithic, right after the last of the Neandertals died and left just us.

I almost stopped doing yoga, feeling the glacial snow chill me through the glass, but was saved by the best part of the story, when one of the Neandertal men fell in love with a beautiful svelte Cro-Magnon woman; locals use the term "Cro-Mignon" when a local woman is as cute as a button (or delectable as the cut of meat). Sadly, this was a story of unrequited love: he was separated from her and would soon die anyhow.

As a final poetic gesture before the credits rolled, he calmed his aching heart—his pining love for the Cro-Mignon, He closed the film by playing a soulful lament on a thick bone flute made from the femur of an animal that the Mignonette had shown him how to play.

He had to blow hard to get any sound from it, so thick was the interior, but blow he did, so heavy was his heart. The score of the film then took over with the soulful lament of what sounded like the Armenian wooden flute, poetically taking it home to my own family's ancestry and to a place in and around the Caucasus where much of this exotic mingling may have first taken place. The Armenian flute is all the more poetic to me, as I had watched as a child some relatives recite mystical poetry, with the flute in the background, and stopping to sip strong black tea, and sometimes stronger arak (anis-seed liquor like ouzo).

Just before the Neandertal man in the movie died, he lay down his flute and let it be known through body language that he gave it to the earth as a gesture of love for the Cro-Mistress. "She was the one he wanted to have children with," said the voiceover narrator. *But that was not to be his fate.* The image then faded to black and the music grew even more mournful. The credits rolled. I sat frozen. I had by now given up trying to do yoga, halted too many times as I took in the imagined last days of love and loss of our closest cousins.

In my movie, with the later breaking news from Bruniquel Cave, I would have had my Neandertal take that flute deep into the earth and sit in the larger circle and play his lament to the mournful echo of the cave, reconnecting with the ancestors who had built the stone circles and weaving himself, the last Neandertal, into their fabric. I might even have him lie down with the flute in hand, but, that would be outside of the current evidence, so I could already hear the director cry, *Cut!*

I looked up the filmmaker, Jacques Malaterre, who also made another Neandertal drama, *Ao, le Dernier Neandertal,* Ao, the Last Neandertal, another splendid tragic drama that perfectly captured the French romance with the last Neandertals and their ideas about Neandertal and *Homo sapiens* romance. (Later, I found the film and watched it. After a lot of hell, the worst of it losing all his kin, Ao ends up in a remote part of Europe—we imagine southern Iberia, possibly Gibraltar—with his lady love, a Cro-Magnon woman, and her child from a prior match whom he loves as his own; and soon, for she is pregnant, a second child is on the way with him.)

Even Sunday lunch in the southwest cannot escape Café Neandertal and the French obsession with prehistory. But it was also clear that the old bias was there. Why not a romance between a Neandertal woman and a *Homo sapiens* man?

*Because,* said Madame La Ferrassie, rolling her eyes, *modern men talk too much, make too much of a deal about language, and have way too much stuff. We prefer the strong silent types who don't clutter the home with things. Voilà. Touché.*

I NEXT SAW Bernadette a few days later for our ritual of late-morning coffee at Sarlat's Wednesday market.

"*Comment ça va avec tes Neandertals?*" she asked.

"*Ça va, ça va.* It's a lot to sort through, all the stones, bones, debates, labels, and data, to get at who they were and how that might have been similar to us or different from us."

She smiled and gazed at her coffee as if looking into a scrying bowl. "Just remember, it's all interconnected, all life, all that happens on this planet. The labels are artificial. In all the infinite diversity is the common bond of oneness. Don't forget that. It's all interconnected and we are a part of the fabric, not separate from it."

The metaphoric sweater stopped unraveling, and instead, began to knit again, as did many of the gems of wisdom gleaned from the specialists along the way.

*Tomato, potAto.*

*Stick to the evidence.*

*We're looking for an Edenic moment.*

*It's good! If you had scars, you survived!*

*Origins are very important to us; everyone has an origin story.*

*To touch a mammoth.*

Les Homo sapiens, ils sont jamais contents.

*Why do they have to be like us to be considered smart?*

*They adapted to each environment; we adapted each environment to ourselves.*

*Look inside yourself.*

*You can't remain a worm in your own turnip.*

I LOOKED OUT at the view from Jean-Jacques's office in Paris and by now the sun had fully set. *L'heure bleue* was turning the city of pale gray, silver, and slate blue by day into one of deep cobalt speckled with golden thread from lamps by night. The Seine was mirroring this blue gold in its body and Notre Dame Cathedral was fully illuminated by floodlights.

Jean-Jacques needed to gather his things and prepare for an evening engagement, but we could continue the conversation and walk together. It had been one of those weeks, as we seem to be having more and more of, where genetic information was coming in faster and causing everyone to rethink everything they thought before a decade ago, a year ago, last week, yesterday, sometimes even just a few hours ago.

"Based on what we have now before us," I asked, sweeping to that amazing view, "what do you think was going on with early modern humans, Neandertals, Denisovans, and even the other as-yet-unidentified archaic humans?"

"The problem we have with this story," he said, "is that we know a lot of things now about Neandertals, Neandertals' origins, we have discovered the Denisovans. . . . Basically, we know a lot about the margins, but the core, we don't know it. For example, what is the mechanism of the emergence of our own species in Africa? We have no clue exactly how it worked. There are geneticists giving stories, but I think in this domain often the geneticists are wrong because they make assumptions, like the notion that all living populations in the past have descendants today— which is wrong. Or assumptions, like, basically, the ancestors of present-day populations lived where these populations live today. Many geneticists have no clue, for example, of what were the environmental changes, the changes in geography and landscapes at the scale of Africa, and the possible movement of people, etcetera. At the moment, let's say for eighty percent of Africa, we know almost nothing about archaeology and paleoanthropology. We know a lot about East Africa, South Africa, a little bit about northwest Africa, but the rest of Africa, we know nothing. There is a complex story in Africa that is still to be discovered."

Chris Stringer, a prominent paleoanthropologist based in London, in a recent talk as a part of a series called "Behaviorally Modern Humans: The Origins of Us" at the Salk Institute at UC San Diego, told the audience that we also can't think in terms of there being any one source of origin in Africa. Like Jean-Jacques, who cautioned about trying to find Edenic moments of origins, Stringer was also saying we couldn't even seek the Eden, the place where it all began. "There isn't a single center of evolution for humans in Africa," he said. "There isn't a garden of Eden in South Africa or East Africa. Different parts of Africa contributed to what we call modern humans, through movements of populations, gene flow, and exchanges of ideas."

Africa is the second-largest continent in the world (after Asia), and today, as in the past, has the greatest diversity of any continent. It is a vast geography that had to have facilitated a lot of population migrations, movements, and the exchange of genes and ideas, within the continent and then moving beyond it into Eurasia and the rest of the world. Some of those migrations took place earlier than 60,000 or 50,000 years ago. But it's the 60,000-years-ago marker and its migrations that seem to be connected to the people we're all related to today: the ones who survived, reproduced, and multiplied so successfully that here we are, all 7 billion of us and counting.

"Was there some sort of an intensification around fifty thousand years ago?" I asked Jean-Jacques as he grabbed his jacket and we stepped into the hall, heading toward the stairs and the courtyard below.

"It's clear that there is a sort of intensification of this out-of-Africa movement that led to the colonization of the whole planet by one form of humans, replacing [all the others]. I think the truth is probably more complicated. Guys like Richard Klein," a paleoanthropologist at Stanford, "they think that there was like one mutation that made human become human. I think there was something like that that happened, but it's not one mutation, it's probably several."

He held the door open for me and we stepped out into the Parisian evening. I smelled roses and coffee and felt the sudden rush of all those many billions of humans on the planet rushing around us in commuter traffic and the thousands of pedestrians leaving work and heading to cafés and home. We turned left and walked past the Cluny Museum and medieval herb gardens planted in neat rows. Inside, the six garnet red and floral *millefleurs* panels of *La Dame à la licorne*, the Lady and the

Unicorn, pointed to another time and another way of knowing the world, both equally caught up in the mystery.

"It's probably a process that took some time. What happened probably is that in this process that is the result of a complex interaction between cultural and social evolution and biology—the two interacting together—and also the interaction between different populations within Africa, there was a sort of a threshold that has been passed at some point that explained this expansion. I think the notion of a threshold is more accurate than the notion of a *click*," he snapped his fingers, "that makes everything different. I think it's like water rising and at some point spilling out. Yes, something happened, but in this sense. It's the end of a process that had been lasting for a while."

We had just passed a café where the waiter was pouring a glass of wine and I imagined it continuing to the lip and slipping over. Something happened, but it was thanks to many somethings happening in a complex mix that culminated in a confluence that together hit the threshold and flowed into full expression.

Too soon we arrived at the corner of Boulevard Saint-Michel and Boulevard Saint-Germain—for I was in heaven, talking Neandertal with the likes of Jean-Jacques in one of the most beautiful cities in the world. It was time to say good-bye.

"Any parting wisdom in making sense of all this?" I asked.

He smiled warmly. "We need to remain humble, and know we will never know everything. We'll never unlock the entire mystery of human evolution."

It was poetic, it was beautiful, and it was not satisfying, but then, he wasn't finished. I held my breath, as if waiting for the mystery of life to be explained. I noticed that the world around me had come to a standstill, that all the cars, buses, taxis, and pedestrian traffic froze in a blurred fog.

"That is also what makes all this so exciting," he said.

I took a deep breath.

He *had* unlocked the mystery of life. We love the mystery and are excited by it; this is what makes us get up in the morning and push on.

The world zoomed back into motion and for a split-second I saw in Jean-Jacques's eyes and face the young boy who landed here as a preadolescent and lost himself in the beauty of nature and the past. We gave each other the formal cheek kiss of *au revoir* and I watched him walk west on St-Germain as I turned north on St-Michel and toward the Seine.

I felt the rush and press of people all around, but also the mystery, and I was so happy to be in the midst of all this as it unfolded. I reached the river and joined the flow.

# ACKNOWLEDGMENTS

THERE ARE MANY, many people, places, and beings to thank, past and present, for their support and influence in this work. First and foremost, a hearty thanks must go to Harold Dibble and Dennis Sandgathe for walking past the shallot seller's stand in Sarlat that market day in May 2010 and changing the course of the last few years of this writer's life. (And thanks also to the shallot seller, because his timing in making change for my purchase of those little alliums orchestrated the synchronicity of seeing Harold's figure and profile whisk through the square at just the right time.)

Thank you next to the core team along with Harold and Dennis who let me into their lives and work: Shannon McPherron, Paul Goldberg, Vera Aldeias, Alain Turq, Jean-Jacques Hublin, and Virginie Sinet-Mathiot—all who let me ask them endless questions over several years toward learning as well as possible the nature of their fields, work, and most importantly, what we can say about Neandertals.

A very special thanks to Cécile Bordes for folding me into the deep tradition of the Bordes family and of archaeology in Carsac, along with the "Carsac sisters" Françoise and Hélène.

Thank you to the many friends, locals, and natives of the Dordogne and southwestern France and northern Spain who all contributed in their own unique ways toward bringing this book together. A particular thanks to Alain Fournier, Didier and Viviane Sebastianutti, Françoise, Bernadette, Béa, Bruno, Nadiya, Nicolas (the expert knapper, firemaker, and spear-thrower), Aurelie Delpeyrat and her whole family, Christian and Fabienne, Michel, Annie Taylor, Petra, Jean, Eric, Patricia Mercier,

## ACKNOWLEDGMENTS

Adrian Mialet, Fabien, Carlos, Vincent, and Bernard with George & Co. Thanks to Ana and Whit for tooling around Neandertal sites in Catalonia with me and letting me crash at the baronial castle.

Thank you to many other generous professionals who cheerfully made time for me to interview them and ask them my many questions about prehistory and Neandertals as they have come to understand them. There were many and I am afraid I may miss noting everyone here but special thanks must go to Ofer Bar-Yosef, João Zilhão, Randall White, Jean-Jacques Cleyet-Merle, Antoine Balzeau, Teresa Steele, Tim Weaver, Zenobia Jacobs, Theodore G. Schurr, Michael Chazan, Francesco Berna, Isabelle Crevecoeur, Asier Gómez-Olivencia, Gilliane Monnier, James C. Ahern, Isabelle Castanet, Bruno Maureille, Laurent Chiotti, Laurent Bruxelles, Dana Walrath, Janet Monge, Alan Mann, Kate Britton, Amanda Henry, Ainara Sistiaga, Sahra Talamo, Wil Roebroeks, Paul Mellars, Svante Pääbo, Sophie Cattoire, Vincent Lesbros, Albert Harris, Aylar, Dafne, Naomi, Anna, Susan, Jonathan, Matt, Sam, Amir, the entire crew of each year at La Ferrassie, the crew at Cova Serinya, the guides at La Chapelle-aux-Saints and Atapuerca, and all the professional guides in Les Eyzies for the various regional prehistoric sites.

Thank you to the people of Carsac, Sarlat, Les Eyzies, Villamayor, Atapuerca, and along the Camino de Santiago, as well as all those who welcomed me and shared their Neandertal prehistory with me in Cornwall, England, eastern Germany, Portugal, other areas of France and Spain, Iran, and into Stone Age *Homo sapiens* territories in Morocco and Egypt that were contemporary to Neandertal sites in Eurasia.

Thank you to the museums, institutions, and libraries that are the treasuries of our human heritage. Among museums, special thanks to the Musée de la Préhistoire and the Pôle International de Préhistoire both in Les Eyzies, the Musée de l'Homme in Paris, the Musée d'Aquitaine in Bordeaux, the Museo de la Evolución Humana in Burgos, the Neues Museum in Berlin, and the Penn Museum of Archaeology and Anthropology in Philadelphia. Thank you to the public libraries of Sarlat-la-Canéda,

Boulder, and Ocean City, and to the Collège de France in Paris and to the Salk Institute at UC San Diego for the excellent broadcasted series on human evolution that allowed me to listen via the internet to some of the world's most renown investigators in Neandertal research.

Thanks to the birds, *les rouges gorges* and *les mésanges bleues*, as always, and the many frogs, dogs, and cats, especially of Chez Bordes (and Mr. Stripes of Sarlat), and above all, Gary the dog of Camp Carsac.

Thank you to my parents who gave me the deep love for prehistory and access to three great continents growing up on which to explore humanity's walk on earth. Thank you to Birch Miles, my husband, who supported all this research even though it took me away from modern *Homo sapiens* and him (and even when he claimed with exaggeration to possess 5 percent Neandertal DNA to entice me to stay). He only registered a complaint once, poetically delivered via email to the field as a song he wrote titled "Neandertal Blues" and cut in one take in the studio with his fellow musician friends. It cast aspersions on one person only, Harold, the root source of all the troubles. (Visit my blog post, "Neandertal Blues," at cafeoc.blogspot.com, to hear the song produced by Birch Miles and the Bardas Band.)

Particular thanks also to John Prendergast and Samuel Hughes, the editors at the *Pennsylvania Gazette* who first commissioned the feature story on Harold and his research in the Dordogne ("On Hearths, Ancient and Modern," Nov./Dec. 2010) and later the feature story about Paleolithic archaeologist Michael Chazan ("Finding an Old Flame," Jan./Feb. 2014), both of which became the seeds for the sprouting of this book. Similarly, great editors and agents make a writer and along with John and Sam are Dan Smetanka, executive editor at Counterpoint Press, whose enthusiasm for this work has been uplifting from the beginning, and my wonderful agent, Laura Strachan, who has championed my writing all along. Thank you both and to the fine team at Counterpoint who brought this book to readers' hands.

## ACKNOWLEDGMENTS

But to all the *Homo sapiens* out there who have helped me and for whom I have strong affection, in the end, the ultimate thanks must go to the Neandertals, for without them and their compelling prehistory and mystery, all of the aforementioned bipeds, other than the shallot seller and the local friends from the Dordogne, would be out of interesting work.

*Merci Madame et Monsieur La Ferrassie et merci à tous.*